PRAISE FOR NORMAN BEIM'S PLAYS

*"Norman Beim is that **rara avis**, a professional playwright. He is what the theatre needs."*

Tony Randall

"Your play (DREAMS) is very well done...simple and moving."

Katharine Hepburn

"THE DESERTER is a moving and compassionate play by a most gifted playwright."

Horton Foote

"The play (SUCCESS) achieves the sublime depths of great universality."

Vlaams Weckblad, Brugge, Belgium

"Norman Beim ranks with the best in America today."

WHBI Radio

BY NORMAN BEIM

PLAYS
Six Award Winning Plays
Plays At Home And Abroad
My Family, The Jewish Immigrants
Giants Of The Old Testament

NOVELS
Hymie And The Angel

NORMAN BEIM

GIANTS

of

The Old Testament

NEWCONCEPT
press, inc.

Emerson   New Jersey

Samuel French
45 West 25th Street
New York, New York 10010

Library of Congress Cataloging-in-Publication Data

Beim, Norman
    Giants of the old testament/Norman Beim
        p.   cm
    Contents: The prince who ate in the morning--Lost in midian--King of the israelites--Looking at the stars--A serpent's tooth--Queen of persia
    ISBN 0-931231-10-8 (alk.paper)
    1. Bible.   O.T.--History of Biblical events--Drama. 2. Bible plays, American. 1. Title.

PS3552.E4224 G5 2001
812'.54--dc21

                                                    2001018334
                                                    CIP

FRONT COVER DESIGN by HOMER GUERRA, New York City

Special Thanks to LARRY ERLBAUM, ART LIZZA, MARTY BEIM

Printed in the United States of America

10 9 8 7 6 5 4 3 2 1

for Frieda

CONTENTS

PREFACE

The epic scope and grandeur of the Biblical tales in the Old Testament are unrivaled in world literature. Religious, political, social and economic issues plus every facet of human relationship is dealt with in these dramatic stories. Creating a coherent plot from these Biblical tales, however, is like solving a puzzle. The Bible gives us tantalizing clues, dots along the way, and it's left to us to connect these dots. Consulting reference books can be more confusing than helpful since each authority has his (or her) own pet theory. There are endless footnotes to the footnotes, each as logical as the one before or after. Some Hebrew scholars spend their lifetime debating the meaning of certain passages. This author felt he had but one recourse...to accept the most logical theory that best served his dramatic purpose.

For example, we know that Moses was raised as an Egyptian prince. We also know that when, as an infant, he was adopted by the young Egyptian princess she was aware of his Hebrew origin and allowed him to be nursed by a Hebrew woman. But we don't know whether she allowed the contact with the Hebrews to continue after the infant was weaned. In THE PRINCE WHO ATE IN THE MORNING the princess sees to it that Moses is kept ignorant of his lowly origin which creates a dramatic situation when the young man finds out the truth and is torn between his loyalty to Egypt and his empathy for his enslaved brethren.

We also know from the Bible that Moses had a Cushite wife but we don't know when he married her. I've taken the liberty of making her an Abyssinian princess whom he met as a young Egyptian general during an expedition to Abyssinia. Decades later, after the exodus, the Bible tells us that Miriam objected violently to the marriage of Moses to this Cushite. (As a matter of fact, God defended Moses and punished Miriam for this by afflicting her with leprosy.) This conflict with Miriam in regard to the marriage of an outsider I've inserted at an earlier date than recorded in the Bible.

***

Moses fled from Egypt after murdering an Egyptian overseer in a fit of rage. He settled in Midian where he took a Midiante wife who

ix

bore him two sons. There's no record of his having confided his criminal past nor his Hebrew origin to members of his Midiante family. As a matter of fact he did not have his two sons circumcised as was the custom among the Hebrews. (Later the Bible tells us that when God was about to kill Moses because of this, it was his Zipporah, his Midiante wife, who took a flint knife and performed the rite.) In LOST IN MIDIAN Moses broods privately about his past, his unwillingness to accept his Hebrew heritage and his reluctance to help the Hebrews even though he feels that's his destiny. This refusal to face his inner self forces him to become uncommunicative and creates a conflict between Moses and Zipporah.

***

In KING OF THE ISRAELITES King Saul, a paranoid, manic-depressive, summons the young David to play and sing for him to lull him out of his black moods. But suddenly the Bible has David back home with his father and visiting Saul on the battlefield, begging the king to allow him to fight Goliath. I had to account for this gap by having young David summoned home by his father. As a matter of fact some scholars believe that David was not the young man that defeated Goliath; and the authenticity of the legend itself, which is dramatized in KING OF THE ISRAELITES, has been questioned.

In KING OF THE ISRAELITES another theme that has been debated among scholars is the nature of the relationship between David and Jonathan. David laments Jonathan's death with the following words:

"Very pleasant has thou been unto me:
Thy love to me was wonderful,
Passing the love of woman."

Does David mean that his relationship to Jonathan was purely spiritual? Is he saying that spiritual love is impossible between man and woman? Saul in his jealous taunts, implies that more than just friendship exists between his son and his rival. This could be ascribed simply to Saul's state of mind. Or was there, perhaps, some justification for these slurs? In KING OF THE ISRAELITES I let the audience draw its own conclusion.

***

When David ran away to escape being killed by King Saul he left his wife, Michal, Saul's daughter, behind. Saul gave her to another man to spite him. When David ascended to the throne he took Michal away from this second husband and Michal was very bitter about this since this second marriage had lasted for ten years and the man had been good to her. Since she was disdainful of David and took pleasure in vilifying him, in LOOKING AT THE STARS it seemed logical to give Michal the role of trouble-maker in regard to David's adulterous affair with Bathsheba, a married woman.

***

The story of Absalom, King David's favorite son, has so many dramatic events that it was a matter of telescoping all these incidents into one coherent whole. In A SERPENTS'S TOOTH, which deals with David and Absalom, I also combined two characters...David's nephew, Jonadab, and his counsellor, Ahithophel, since both were up to no good and served the same purpose. (It's interesting to note that neither King Saul nor King David were exemplary fathers. Saul was paranoid about holding onto his throne and David was an overindulgent parent, letting his sons do as they pleased.)

***

In QUEEN OF PERSIA, which is based upon the Book of Esther, Esther, an orphan, was adopted by her cousin, Mordecai. It was his refusal to bow to Haman, the prime minister, that led Haman to persuade the king to destroy the Jews. There are a number of conflicting theories as to why Mordecai refused to pay homage to Haman. I've chosen to portray Mordecai as a rather arrogant and stubborn man. Also I've played devil's advocate in regard to Haman. I've given him some idealistic reasons for persecuting the Jews and an emotional basis for his bias. (Incidentally it's the Book of Esther that's most easily adaptable into play form since the story is so well constructed. It's also interesting to note that it is the Book Of Esther that is the least holy. There's no mention of God anywhere nor any mention of prayer.)

***

It's ironic that the Bible, this holiest of books, is peppered with violence (continual wars and battles), adultery (David and Bathsheba), rape (David's son rapes his half sister) and murder (Absalom murders his brother. David has Bathsheba's husband murdered. David's general, Joab, murders two rival generals.)

THE PRINCE WHO ATE IN THE MORNING

"Woe to thee, O land, when thy king is a child
And thy princes eat in the morning!
Happy art thou, O land, when thy king is the son of nobles,
And thy princes eat in due season,
For strength and not for drunkenness!"
Ecclesiastes X

CAST OF CHARACTERS

MOSES . . . . An Egyptian prince

THERMUTIS . . . . An Egyptian princess, Moses' mother

MERNEPTAH . . . . An Egyptian prince, Thermutis' brother

RAMESES II . . . . The pharaoh

THARBIS . . . . An Abyssinian princess

NICIAS . . . . Moses' servant, a Hittite

MIRIAM . . . . Moses' sister

AARON . . . . Moses' brother

(If so desired the role of MIRIAM may be doubled with that of
THERMUTIS and the role of AARON may be doubled with that of
RAMESES II.)

SCENE

Moses' apartment in Memphis, the capital of ancient Egypt, and a tent
in Abyssinia.

ACT ONE

Scene One

(Moses' apartment in the royal palace in Memphis. Early morning. MERNEPTAH, a young prince, enters from the exterior and looks about. NICIAS, a middle-aged servant, enters from the interior.)

NICIAS: Your highness...

MERNEPTAH: Is he still asleep?

NICIAS: I'm afraid so, your highness.

MERNEPTAH: Wake him!

NICIAS: I've been given strict instructions.

(MERNEPTAH starts for the bedchamber.)

NICIAS: Now, now your highness, you know what he's like in the morning.

MERNEPTAH: This is outrageous! I mean, after all, I will be pharaoh one day. Or is that what he's banking on? That someone else will succeed my father?

MOSES: *(Offstage)* What's all that noise?

NICIAS: I'll let him know that you're here.

MERNEPTAH: You needn't bother.

NICIAS: I wouldn't, your highness. He got in very late last night.

5

MOSES: *(Offstage)* Nicias?!

NICIAS: Excuse me. *(HE goes off to the bedchamber.)*

MOSES: *(Offstage)* Tell him to go away!

(NICIAS reenters.)

MERNEPTAH: I'm not leaving, and you can tell him that. We had a date to go riding and this is the third time he's disappointed me. *(HE sits.)* I'm not leaving. You can tell him that.

NICIAS: Would your highness care for some breakfast?

MERNEPTAH: I've just had my breakfast, thank you. Where are you going? I'm haven't dismissed you yet.

NICIAS: Your highness.

MERNEPTAH: Keep me company. Sit down. I said sit down.

(NICIAS sits with a sigh.)

MERNEPTAH: Don't you miss your homeland, Nicias?

NICIAS: Egypt's my homeland now, your highness.

MERNEPTAH: What about your family?

NICIAS: All dead, your highness.

MERNEPTAH: What a pity! All of them?

NICIAS: I'm afraid so.

MERNEPTAH: Well, that's war for you. But we're at peace now. With your people, at any rate. Wouldn't you like me to speak to Moses? About releasing you?

NICIAS: That's very kind of you, your highness.

MERNEPTAH: But you're happy here.

NICIAS: I left nothing behind but painful memories.

MERNEPTAH: And Moses treats you well.

NICIAS: I have no complaints.

MERNEPTAH: You have so much in common, you and your master. What I mean to say is, neither of you are of royal blood, though the way he carries on you'd never know it. I don't know why I waste my time with him. I really don't. I feel sorry for him, I suppose. Not that he deserves it. It's all my sister's fault, of course. She spoils him dreadfully. I mean, the way he struts about the palace you'd think he owned it. I don't know how you put up with it. I really don't. What I mean to say is it's not as if you were born a servant. You come from a very good family, don't you? Don't you?

NICIAS: We were free men.

MERNEPTAH: It might interest you to know that I've always had the greatest respect for your people.

NICIAS: Thank you, your highness.

MERNEPTAH: As a matter of fact, I've often thought that you Hittites were so much more civilized than we Egyptians. Just between the two of us, Nicias, I find your master an embarrassment. I really do. And, of course, there's no use speaking to my sister about it. She's obviously besotted with this so-called progeny of hers. But I was just wondering…

NICIAS: Your highness?

MERNEPTAH: You don't think he's under any misconception that he's in line for the throne? Do you?

(*MOSES appears in the doorway in a lounging robe.*)

MOSES: Well, Nicias? What do you think? What are my chances of succeeding the pharaoh?

MERNEPTAH: Do you know what time it is?

NICIAS: I'll get your breakfast. (*HE goes off.*)

MOSES: Aren't you ashamed of yourself?

MERNEPTAH: I don't know what you're talking about.

MOSES: Stooping to grill the servants?

MERNEPTAH: We were supposed to go riding this morning.

MOSES: Were we?

MERNEPTAH: Yes, we were. I don't know why I bother with you. I really don't.

MOSES: I'm such good company?

MERNEPTAH: You're disgraceful. That's what you are.

MOSES: Oh, please!

MERNEPTAH: What on earth has gotten into you?

MOSES: Whatever it is it's given me a violent headache.

MERNEPTAH: You've got a hangover, that's what you've got.

MOSES: All right, all right. You needn't shout.

MERNEPTAH: You ought to be ashamed of yourself. Drinking and brawling. Frequenting all those low places with all those disreputable... riffraff.

MOSES: They speak well of you.

MERNEPTAH: You're absolutely impossible.

MOSES: Improbable, perhaps.

MERNEPTAH: You may be adopted but your behavior still does reflect upon us all. Look at you. Just look at you.

MOSES: What?

MERNEPTAH: You look like death warmed over. You call that having a good time?

MOSES: Must you shout like that?

NICIAS: It's pointless. Absolutely pointless. Well, it's none of my business...

MOSES: Exactly.

MERNEPTAH: But the pharaoh's very angry with you.

MOSES: What about?

MERNEPTAH: *(Loudly)*What about?!

MOSES: *(Putting his hands to his ears.)* Please.

MERNEPTAH: Don't you remember?

MOSES: Did I do something naughty?

MERNEPTAH: You caused a riot. That's what you did.

MOSES: Oh, come now.

MERNEPTAH: I only know what I heard.

MOSES: And what exactly did you hear?

MERNEPTAH: There was a brawl. Some officers stepped in and tried to quiet things down and you put two of them into the hospital.

MOSES: Only two?

MERNEPTAH: It isn't funny. You go berserk whenever you drink. You're absolutely frightening. You ought to know that by now. This terrible temper of yours is going to be the death of you yet. You just wait and see.

> (*NICIAS reenters with a goblet, which he hands to MOSES. MOSES takes a sip, makes a face then gulps the mixture down. NICIAS goes off.*)

MERNEPTAH: What's that you're drinking?

MOSES: I don't know.

MERNEPTAH: What do you mean, you don't know?

MOSES: It something that clears my head.

MERNEPTAH: What's in it?

MOSES: I don't know.

MERNEPTAH: You could be drinking poison, for all you know.

MOSES: I don't think I'm important enough to poison.

MERNEPTAH: Quite possibly, but you do live here in the palace. You are considered royalty and there are all sorts of crackpots out there. These are dangerous times we're living in.

MOSES: Dangerous?

MERNEPTAH: Yes, dangerous. It's like living on top of a volcano. Haven't you noticed the way the Hebrews have been behaving?

MOSES: Not really, no.

MERNEPTAH: Sulking. Recalcitrant. You can hear them muttering under their breath.

MOSES: What are they saying?

MERNEPTAH: It isn't funny. One of these days that volcano is going to erupt, and then where will we be?

MOSES: Swimming in lava?

MERNEPTAH: Every time I look at them they give me the creeps.

MOSES: Don't look at them. I am absolutely starved. Ah, here we are.

> *(NICIAS enters with a tray of food which he places on a table.)*

MOSES: Would you care for some breakfast?

MERNEPTAH: Breakfast? It's almost time for lunch.

> *(NICIAS goes off. MOSES starts to eat.)*

MERNEPTAH: The pharaoh's really furious.

MOSES: It won't be the first time.

MERNEPTAH: It may be the last as far as you're concerned.

MOSES: What's he going to do? Chop my head off?

MERNEPTAH: You're supposed to set an example. Privilege carries with it certain responsibilities.

MOSES: You're absolutely right.

> *(MOSES continues to eat. THERMUTIS, an attractive woman in her late thirties, enters from the exterior. MOSES rises.)*

MOSES: Well, well, well. This is a red letter day.

THERMUTIS: *(Grimly)* Good morning.

MOSES: Uh, oh!

THERMUTIS: *(To MERNEPTAH)* Would you excuse us, please?

MERNEPTAH: We had a date to go riding.

THERMUTIS: Please.

MOSES: Tomorrow. I give you my word.

MERNEPTAH: Such as it is. *(HE goes off.)*

MOSES: *(HE kisses her.)* Please don't look at me like that.

THERMUTIS: What did I do wrong? Tell me.

MOSES: "I've given you every advantage and this is the way you pay me back. You wanted to study architecture, I let you study architecture. You wanted a commission in the army. I got you a commission in the army."

THERMUTIS: What do you want?

MOSES: My place in the sun.

THERMUTIS: Meaning what?

MOSES: I'm bored. Don't you understand? I'm bored, bored, bored.

THERMUTIS: I see.

MOSES: I am not of royal blood, I'm aware of that. But then, what am I? I attend state functions. I nod, I smile and I make small talk. From time to time I'm even allowed to entertain some visiting dignitaries. And, oh yes, every six months or so I'm permitted to leave the palace and conduct some maneuvers somewhere out in the desert. And what a joke that is!

THERMUTIS: Go on.

MOSES: I look about and I see others far less qualified than myself being given positions of authority and it's humiliating. I am not a child anymore.

THERMUTIS: What would you like to do?

MOSES: I think I ought to be given some sort of responsibility. I don't care about titles and that sort of nonsense...

THERMUTIS: The pharaoh has asked me to make a tour of the Upper Valley? Would you care to accompany me?

MOSES: As what? As your appendage? As your play thing?

THERMUTIS: You mustn't pay attention to gossip. There will always be small minded people. Envious people. Especially here at court.

MOSES: The fact of the matter is...

THERMUTIS: The fact of the matter is you're too sensitive. You take everything personally. It just so happens that the pharaoh's very fond of you. As a matter of fact, if the truth were known, he likes you better than he does his own son. But you must be patient. Let me finish please. It's true. You are not my flesh and blood, nor are you his.

(RAMESES II, the pharaoh, enters from the exterior.)

MOSES: Your majesty.

THERMUTIS: I've had a long talk with him.

RAMESES: Wait outside. I said...

THERMUTIS: Yes. Yes, of course. I'll wait outside. *(SHE hesitates then goes off.)*

RAMESES: Well, I must say, you certainly don't look the worse for wear.

MOSES: Things got out of hand apparently.

RAMESES: Apparently. Is that your breakfast?

MOSES: May I offer you something?

RAMESES: I've had my breakfast, thank you.

MOSES: I'm sorry about last night.

RAMESES: *(Ironically.)* And it'll never happen again.

MOSES: You have every right to be angry with me.

RAMESES: Apparently you don't know your own strength.

MOSES: It's just that I don't hold my liquor well.

RAMESES: Nor your temper as well. I had the same problem once. The drinking, that is.

MOSES: And how did you solve it?

RAMESES: I was fortunate. Too much liquor made me ill. How's my son doing?

MOSES: His riding's improving?

RAMESES: And his archery?

MOSES: His wrists are weak and I've given him some exercises to do.

RAMESES: And does he do them?

MOSES: I'll keep after him.

RAMESES: Good. Good. *(HE sits with a sigh.)*

MOSES: You don't look well, sire.

RAMESES: It's been a hectic morning. And the day's just begun.

RAMESES: *(After a moment)* I'm sending some troops to the southern border. Would you care to lead them?

MOSES: Abyssinia?

RAMESES: *(HE nods.)* Well?

MOSES: You mean I'd be in charge of the expedition?

RAMESES: *(HE nods.)* Well?

MOSES: Well...yes!

RAMESES: Good, good.

MOSES: I won't disappoint you, sire.

RAMESES: I'm sure you won't.

MOSES: When do I leave?

RAMESES: The end of the week. Time enough to say your good-byes.

MOSES: Does my mother know?

RAMESES: Not yet. Love's a peculiar thing, my boy. It can be nourishing. It can also suffocate. However we are what we are. Needy creatures, in spite of our exalted position, in spite of our lofty aspirations. Perhaps, because of them. And it doesn't get any easier, my boy. It doesn't get any easier. Just remember one thing. Those of us who are strong must remember to be gentle. My son's very fond of you, you know. He looks up to you and someday he's going to be pharaoh. And you know, my boy, it's possible to have great power without all that fuss and bother.

MOSES: I understand.

RAMESES: I ran into him, sulking in the courtyard.

MOSES: We were supposed to go riding this morning.

RAMESES: The day's still young. Go talk to him. And send in your mother.

MOSES: Thank you, sire. Thank you.

(MOSES goes off. RAMESES walks about impatiently, sits then rises and is suddenly taken with a coughing fit as THERMUTIS reenters.)

THERMUTIS: Are you all right?

RAMESES: As all right as I'm going to be. You're going to succeed me, you know. You and your brother.

THERMUTIS: You've resented him from the very first.

RAMESES: If I had, you wouldn't have been allowed to keep him.

THERMUTIS: You're sending him to his death.

RAMESES: Nonsense.

THERMUTIS: But why Abyssinia?

RAMESES: It's a minor skirmish.

THERMUTIS: He's all I have.

RAMESES: And if you really want to keep him let him go.

THERMUTIS: It's so far away.

RAMESES: He'll come back, my dear, a man perhaps.

THERMUTIS: And suppose he does come back? Suppose he comes back in triumph?

RAMESES: Once and for all...

THERMUTIS: You said yourself...

RAMESES: Now look. For your sake I have bent over backwards. And I will admit he's turned out better than I expected.

THERMUTIS: There you are.

RAMESES: That does not detract from the fact that you have done the boy a great disservice. You've allowed him to live a lie. You've allowed him to hope for things that are beyond his reach.

THERMUTIS: You gave me your word.

RAMESES: My dear child, he is bound to find out the truth one day and what, my dear, will he think of you then?

THERMUTIS: I saved his life, didn't I?

RAMESES: That you did, and the lives of his people.

THERMUTIS: They are not his people. Don't say that. We are his people. You promised.

RAMESES: I will keep your deep dark secret. Don't worry. Though it's questionable how much of a secret it really is. You did a great service for both Egypt and these people by persuading me to rescind that edict. I'm very grateful to you for that. It was a moment of panic and I regretted it. We need these people and killing them off was, to say the least, counter-productive. The fact of the matter is, however, this boy could be most useful as a liaison between the government and...the Hebrews.

THERMUTIS: No!

RAMESES: All right, all right. But you know, my dear, there comes a time in ones life, as it's come for me now, when one looks back and passes judgement on oneself. When that time comes for you you'll want the pluses to outweigh the minuses. Think about it. That's all I ask.

> (RAMESES kisses her on the forehead and goes off. THERMUTIS sits, visibly shaken. After a moment NICIAS reenters and starts to clear the table.)

THERMUTIS: Nicias?

NICIAS: Your highness?

THERMUTIS: When he does find out the truth, will he hate me then, do you think?

NICIAS: That's difficult to say.

> *(THERMUTIS sighs and goes off. NICIAS picks up the breakfast tray, stands lost in thought for a moment then goes off to the interior as the lights slowly fade.)*

Scene Two

(Martial music is heard and fades as the lights come up on Moses' tent in Abyssinia. Evening. THARBIS, an Abyssinian princess is discovered waiting impatiently. MOSES enters. THEY stand looking one another over.)

MOSES: You wanted to see me?

THARBIS: Your highness! One addresses me as your highness.

MOSES: Your highness. What can I do for you?

THARBIS: The question is, what can I do for you?

MOSES: All right. What can you do for me?

THARBIS: For one thing, I can save you many lives.

MOSES: You're here to negotiate a surrender?

THARBIS: In a sense.

MOSES: Meaning?

THARBIS: There are surrenders and there are surrenders.

MOSES: Why yes, I suppose there are.

THARBIS: In order to end this ridiculous little war you are to surrender...to me. You find that amusing?

MOSES: You're not serious?

THARBIS: Do I look like a frivolous person? I saw you from the city wall and I was impressed. In return for marriage my father, the king, is willing to come to terms with you.

MOSES: That's very generous of you, but we happen to be winning this ridiculous little war.

THARBIS: For the moment, perhaps. But this is our home. We know this terrain. And we haven't even begun to fight.

MOSES: I see.

THARBIS: You don't have to give me your answer now.

MOSES: Thank you. That's very generous of you. May I offer you some refreshment?

THARBIS: Like what?

MOSES: Some fruit, perhaps. Some beer.

THARBIS: Beer?

MOSES: You don't drink beer?

THARBIS: We drink wine.

MOSES: In Egypt we use wine for ceremonial functions.

THARBIS: You mean religious ceremonies?

MOSES: Isn't that what I said?

THARBIS: No, that's not what you said, and my visit here is an official one.

MOSES: I'm terribly sorry. There is no wine. May I offer you a chair instead?

THARBIS: Thank you. *(SHE sits.)* You may join me.

MOSES: Thank you. *(HE sits.)* So?

THARBIS: So?

MOSES: Marriage to me would mean leaving your homeland.

THARBIS: Yes, of course.

MOSES: And you're ready to do that?

THARBIS: I may be young but I'm not a child.

MOSES: And you know nothing about me.

THARBIS: You're an Egyptian prince and a general, are you not? And our marriage would cement an alliance between your country and mine, which is why my father has given his consent.

MOSES: In other words this would be a political alliance.

THARBIS: Yes, of course. I'm not a silly school girl. I would return with you to Egypt to represent my country at court.

MOSES: Yes, well it just so happens that I am not a politician.

THARBIS: You're not a fool, unless I'm mistaken. An easy victory for one as young as you are would do your reputation no harm. What are you smiling at?

MOSES: How old are you, by the way?

THARBIS: Age has nothing to do with it.

MOSES: And besides, when it came to marriage I thought somehow the situation would be reversed. I mean that I would do the choosing.

THARBIS: Have I wounded your masculine vanity?

MOSES: I have no masculine vanity. What I mean to say...

THARBIS: What do you mean to say?

MOSES: *(HE laughs.)* I am not of royal blood, you know.

THARBIS: You're not?

MOSES: I was adopted.

THARBIS: By whom?

MOSES: The pharaoh's daughter.

THARBIS: Then you're a prince.

MOSES: Technically, perhaps.

THARBIS: And you carry yourself like a prince. How many wives do you have?

MOSES: I don't have any, as yet.

THARBIS: None?

MOSES: Isn't that what I said?

THARBIS: Why?

MOSES: We haven't gotten around to it.

THARBIS: We?

MOSES: My mother, the pharaoh and myself.

THARBIS: You're an only child?

MOSES: What has that got to do with it?

THARBIS: It was just a simple question.

MOSES: Yes, I'm an only child.

THARBIS: I didn't mean to pry...

MOSES: Which comes first? Your surrender or mine?

THARBIS: Actually we're talking about a truce, to begin with. And, of course, the truce comes first. We wouldn't want you taking an enemy as a wife. Now would we?

MOSES: Are you...laughing at me?

THARBIS: Does that disturb you?

MOSES: I don't like to be laughed at.

THARBIS: I'll keep that in mind. Are you really that insecure?

MOSES: Apparently.

THARBIS: We'll have to work on that. You have until morning to decide. *(SHE starts off.)*

MOSES: Just a moment...

(THARBIS continues to leave.)

MOSES: Your highness.

THARBIS: *(SHE stops, turns and faces him.)* Yes, general? What is it?

MOSES: *(HE blushes.)* I forgot what I was going to say.

THARBIS: *(SHE smiles.)* Until morning then.

(THARBIS goes off. MOSES watches her leave then sits thoughtfully as the lights come down. Wedding music is heard and fades.)

Scene Three

(Moses' apartment. One month later. THARBIS enters from the outside, looks about, goes off to the interior then reenters and stands looking out onto the terrace. MOSES enters from the outside.)

MOSES: At any rate, welcome to Egypt.

THARBIS: You call this a welcome?

MOSES: I don't understand it.

THARBIS: It's an insult.

MOSES: I'm sure there must be some sort of an explanation.

THARBIS: Abyssinia may not be as magnificent as Egypt, but we are a power to be reckoned with, and this sort of treatment is unacceptable. Absolutely unacceptable!

MOSES: All right, all right. Calm down.

THARBIS: I am the daughter of a king.

MOSES: Yes, my dear, I know.

THARBIS: And if my father hears about this...

MOSES: There's something's wrong somewhere. It's just too quiet.

THARBIS: It's an insult to you as well. You return victorious, a conquering hero, and absolutely no one here to greet you! Aren't you offended? If you're not you ought to be.

MOSES: As soon as we get settled I'll look into it. As a matter of fact, I'm rather concerned. We're really very fussy about protocol. At any rate, what do you think of Memphis, aside from our poor reception?

THARBIS: Very impressive.

MOSES: Come, come, come. It's a magnificent city and you know it. When have you ever seen such splendor? The architecture, the statuary. The way the streets are all laid out. As soon as we're settled we'll take a walk around the city. The Temple of Isis is my favorite. These quarters are not very spacious, I know. But we can arrange for larger ones.

THARBIS: This will do fine.

MOSES: The bedroom's right through there...

THARBIS: Yes, I know.

MOSES: What happened to our luggage?

THARBIS: Your men dumped all of our bags into the bedroom.

MOSES: It's really strange. I thought surely Nicias would be on hand to greet us.

THARBIS: He's your servant?

MOSES: My servant, my friend and my mentor.

THARBIS: You did send word ahead, didn't you?

MOSES: Yes, of course.

THARBIS: And they are aware of our marriage, aren't they?

MOSES: As a matter of fact the pharaoh wrote me this glowing letter. That's why I think it's so odd...

THARBIS: And your mother knows...

MOSES: Well, of course, she knows and she's looking forward to meeting you. And I thought surely Merneptah would be sniffing around.

THARBIS: Merneptah?

MOSES: The heir apparent.

THARBIS: And what is he like, this heir apparent?

MOSES: One never knows from day to day. You must be tired.

THARBIS: And dirty. I would like a bath.

MOSES: It's...

THARBIS: I know where it is.

MOSES: Still angry?

THARBIS: Yes.

MOSES: Good. I love you when you're angry.

> *(HE kisses her. SHE responds then restrains herself.)*

THARBIS: My bath.

MOSES: I was just about to suggest it myself.

> *(SHE pushes him away and starts off. HE pats her on the rear as she leaves then looks about the room. NICIAS enters from the outside. MOSES embraces him.)*

MOSES: Nicias! Where is everyone?

NICIAS: You haven't heard?

MOSES: No. What?

NICIAS: The pharaoh's on his death bed.

MOSES: Why wasn't I told?

NICIAS: It was kept hush-hush.

MOSES: How imminent is it?

NICIAS: Any minute now.

MOSES: I should pay my respects.

NICIAS: He's unconscious...and no one's permitted.

MOSES: Is my mother with him?

NICIAS: And Merneptah. Where's your bride?

MOSES: She's taking a bath. She's very upset. About our reception I mean.

NICIAS: I'll do my best to make her feel at home.

MOSES: She is a princess, you know.

NICIAS: Yes, I know. As a matter of fact the pharaoh had a hero's welcome all planned. Under the circumstances, however...

MOSES: Yes. Yes, of course. And the princess, my mother? How is she taking it?

MOSES: It's difficult to tell.

MOSES: I mean my marriage,

NICIAS: Oh, that. She's very proud of you.

MOSES: She's really a very remarkable young lady.

NICIAS: I'm looking forward to meeting her.

MOSES: The one woman she was attached to, her wet nurse, was too old and too fragile to travel. So she's here all alone...in a strange country.

NICIAS: Yes, I know the feeling.

MOSES: And how's Merneptah these days?

NICIAS: Merneptah's changed quite a bit.

MOSES: For the better, I hope.

NICIAS: That remains to be seen

(THARBIS reenters.)

THARBIS: I can't find...my dressing gown.

MOSES: It's probably mixed in with my things. Tharbis this is Nicias.

NICIAS: Your highness. It's an honor.

THARBIS: I've heard a great deal about you. *(To MOSES)* Would you...?

MOSES: Yes. Yes, of course. *(HE goes off to the interior.)*

NICIAS: I must apologize for your reception. The pharaoh is deathly ill, you see.

THARBIS: I'm sorry. Perhaps we should pay our respects.

NICIAS: The funeral, I'm afraid, will be the proper time.

THARBIS: I see. My father sent along a gift for the pharaoh.

NICIAS: That will probably be the prince, Merneptah.

THARBIS: Probably?

NICIAS: It's almost a certainty.

THARBIS: I see. You're not Egyptian, are you?.

NICIAS: I'm a Hittite.

THARBIS: We're both of us aliens then, are we not? Until I find an attendant you're going to have to do double duty. Would you mind?

NICIAS: It will be my pleasure.

> *(MOSES reenters holding a dressing gown which he hands to THARBIS.)*

MOSES: Here you are.

THARBIS: Thank you. *(SHE kisses him and goes off.)*

NICIAS: Charming.

MOSES: And she does have a mind of her own.

NICIAS: I can see that.

> *(MERNEPTAH enters from the outside.)*

MERNEPTAH: So, you're back.

MOSES: Apparently.

MERNEPTAH: My sister's been asking for you, Nicias.

NICIAS: Your highness. *(HE starts off.)*

MERNEPTAH: Your majesty!

NICIAS: Your majesty. *(HE hesitates and goes off.)*

MOSES: How's the pharaoh?

MERNEPTAH: Didn't you just hear what I just said? I'm the pharaoh now.

MOSES: I'm sorry. What I mean to say is...

MERNEPTAH: I know what you mean to say.

MOSES: I shall miss him.

MERNEPTAH: We shall all mourn his passing. So, you found yourself a princess, I hear.

MOSES: Well, actually...

MERNEPTAH: I know the story. Romance and derring-do. The kind of a tale that myths are made of. Congratulations.

MOSES: Thank you, I think. Have all the preparations been made?

MERNEPTAH: The coronation will take place tomorrow.

MOSES: I meant the funeral.

MERNEPTAH: The end of the week. The body will be on display for those who care to pay their respects, and in two days time he will enter his tomb. Things will be moving more quickly from here on in. The pharaoh was getting senile these past few years.

MOSES: Senile?!

MERNEPTAH: His tomb would never have been completed in time if I hadn't rushed things along. The way he indulged those Hebrews. We're going to pay for it, you know. You just wait and see. Last week we almost had an uprising.

MOSES: What happened?

MERNEPTAH: Well, it could have turned into one. One of the slaves attacked an Egyptian overseer.

MOSES: Why was that?

MERNEPTAH: What?

MOSES: Why did he attack the overseer?

MERNEPTAH: What difference does it make?

MOSES: I should think it would make a great deal of difference. Did you look into it?

MERNEPTAH: Of course, I looked into it.

MOSES: And?

MERNEPTAH: The slave was disposed of. It was most unpleasant. My stomach was queasy for a week. And here you bring home an Abyssinian.

MOSES: She is of royal blood, you know.

MERNEPTAH: They're savages.

MOSES: They fought very bravely for savages.

MERNEPTAH: And did you have to marry her?

MOSES: It was part of the agreement.

MERNEPTAH: And bring her home with you?

MOSES: She's my wife. And she is the official representative of Abyssinia.

MERNEPTAH: Yes, well we'll see about that. The fact of the matter is you should have written for permission.

MOSES: The pharaoh, your father, put me in charge.

MERNEPTAH: A royal wedding is...a royal wedding. You were in no position to make that sort of decision on your own. Not that you're really royalty...

MOSES: And your father, the pharaoh, gave the union his blessing.

MERNEPTAH: That was after the fact. What else could he do? And just remember I'm the pharaoh now.

MOSES: How could I possibly forget?

MERNEPTAH: Don't be impertinent. And how do you think my sister felt? Your mother?

MOSES: It was a matter of state.

MERNEPTAH: A matter of state?! Well, well, well! Aren't we the one? A matter of state. Well, from here on in you will consult me personally in matters of state. *(HE laughs.)* A matter of state. And from here on in, if I were you, I would save my diplomacy for the bedroom, where I presume you must be very proficient.

MOSES: I've had no complaints.

MERNEPTAH: I'm sure you haven't.

MOSES: At any rate I hope I can serve you the way I served your father.

MERNEPTAH: Oh, now really! Who do you think you're fooling? You did nothing for years but drink and brawl and make an utter fool of yourself. And now, by some miracle, you've managed to win a minor campaign. I wouldn't even call it that. A minor skirmish. And how, exactly, did you win it? By selling your sexual favors. That's not the way I mean to rule this empire.

MOSES: At any rate I shall do what I can.

MERNEPTAH: What you've done so far is drive a stake through my sister's heart.

MOSES: She expected me to marry one day.

MERNEPTAH: Not some heathen.

MOSES: Is she well?

MERNEPTAH: As well as can be expected, under the circumstances.

MOSES: I should like to pay my respects to the pharaoh.

MERNEPTAH: He's being prepared for burial. Unless, of course, you'd care to assist with the embalming.

>*(THERMUTIS appears in the doorway.)*

MERNEPTAH: He's back. *(HE goes off.)*

THERMUTIS: You may kiss me, if you like.

>*(MOSES kisses her on the cheek. SHE clings to him and sobs uncontrollably. THEY sit.)*

MOSES: It's all right, it's all right.

THERMUTIS: I feel so alone.

MOSES: Now, now, now. You still have me. And Merneptah.

THERMUTIS: Where's your wife?

MOSES: She's taking a bath. How long had he been ill?

THERMUTIS: He'd been ill for years. No one was supposed to know about it.

MOSES: He loved you very much. Merneptah's succeeded him, I gather.

THERMUTIS: We're to share the throne.

MOSES: Oh? And how does he feel about that?

THERMUTIS: I should think he'd be greatly relieved, He'll need all the help he can get. *(SHE studies his face and caresses his forehead and hair.)*

MOSES: What are you smiling at?

THERMUTIS: Nothing.

MOSES: You found something amusing.

THERMUTIS: So you're a married man.

MOSES: I think you'll like her.

THERMUTIS: I'm sure I shall.

MOSES: I'm very angry with you. I wrote you almost every single day.

THERMUTIS: Yes. Yes, I know.

MOSES: And you never bothered to answer.

THERMUTIS: I never received them.

MOSES: Then how...?

THERMUTIS: I came across your letters this morning for the first time in the pharaoh's desk. I was looking for some papers and there they were, all wrapped up in a bundle. He thought I was being unfair to you. That I was holding you back.

MOSES: I see. So, what can I do? How can I help?

THERMUTIS: There are the preparations for the funeral.

MOSES: Yes, of course.

THERMUTIS: There'll be a formal ceremony involving officials from all over the kingdom and the neighboring countries as well. I've made up a list. There'll be invitations to send out. Preparations to house and entertain the visiting dignitaries. Seating arrangements, etcetera. I want to make sure it's all conducted properly. I don't trust anyone.

MOSES: I'll take care of it. May I see him?

THERMUTIS: Yes, of course. Come along. *(SHE takes his arm and kisses him.)* You've gained some weight.

MOSES: A little.

THERMUTIS: It's very becoming.

MOSES: Thank you, your majesty.

> *(HE kisses her as THEY go off together arm in arm.
> THARBIS reenters in a lounging robe.)*

THARBIS: I feel like a new...person. Moses? Moses?

> *(SHE looks about, then looks out towards the terrace.
> NICIAS enters.)*

THARBIS: Nicias. Have you seen Moses?

NICIAS: He's with the princess, his mother.

THARBIS: Did she send for him?

NICIAS: She was just here.

THARBIS: They must have gone to pay their respects to the pharaoh.

NICIAS: The pharaoh is dead.

THARBIS: I see.

NICIAS: If there's anything I can do...

THARBIS: What's that?

NICIAS: May I help you unpack?

THARBIS: Thank you.

> *(NICIAS goes off. THARBIS sits and looks about
> uneasily as the lights come down.)*

Scene Four

(Moses' apartment. Early morning. One month later. MOSES and MERNEPTAH enter from the outside in riding clothes.)

MOSES: Nicias!

(NICIAS enters.)

MOSES: Some fruit.

(NICIAS goes off.)

MERNEPTAH: So, what do you think?

MOSES: What does Thermutis say?

MERNEPTAH: What difference does it make? The fact of the matter is we're way behind schedule.

MOSES: What's the rush?

MERNEPTAH: I want the new municipal center ready by Spring. And that's two months away.

MOSES: Why Spring?

MERNEPTAH: Because I say so.

MOSES: What's so important about the municipal center? And besides they're working day and night, as it is.

MERNEPTAH: They're lazy, sullen brutes. And I want someone forceful in charge. Someone who can get things done. Someone I can trust.

MOSES: Well, I have studied architecture...

MERNEPTAH: This has nothing to do with architecture. The plans are all laid out. The work is underway. I just need someone who can handle men.

> *(NICIAS enters with a tray containing a bowl of fruit and two plates. HE sets the tray down on a table.)*

MOSES: Nicias, where's my wife?

NICIAS: She's still asleep. *(HE goes off.)*

MERNEPTAH: As usual.

MOSES: Why are you so nasty to her?

MERNEPTAH: When have I ever been nasty to her?

MOSES: Every time you see her. She is the ambassador for Abyssinia.

MERNEPTAH: She has yet to produce the proper papers.

MOSES: She's sent for them and, in addition to that, she is my wife. She's here all alone in a strange land.

MERNEPTAH: Whose fault is that? And please don't change the subject. Will you or will you not take over?

MOSES: What exactly would you like me to do?

MERNEPTAH: I've just told you. All you've got to do is supervise. That's all. Would you believe it, those wretches haven't even laid the foundation for my tomb?

MOSES: You're planning an early departure, are you?

MERNEPTAH: Please don't try to be clever. It doesn't suit you.

(THARBIS enters in a dressing gown.)

MOSES: Good morning.

THARBIS: Good morning. *(SHE kisses MOSES.)* Good morning, your majesty.

MERNEPTAH: Good morning.

THARBIS: Did you enjoy your ride?

MERNEPTAH: Is there any reason why I shouldn't?

THARBIS: I suppose that all depends on what sort of a temper you're in.

MERNEPTAH: A good one, up until now.

THARBIS: Perhaps you'll improve as the day wears on.

MERNEPTAH: *(HE rises and turns to Moses)* I have some things to attend to. Think about it. What we've talked about!

MOSES: What's that? Yes. Yes, I will.

(MERNEPTAH goes off.)

THARBIS: What a nasty man!

MOSES: He's very insecure.

THARBIS: And you're always defending him.

MOSES: What choice do we have? He is the pharaoh. Did you sleep well?

THARBIS: Eventually.

MOSES: Bad dreams?

THARBIS: No. Just restless.

MOSES: Homesick?

THARBIS: A little.

(SHE rings the bell. NICIAS enters.)

THARBIS: I'll have my breakfast, Nicias.

(NICIAS goes off.)

MOSES: What did your sister say? In her letter? When does she plan to visit us?

THARBIS: She's not coming.

MOSES: Why not?

THARBIS: I asked her not to.

MOSES: I thought you were looking forward to her visit.

THARBIS: And have her treated like an outcast?

MOSES: Would you care to pay her a visit?

THARBIS: Are you trying to get rid of me?

MOSES: *(HE kisses her.)* It hasn't been easy for you, I know.

THARBIS: I'm not used to being treated like a servant. Less than a servant. If I were back home and someone spoke to me like that I'd have them drawn and quartered. You think that's funny?

MOSES: They'll come around. Have you tried making friends with the women at court?

THARBIS: They're all afraid of offending the pharaoh.

MOSES: My mother's been friendly to you, hasn't she?

THARBIS: When she has the time. Oh, I'm not blaming her. She does have a great deal of responsibility, and that idiot to cope with. It's just too bad...

MOSES: What?

THARBIS: That this empire's burden with a nincompoop like that. I'm sure your mother would much prefer sharing the throne with someone she can respect. Someone she can look up to. Don't look at me like that.

MOSES: I've told you...

THARBIS: I know what you've told me. But the world is changing.

MOSES: Not that much.

> (NICIAS enters with a breakfast tray. HE places the tray
> on the table and goes off.)

THARBIS: I just don't see why you must live in the shadow of that...that...

MOSES: Eat your breakfast. He wants to put me in charge of the municipal works.

THARBIS: Doing what?

MOSES: Supervising the construction.

THARBIS: A supervisor, in charge of slaves?

MOSES: I know, I know.

THARBIS: You know what the problem is. You're too popular. That's what the problem is. What about your mother?

MOSES: What about her?

THARBIS: Have you spoken to her about it? Your position here at court.

MOSES: Not really, no.

THARBIS: Why not?

MOSES: She's got enough on her mind.

THARBIS: Then perhaps you can ease her mind.

MOSES: You're so considerate.

THARBIS: Oh, go take your bath. You smell like a stable.

(MOSES laughs and kisses her.)

THARBIS: Phew!

(SHE pushes him away and HE goes off. THARBIS sits lost in thought. NICIAS reenters.)

THARBIS: Nicias...?

NICIAS: Your highness?

THARBIS: What am I doing wrong?

NICIAS: These things take time.

THARBIS: I feel like an outcast.

NICIAS: I know, I know.

THARBIS: You're a cultivated man. How can you bear to be subservient to these...boors?

NICIAS: We're all here to serve, in one way or another.

THARBIS: All this hypocrisy. All this pretention. All they really live for is this other world of theirs. It's as if they were already embalmed and just waiting to be laid to rest in their beautiful mausoleums.

NICIAS: Ah well, I suppose there is some comfort in looking forward to a pleasant hereafter.

THARBIS: And that master of yours... I just want to shake him.

(THERMUTIS appears in the doorway. THARBIS rises.)

THARBIS: Thank you, Nicias.

(NICIAS goes off.)

THARBIS: Good morning.

THERMUTIS: I'm interrupting your breakfast.

THARBIS: Moses is bathing at the moment. I'll go fetch him.

THERMUTIS: There's no rush. That's a very pretty robe.

THARBIS: Thank you.

THERMUTIS: I love the colors.

THARBIS: I have another just like it if...

THERMUTIS: No, no, no. That's very kind of you. Sit down, please.

(THEY sit.)

THERMUTIS: I thought they were going to find you larger quarters.

THARBIS: We're quite comfortable here.

THERMUTIS: You're sure?

THARBIS: This is fine.

THERMUTIS: Are you happy, my dear?

THARBIS: I don't feel very welcome. Here at court, I mean, if you really want to know.

THERMUTIS: You must give us time. People here aren't used to speaking their mind.

THARBIS: In other words keep my mouth shut.

THARBIS: On the contrary. Stand your ground, my dear. You're like a breath of fresh air. You'll win them over and, in time, I promise you you're going to be very popular.

THARBIS: And that will solve everything.

THERMUTIS: What do you mean?

THARBIS: Look at Moses and look at the way he's treated. And he is in line to succeed you, is he not?

THERMUTIS: Succeed me?

THARBIS: As co-regent I meant. What I mean to say is he is your son.

THERMUTIS: It's not as simple as that.

THARBIS: It's no secret that you're the one that's ruling this country.

THERMUTIS: You're mistaken, my dear. And, if I were you, I would not encourage my son to think along those lines. I'm speaking as a friend.

THARBIS: And as my mother-in-law?

THERMUTIS: As your mother-in-law as well. He is not of royal blood. Or weren't you aware of that?

THARBIS: It's the first thing he told me.

THERMUTIS: And it madc no difference?

THARBIS: In my country royalty is a matter of character.

THERMUTIS: Yes. well, that's all very admirable...

(MOSES enters in a lounging robe.)

THERMUTIS: *(To Tharbis.)* I'm on my way to inspect the new temple. I'd like you to join me. Why don't you get dressed? I'll wait for you. And Tharbis...

THARBIS: Your majesty?

THERMUTIS: There's no rush.

(THARBIS nods and goes off.)

THERMUTIS: No kiss?

MOSES: *(HE kisses her on the cheek.)* I hardly get to see you anymore. To what do I owe this honor?

THERMUTIS: The new temple's been completed and I thought you might like you to see it.

MOSES: All right.

THERMUTIS: You don't have to if you don't want to. Moses?

MOSES: Yes? What is it?

THERMUTIS: You've been offered the position of building supervisor.

MOSES: Taskmaster to a bunch of Hebrew slaves?

THERMUTIS: I'd like you to accept the position.

MOSES: Oh, now really!

THERMUTIS: It was my idea.

MOSES: I see.

THERMUTIS: Sit down. I said, sit down.

MOSES: *(HE sits.)* So that's what you've had in mind for me all along.

THERMUTIS: The fact of the matter is we're having all sorts of problems with the Hebrews and we're at a loss to know what to do about them.

MOSES: Why me?

THERMUTIS: With your military background, with your war experience... I think you'll know how to handle these people. And it is an important issue, of great concern...

MOSES: I'm not interested.

THERMUTIS: As a favor to me?

MOSES: No! *(HE rises and paces about.)* Don't you realize how demeaning this is? Don't you realize...?

THERMUTIS: Sit down! I have something to say to you and I want you to hear me out, quietly and calmly. Did you hear what I said?

MOSES: I heard you. *(HE sits.)*

THERMUTIS: At one time there was an edict to the effect that all male children born to the Hebrews were to be put to death. Did you know about that?

MOSES: Vaguely. It was some time ago, wasn't it?

THERMUTIS: Not that long ago. As a matter of fact it was shortly before you were born. It was my father's idea and I persuaded him to rescind it. And the fact of the matter is Merneptah's been ranting and raving about the Hebrews.

MOSES: And you think that he might try to revive this edict?

THERMUTIS: It has come up.

MOSES: It would be cutting off one's nose to spite one's face.

THERMUTIS: Exactly, and I hope it never comes to that. It was an awful time. Children were found everywhere. In the temples, on street corners, in trash bins. Some were given away to friendly Egyptians. There was one family...they placed their son in a waterproof basket and placed the basket in the reeds along the river. A beautiful child.

MOSES: Now how would you know that?

THERMUTIS: I found the child near the riverbank.

MOSES: And...? What did you do with it?

THERMUTIS: I adopted it.

MOSES: You adopted it?

THERMUTIS: I was a child myself but I fell in love with this beautiful infant and I decided that I must have it.

MOSES: And the pharaoh let you?

THERMUTIS: If I wanted something badly enough...

MOSES: What happened to this...? Was it a boy or a girl?

THERMUTIS: A boy.

MOSES: What happened to this boy?

THERMUTIS: He grew up to be a handsome general, the commander of an Egyptian army.

MOSES: What are you saying? Are you saying that I am that child? Is that what you're saying? Are you saying that my parents were Hebrews? Is that what you're saying?

(THERMUTIS nods.)

MOSES: What about that maidservant of yours? The one who died in childbirth, the one who was supposed to be my mother? What about that lover of hers, that soldier who was killed in battle, the one who was supposed to be my father?

THERMUTIS: Fiction, my dear. Pure fiction.

MOSES: I see. Who knows about this? The world, I suppose. Everyone but me?

THERMUTIS: No one knows.

MOSES: What do you mean no one knows? How could you possibly keep something like that a secret?

THERMUTIS: Except for the pharaoh, of course. My father, that is.

MOSES: What about your servants?

THERMUTIS: They were sworn to secrecy. And so was Nicias.

MOSES: You mean to tell me that Nicias has known about this all along? And Merneptah as well, I suppose?

THERMUTIS: Merneptah hadn't been born yet.

MOSES: Why are you telling me this?

THERMUTIS: You were bound to find out eventually.

MOSES: Why now? Why have you waited all these years?

THERMUTIS: I've been meaning to tell you. I've been meaning to tell you for quite some time...

MOSES: But why now?!

THERMUTIS: You want to be of use, my dear. Well, here's your chance.

MOSES: Of use? Of use to whom?

THERMUTIS: To us, and to them.

MOSES: Who is us? And who is them?

THERMUTIS: You're an Egyptian prince. And Egypt needs your help.

MOSES: All these years... All these years I've been living a lie.

(THARBIS enters dressed for the day.)

THARBIS: I'm ready.

THERMUTIS: Good.

THARBIS: *(To MOSES)* Are you joining us?

MOSES: I haven't had my breakfast yet.

THARBIS: We can wait. *(To THERMUTIS)* Can't we?

MOSES: I'm not in the mood for temples.

THERMUTIS: He can join us later on. I'd like you two to have dinner with me this evening. *(To THARBIS)* Come along, my dear. Come along.

(THERMUTIS takes THARBIS's arm and THEY go off together. MOSES stands stunned and confused. HE sits, rises, walks about, then rings for NICIAS who enters a moment later.)

NICIAS: Your breakfast?

MOSES: Never mind my breakfast.

NICIAS: Is there anything wrong?

MOSES: And here I thought you were my friend.

NICIAS: Have you any reason to doubt it?

MOSES: Why haven't you ever told me?

NICIAS: Told you what?

MOSES: You know what! My lovely mother's just told me the whole charming story.

NICIAS: And what story is that may I ask?

MOSES: The one about the Hebrew baby in the basket.

NICIAS: I see.

MOSES: But why? Why did she have to tell me? If I lived this long without knowing...?

NICIAS: You were bound to find out eventually?

MOSES: But why now? Now, after all these years?

NICIAS: Can't you guess, my boy? She's dying.

MOSES: What's wrong with her? She looks perfectly healthy to me.

NICIAS: Well she's not, according to her doctors. And your secret's safe as long as she's alive.

MOSES: You should have told me, Nicias.

NICIAS: It would have meant my life.

MOSES: I'll never forgive her for this. Never!

NICIAS: For saving your life? For saving the life of your people?

MOSES: Please! Don't call them my people. And what am I supposed to do? Am I supposed to be their champion? These wretches? Is that what she has in mind for me?

NICIAS: Is that so terrible?

MOSES: People snickering at me behind my back. All this time. The pharaoh knew all along and he said nothing.

NICIAS: He was fond of you. At least he grew to be.

MOSES: And when she's gone they'll all be free to snicker at me openly.

NICIAS: You've nothing to be ashamed of.

MOSES: How can you say that?

NICIAS: They're an ancient people, my boy, with a noble tradition, an honorable heritage.

MOSES: Honorable?!

NICIAS: Yes, honorable.

MOSES: How long ago was that?

NICIAS: And perhaps someday, with your help, they can regain their place in society.

MOSES: Not with my help, they won't.

NICIAS: Would you care to meet them?

MOSES: Them? Who is them?

NICIAS: Your family. Your brother and your sister for one.

MOSES: That's all I need. A Hebrew brother and a Hebrew sister. And what about my Hebrew mother and my Hebrew father?

NICIAS: Your father's dead. He was crushed by a boulder in a building accident. Your mother's still alive, bed ridden and half crippled. She was the one who nursed you. When the princess found you your sister was nearby and she offered to find a wet nurse for you.

MOSES: And that was my mother. What a charming fable! And you've been in touch with them all this time, I suppose. I don't want to hear.

NICIAS: Your brother's name is Aaron.

MOSES: I said...

NICIAS: And your sister's name is Miriam.

MOSES: I don't want to know.

NICIAS: Moses…

MOSES: I'll never forgive her for this. Never!

> *(MOSES strides off. NICIAS sighs as the lights come down.)*

ACT TWO

Scene One

(The apartment. Early afternoon, two weeks later. THARBIS and MERNEPTAH enter from the outside. They are dressed somberly. THARBIS looks about, goes off to the interior and reenters, then shakes her head.)

THARBIS: He's not here.

MERNEPTAH: Shameful! Absolutely shameful!

THARBIS: I'm beginning to worry.

MERNEPTAH: Oh, he'll show up eventually.

THARBIS: But it's been almost two weeks now.

MERNEPTAH: I can assure you. There is nothing to worry about.

THARBIS: Has he done this before?

MERNEPTAH: With sickening regularity. He'd disappear for weeks at a time and then he'd show up filthy and ragged, smelling to high heaven. Of drink, my dear, of drink.

THARBIS: I didn't know that he drank.

MERNEPTAH: He used to. He used to wallow in it.

THARBIS: But he doesn't any more, and he hasn't for quite some time now. And he loved her very much.

MERNEPTAH: Love?! He doesn't know the meaning of the word. He's a monster. As long as I live I shall never forgive him for this. I'll never forget the look on her face. And they say that no one dies of a broken heart.

THARBIS: I thought it was her lungs.

MERNEPTAH: There was nothing wrong with her lungs. You know, of course, that he's a Hebrew.

THARBIS: Yes. Yes, I know.

MERNEPTAH: He told you?

THARBIS: Your sister did before she died.

MERNEPTAH: Nevertheless she worshipped the ground he walked on. That was the problem, of course. She spoiled him, gave him false hopes. What I mean to say is he is not of royal blood. and he is rather common when you come right down to it. If you look closely enough you'll see that he does have that Hebrew look about him. Oh, I don't blame her. He could be a charmer, when he wanted to be. Even my father came under his spell. Nevertheless he can be of use...as a liaison between us and those wretched Hebrews. That's what my sister wanted for him and that's what my father wanted too. But oh no, he's too proud. He's actually deluded himself into thinking that he's royalty. You must find all of this rather embarrassing.

THARBIS: What's that?

MERNEPTAH: Being married to a Hebrew. I can have the marriage annulled if you like. Actually it is illegal, the marriage I mean, to a Hebrew, that is. But then again you are an Abyssinian.

(NICIAS enters.)

MERNEPTAH: Well?

(NICIAS shakes his head.)

MERNEPTAH: Did you look in the Hebrew quarter?

NICIAS: I looked all over.

MERNEPTAH: Shameful! Absolutely shameful! *(HE strides off.)*

THARBIS: He never spoke about them, did he? The Hebrews, I mean.

NICIAS: I doubt if he was even aware of them. We're all of us sort of invisible, are we not, we slaves?

THARBIS: And now that he knows...?

NICIAS: He'll come around...after he gets over the initial shock, that is. He's a sensible boy. You must be hungry.

THARBIS: I couldn't eat a thing. I'm going to lie down for a while. If you hear anything let me know.

NICIAS: I'll keep looking.

> *(NICIAS goes off. THARBIS sighs and goes off. After a moment MOSES, disheveled and dirty, enters from the terrace. HE looks about then sits.)*

THARBIS: *(Offstage)* Moses? *(SHE reenters.)* Moses, I was so worried about you.

MOSES: I'm sorry.

THARBIS: Are you all right?

MOSES: I'm fine.

THARBIS: You've heard about your mother, of course.

MOSES: Yes, of course.

THARBIS: She kept asking for you. We thought surely you'd turn up for the funeral.

MOSES: I'll never forgive her, never.

THARBIS: She did what she thought was right.

MOSES: She lied to me. She deceived me.

THARBIS: About your heritage you mean?

MOSES: You know about that? When did you find out?

THARBIS: She told me, the day she took me to see the new temple. The day you disappeared. She took to her bed right after that.

MOSES: And it doesn't bother you? Married to a Hebrew? A race of slaves?

THARBIS: They weren't always slaves.

MOSES: For as long as I can remember.

THARBIS: Where have you been all this time?

MOSES: I wandered about the Hebrew quarter. I wanted to see what ...my people were like.

THARBIS: Did you visit your family?

MOSES: You know about them too?

THARBIS: Nicias told me. There's your brother, Aaron, and your sister, Miriam.

MOSES: Ironic, isn't it? A Hebrew brother and a Hebrew sister, and a Hebrew mother who's bed-ridden.

THARBIS: Did you meet them?

MOSES: No. I did locate them though. I wanted to take a look at them.

THARBIS: And?

MOSES: Actually my brother's quite presentable. Well dressed, and rather well spoken, and he carries himself with a certain amount of dignity.

THARBIS: And your sister?

MOSES: Miriam? Apparently she's something of a firebrand. Rather imposing, as a matter of fact.

THARBIS: Where did you stay? Where did you sleep?

MOSES: In the street. In doorways. I wanted to see what their living conditions were like. Actually they're pretty grim. Yet somehow or other they seem to take it in their stride. They cling to this one god of theirs and, for some unknown reason, it seems to sustain them.

THARBIS: I've been thinking.

MOSES: What?

THARBIS: You may look upon this as a calamity, my dear, but actually this could be the opportunity we've been looking for. I'm perfectly serious. The Hebrews are a vital element in this country's economy. If you could organize these people and represent them...

MOSES: And then what?

THARBIS: It would give you a position of authority.

MOSES: Pharaoh to a bunch of slaves?

THARBIS: A work force, without which there would be no municipal center, no pyramids, no temples...

MOSES: That would take some doing, I'm afraid.

THARBIS: You don't think you can?

MOSES: I never said that.

THARBIS: *(Daring him)* Why not?!

MOSES: It's something to think about, I suppose . They'd be suspicious, of course. An Egyptian prince suddenly coming to their rescue.

THARBIS: But you're one of them, aren't you? And then there's your sister and your brother. I should think they'd want to help.

MOSES: What do they think of me, I wonder. What have they thought about me for all these years?

THARBIS: You are their flesh and blood, and Nicias has been in touch with them. Perhaps he can arrange a meeting.

MOSES: Since I bear the stigma why not take advantage of it? Why not indeed? Then you think I ought to accept the pharaoh's offer?

THARBIS: Do you have any choice?

MOSES: Building supervisor! Fancy title for an ignominious position!

THARBIS: It needn't be.

MOSES: You're a clever little devil, aren't you, my Abyssinian witch. I've missed you so. *(HE embraces her.)*

THARBIS: And your bath as well.

MOSES: Come along. You can wash my back.

THARBIS: You're so kind.

　　　　(THEY kiss and go off together.)

Scene Two

(Early evening two days later. NICIAS enters from the terrace followed by MIRIAM and AARON who look about in awe.)

NICIAS: Make yourself comfortable.

AARON: What's he like now, Nicias?

NICIAS: Much calmer now since his marriage.

MIRIAM: What does he want to see us about?

NICIAS: You'll have to ask him. Sit down, sit down.

> *(NICIAS goes off. MIRIAM and AARON remain standing.)*

AARON: Well, at least he knows.

MIRIAM: Yes, but how has he taken it?

AARON: He's come back. He's sober and he wants to see us. Maybe he wants to help us.

MIRIAM: I wouldn't count on it.

AARON: Then why would he want to see us?

MIRIAM: He's an Egyptian prince. Don't forget that. At least, that's the way he sees himself.

AARON: He's still our flesh and blood.

MIRIAM: Aaron, this is not the same child we put into that basket over twenty years ago. We mustn't hope for too much.

(MOSES enters. There's an embarrassed silence.)

MOSES: Miriam. Aaron. Thank you for coming. Sit down, please. Can I get you something to eat? Some fruit, perhaps. Something to drink?

AARON: Nothing, thank you.

MOSES: Miriam?

MIRIAM: *(SHE shakes her head.)* Nothing.

MOSES: Sit down, please.

(THEY all sit.)

MOSES: Well...

AARON: Well...

MOSES: I don't know...

AARON: *(At the same time)* Nicias said that you...

MOSES: I'm sorry.

AARON: No, no. Please.

MOSES: I don't know what Nicias has told you.

AARON: He's told us that you're now aware of your parentage.

MOSES: Yes, I've just learned about it. I understand my mother is bedridden. Is there anything I can do?

MIRIAM: A new body perhaps?

MOSES: How can I help?

AARON: There's this new edict.

MOSES: What edict is that?

AARON: You haven't heard?

MOSES: Actually I've just been put in charge of construction. As a matter of fact I haven't started yet.

AARON: Every man has a quota of bricks that he must produce.

MOSES: Yes, I know.

AARON: Well, occasionally a man falls behind. So now the pharaoh has decreed that if someone falls behind he must take his own child and use the child in place of the bricks.

MOSES: I'll put a stop to it at once.

AARON: And, of course, there are the working conditions and the hours.

MOSES: I'll look into that.

AARON: And we've barely enough to live on.

MIRIAM: If you really want to help...

MOSES: Yes? What is it?

AARON: Miriam, please.

MIRIAM: Forget about the working conditions. Forget about the hours.

AARON: She has these crazy ideas.

MOSES: No, please. Let her speak. I'd like to hear what she has to say.

MIRIAM: You don't fool with the symptoms. You don't put a bandage on a disease.

MOSES: And what exactly is this disease we're talking about?

AARON: Don't listen to her.

MIRIAM: Slavery!

MOSES: You want me to put an end to slavery?

AARON: She's talking nonsense.

MIRIAM: We're human beings. We have a right to live like human beings.

MOSES: You want me to turn an entire society upside down? Is that what you want? You want me to change the course of history?

MIRIAM: You're a man aren't you? Who makes history?

AARON: Come on, Miriam!

MIRIAM: *(To AARON)* Where do you want me to go? You think it's right that we're treated like animals? That we have to slave day and night for nothing? He's a prince, isn't he? An Egyptian general, a war hero...

AARON: He may be all of that, but he's not a magician.

MOSES: There's no way you're going to eliminate slavery. Our whole economic system would collapse.

MIRIAM: So let it.

AARON: And how would that benefit us?

MOSES: Exactly. We're Egyptians as well as Hebrews, are we not?

MIRIAM: No, I am not an Egyptian.

AARON: *(Throwing up his hands)* What can I tell you?

MIRIAM: I may live in this country. I beg your pardon, exist, but no, I am not an Egyptian. Not in my heart, not in my mind and certainly not in my soul. *(To MOSES)* What you do, perhaps, you do for the good of Egypt.

MOSES: What benefits Egypt benefits you as well. *(To AARON)* Don't you agree?

AARON: Well, of course. Miriam, be reasonable.

MIRIAM: I am sick and tired of being reasonable.

MOSES: You want a revolution? Is that what you want?

MIRIAM: If that's what it takes.

MOSES: A revolution would take planning. A revolution would take money. A revolution would take weapons.

AARON: To say nothing of lives.

MOSES: And even if we had all that we would never be strong enough to fight the entire Egyptian army.

MIRIAM: Then we can die trying.

AARON: Who wants to die? I want to live.

MIRIAM: You call this living? Slaving away day after day without any hope, without any self respect?

AARON: If you want to die a martyr, that's your privilege.

MOSES: I can certainly do something about that edict and the working conditions as well.

MIRIAM: You're friends with the pharaoh, aren't you? You grew up together, didn't you?

MOSES: The pharaoh has his own ideas about the Hebrews and they're pretty inflexible.

MIRIAM: Very well then, if we can't live as free men here in Egypt ...

AARON: Then what?

MIRIAM: So let's leave.

AARON: Leave? Leave where? Leave what?

MIRIAM: Leave Egypt.

AARON: What a brilliant idea! And then what? What do we do? Where do we go?

MIRIAM: We go to Canaan. The land that was promised to us by God. The land that was promised to Abraham and Isaac and Jacob.

    (THARBIS enters from the interior. THEY all stand.)

THARBIS: I'm sorry. I don't mean to interrupt.

MOSES: Come in, come in. I'd like you to meet my sister and my brother. This is my wife, the princess Tharbis. This is Aaron.

AARON: *(HE bows.)* Your highness.

MOSES: And this is Miriam.

THARBIS: How do you do.

    (MIRIAM turns away.)

THARBIS: I won't disturb you.

MOSES: That's quite all right. Would you care to join us?

THARBIS: *(After a moment.)* Thank you, no. I was just on my way out. It's been nice meeting you. *(SHE kisses MOSES.)* Have a good evening. *(SHE goes off.)*

MIRIAM: If you're really one of us you'll get rid of that woman.

MOSES: I beg your pardon?

AARON: Miriam!

MIRIAM: He's a Hebrew, isn't he? Hebrews don't marry black savages.

AARON: You mustn't pay any attention to her.

MOSES: That savage, as you call her, happens to be my wife. And, incidentally, she happens to be a princess as well.

MIRIAM: In Abyssinia, perhaps.

MOSES: She's also happens to be the Abyssinian ambassador here at court.

AARON: Don't listen to her.

MIRIAM: I'm sorry, but as long as you're married to that woman we want nothing to do with you.

AARON: Just a minute.

MOSES: What kind of nonsense is this?

MIRIAM: It may be nonsense to you, having been brought up as an Egyptian.

AARON: And whose fault is that?

MIRIAM: The fact remains that there are many of us that feel as I do.

AARON: She does not speak for all of us.

MIRIAM: Especially among the council of elders.

MOSES: Look, I am willing to risk everything to help you people, my position, my reputation, such as it is, but if such pettiness exists among you people...

MIRIAM: You may call it what you like.

MOSES: Such bigotry.

MIRIAM: I'm sorry.

MOSES: Then there's nothing more to be said.

AARON: Miriam... Moses... This is madness. Miriam, please. Sit down. Let's talk this over.

MIRIAM: *(To AARON)* Tell me something, honestly.

AARON: What?

MIRIAM: Do you really trust this man?

AARON: What are you talking about?

MIRIAM: I will say what has to be said, whether you like it or not. We came here with an open mind. We were willing to welcome you with open arms, our dear lost brother. We put such hope in you, such faith. One day, we prayed, he will come to our rescue, this prince of our dreams. Our savior. All these years we've been waiting, waiting. And now that we're here and I see with my own eyes...I look around at this room. I look at this palace built with our sweat and our blood. And I look at this Egyptian prince! This royal hero! And I ask myself why is this man, this stranger, going to help us? Why is this conquering general going to bother with a bunch of slaves?

MOSES: I don't blame you for being suspicious...

AARON: What has he got to gain?

MIRIAM: Don't be a fool! His protectress is dead. Who's he going to turn to now?

MOSES: I never knew...

MIRIAM: You never knew what? All these years you never knew that you were a human being? You had no eyes? You had no heart? You never saw the way other human beings were being treated? The way they were being abused?

MOSES: I guess I just took things for granted.

MIRIAM: He just took things for granted.

MOSES: I am not a saint. I've never claimed to be.

AARON: Miriam, please. Give the man a chance.

MIRIAM: Why this sudden change of heart? Tell me that?

MOSES: I've suddenly come face to face...

MIRIAM: With what?

MOSES: With the way things are. And it's not only because I'm one of you which, I swear to you, I never knew up until just a few weeks ago and I am appalled...

AARON: Let him finish.

MOSES: I am appalled at the way...at the way my people are being treated.

MIRIAM: His people! Suddenly...

MOSES: I spent the last two weeks wandering about the Hebrew quarter. Taking everything in. Looking at your working conditions. My eyes have been opened.

MIRIAM: His eyes have been opened.

MOSES: And you, Aaron? Is that the way you feel, too?

MIRIAM: Yes, my dear Aaron. Let's hear from that silver tongue of yours. Let's hear what you have to say. Do you trust this Egyptian prince...?

AARON: It's not a matter of trust, my dear.

MIRIAM: What is it then?

AARON: First of all we are not in a position to be so choosey. We're in a bad way and we need help. And when someone offers to help you don't get up on your high horse and turn up your nose. And second of all this man happens to be our brother, our own flesh and blood. But even if he were the devil himself I'd say, "Fine. What can you do for us?"

MIRIAM: Then you can stay here if you want, and you can deal with the devil himself. *(SHE starts off.)*

AARON: Miriam!

MOSES: Let her go.

MIRIAM: *(SHE stops and turns.)* Are you coming or aren't you?

AARON: *(To MOSES)* Not all of us feel this way.

> *(MIRIAM starts toward the terrace.)*

AARON: Miriam. *(To MOSES)* I'll see what I can do.

MOSES: Don't bother.

AARON: Miriam...

> *(AARON follows MIRIAM off. NICIAS reenters.)*

NICIAS: Where are they? Where have they gone?

MOSES: They can go to hell, for all I care!

> *(NICIAS runs off through the terrace. MOSES kicks over a chair and strides off as the lights come down.)*

Scene Three

(Early morning. Two weeks later. MERNEPTAH, holding some papers, enters from the outside. Seeing no one about HE rings the bell. NICIAS enters a moment later tying the belt of his robe.)

NICIAS: Your majesty?!

MERNEPTAH: Where is everyone?

NICIAS: It's rather early, your majesty.

MERNEPTAH: It's not that early.

(THARBIS enters.)

THARBIS: Good morning, your majesty.

(NICIAS bows and goes off.)

MERNEPTAH: Am I the only one awake in this god-forsaken city?

THARBIS: It is rather early.

MERNEPTAH: Where's Moses?

THARBIS: He's still asleep. I'll wake him.

MERNEPTAH: Never mind.

THARBIS: Is there anything wrong?

MERNEPTAH: You've simply got to talk some sense into him.

THARBIS: What's the problem? What's happened?

MERNEPTAH: The problem is he's rescinded a royal edict. That's what the problem is.

THARBIS: There must be some misunderstanding.

MERNEPTAH: Oh, no my dear, there is no misunderstanding. I have the report right here. And I will not put up with it. I will not put up with it. Do you hear? He thinks because he was once in charge of some minor skirmish he can do just as he pleases.

THARBIS: I'll have a talk with him.

MERNEPTAH: I would strongly advise it.

THARBIS: You're quite right to be angry.

MERNEPTAH: This is what I get for giving him all that authority. It was only because of my sister. That was her dying wish.

THARBIS: He should have consulted you, of course.

MERNEPTAH: After all we've done for him. Where's his loyalty? I ask you that. Is this how he repays us? And I used to think of him as a friend.

THARBIS: I'm sure it would pain him to hear you say that. That your friendship is part of the past, I mean. As a matter of fact he often speaks about the times when the two of you used to go riding together.

MERNEPTAH: Does he really?

THARBIS: And I think you're mistaken when you question his loyalty. Because whatever he does he does for the sake of Egypt.

MERNEPTAH: By indulging those wretches?

THARBIS: You can catch more flies with honey, they say.

MERNEPTAH: What about "Spare the rod and spoil the child."?

THARBIS: I know for a fact that he takes his position very seriously.

MERNEPTAH: That's the problem, my dear. That's exactly the problem. You can't treat these people as equals. They're children and they must be disciplined. Primitive customs. Primitive religion. One god, mind you! Did you ever hear of anything so ridiculous?

THARBIS: May I ask...?

MERNEPTAH: What? Speak up, speak up.

THARBIS: May I ask what the edict was?

MERNEPTAH: What difference does it make?

THARBIS: Has it slowed up production? What I mean to say is...

MERNEPTAH: That is not the point. It's a matter of discipline. It's a matter of authority. Just the other day one of our overseers, an Egyptian, was found murdered.

THARBIS: Oh, dear.

MERNEPTAH: Exactly. We may wake up one morning to find that we've been murdered in our beds. I'm glad you find that amusing.

THARBIS: I'm sorry. Have they caught the culprit?

MERNEPTAH: Not yet.

THARBIS: Well, there you are. It might have been anyone. I doubt if any Hebrew would be that foolish.

MERNEPTAH: I don't know what's come over him. I really don't. He used to be lots of fun. Witty and charming, when he was sober, that is. Now he's so sober it's frightening.

THARBIS: Perhaps if you sat down and talked to him

MERNEPTAH: Talk to him? He doesn't listen to me anymore. How can I talk to that...sullen brute? I tell you this. If he doesn't pull himself together I'm going to strip him of his authority and he can join his fellow wretches. I mean it.

THARBIS: I was just about to sit down to breakfast. Won't you join me?

MERNEPTAH: I've had my breakfast, thank you. I'm relying on you, my dear.

> *(MERNEPTAH strides off. THARBIS sits with a sigh. NICIAS enters with a breakfast tray.)*

THARBIS: Did you hear all that?

NICIAS: Oh, yes indeed.

THARBIS: What's come over him?

NICIAS: Merneptah?

THARBIS: No. I mean Moses. He's grown so withdrawn, so morose. We used to share things. We used to confide in one another, and now we hardly talk. Sometimes I think it's me. Something I've said, something I've done. I wonder...

NICIAS: What?

THARBIS: Do you think his family may have turned him against me?

NICIAS: He's not in touch with his family.

THARBIS: Are you quite sure?

NICIAS: I'm positive.

THARBIS: What happened?

NICIAS: The Hebrews look upon him as an Egyptian. The Egyptians look upon him as a Hebrew. She may have had her faults, the princess, his mother, but in her own quiet way she was a powerful force in this country. She was the heart of Egypt. And now that she's gone this empire's become a cold, inhuman place.

(MOSES appears in the doorway.)

THARBIS: Good morning.

MOSES: G-good morning.

THARBIS: Just in time to join me for breakfast.

MOSES: I don't have time.

THARBIS: It's still early. Please. Nicias...

MOSES: Never mind, Nicias. I'm not hungry.

THARBIS: Then sit down and talk to me.

MOSES: I really should g-get to work.

THARBIS: Please!

(MOSES sits. NICIAS goes off.)

THARBIS: I hardly get to see you anymore. What do you do all day?

MOSES: Nothing. Absolutely nothing. *(HE rises and starts off.)*

THARBIS: Moses...?!

MOSES: What is it?

THARBIS: Talk to me. Please!

MOSES: What do you want to know?

THARBIS: What's happening.

MOSES: Where?

THARBIS: With the Hebrews? How are you managing?

MOSES: What do you care? You and the pharaoh?

THARBIS: He has been a little nicer to me, it's true.

MOSES: Oh, come, come. You're the darling of the court. People are falling all over themselves to get to you.

THARBIS: I do represent Abyssinia...

MOSES: Oh, I understand. It's important to kiss their behinds, to cater to the whims of a corrupt society.

THARBIS: You're the product of that society.

MOSES: Don't remind me.

THARBIS: And you think that brooding about it will help?

MOSES: You know nothing about what's going on under your very nose?

THARBIS: The situation with the Hebrews is deplorable. I've been aware of that from the moment I came here. But you're now in a position to do some good.

MOSES: You think so, do you?

THARBIS: But you've got to use some tact.

MOSES: Oh, I see. Is that what's called for, tact?

THARBIS: And some common sense. Merneptah was here just now. He's furious about your rescinding that edict of his.

MOSES: How could I possibly rescind a royal edict?

THARBIS: Then he was mistaken.

MOSES: I merely saw to it that the edict was not carried out.

THARBIS: Did it ever occur to you to sit down and discuss this with him?

MOSES: How can you talk to a man who never listens?

THARBIS: Have you tried?

MOSES: Of course I've tried. I've tried till I'm blue in the face. It's gotten to the point w-where every time I see him my stomach gets tied up in knots. Did he tell you what the edict was?

THARBIS: No. What is it?

MOSES: Each man has to produce a certain amount of bricks. And occasionally someone falls behind.

THARBIS: Deliberately?

MOSES: Whatever the reason it does not justify the punishment.

THARBIS: And what is the punishment?

MOSES: The man must use his own child in place of the missing bricks. I had the practice stopped. These people are overworked and underfed.

THARBIS: *(After a moment)* Suppose they all laid down their tools and refused to work?

MOSES: And what would that accomplish?

THARBIS: It might bring Merneptah to his senses. Why not? What have they got to lose?

MOSES: Well it's not going to happen.

THARBIS: Why not?

MOSES: Because something like that would have to be organized. And there is no leader. There's no organization. There's only a slave mentality.

THARBIS: What about your brother and your sister?

MOSES: What about them?

THARBIS: Can't you talk to them?

MOSES: No, I cannot.

THARBIS: Why not?

MOSES: We don't speak the same language.

THARBIS: I thought that...

MOSES: You thought wrong. The Hebrews are ignorant brutes, savages beyond redemption. And now, if you'll excuse me I have work to do. *(HE starts off.)*

THARBIS: Moses?

MOSES: Yes? W-what is it?

THARBIS: I love you.

MOSES: I love you, too.

>*(MOSES smiles weakly, kisses her and goes off. THARBIS starts to eat her breakfast, then stops and sits lost in thought. NICIAS reenters.)*

THARBIS: Nicias...?

NICIAS: Your highness?

THARBIS: What happened between Moses and his sister and brother?

NICIAS: I don't know.

THARBIS: I'd like to pay them a visit.

NICIAS: I wouldn't advise it.

THARBIS: Why not?

NICIAS: The Hebrew quarter is not the safest place in the world.

THARBIS: Then bring them here.

NICIAS: You think that wise?

THARBIS: Will you? Please?

NICIAS: If you insist.

THARBIS: I do.

>   *(NICIAS nods.)*

THARBIS: Thank you.

>   *(NICIAS goes off. THARBIS stands lost in thought as the
>   lights come down.)*

Scene Four

(Late afternoon that same day. MIRIAM and AARON are discovered waiting anxiously.)

AARON: Don't get your hopes up.

MIRIAM: Why else would he have sent for us?

AARON: He wants to talk.

MIRIAM: He knows how we feel.

AARON: Not we, you.

MIRIAM: At any rate he's sent for us.

AARON: And please, whatever you do, don't ask for the impossible.

MIRIAM: Aaron, what sort of a future is there for us here in Egypt?

AARON: All right. Look, it's true our life here at the moment is not a pleasant one. But this is our home. The home of our fathers and our fathers' fathers. We have roots here. Many of us have married Egyptians and, whether you approve of these marriages or not, these men and women are Hebrews. Let me finish, please. We have a place to live, humble as it may be, and some of us have worked our way up to respectable positions.

MIRIAM: Just because you have an easy job...

AARON: That is neither here nor there.

MIRIAM: While most of us are being worked to death.

AARON: The fact of the matter is...

MIRIAM: Yes, my dear?

AARON: The fact of the matter is we are living in a highly civilized society, the most powerful nation in the world with everything civilization has to offer...

MIRIAM: To whom?

AARON: To those of us who have the freedom and the power...

MIRIAM: Exactly.

AARON: Look, if we can arrange to be paid for our work. If we can arrange for decent hours and decent working conditions. If we can be allowed to apply for a job... What are you smiling at? Why do you shake your head? You think it will be easy to leave? You think the pharaoh will just let us go? Good bye and good luck? Come on! We are a gold mine. Manpower for nothing. All right. And if, by some miracle, we are allowed to leave are you prepared to take up a nomadic life? To wander about in the wilderness like our ancestors did?

MIRIAM: There's the land of Canaan...

AARON: Ah, yes, the land of Canaan. What an inspiration! What a brilliant idea! The land of Canaan. The land of Canaan is just standing there, waiting for us. All those people there are going to move over and make room for us. Welcome home! Won't you please come in? Don't talk nonsense. The fact of the matter is we do have a home, right here in Egypt.

MIRIAM: You call this a home? All right, all right. Let's wait and see. Let's wait and see what he has to say.

AARON: And, please...

MIRIAM: I said I will not bring it up.

   (THARBIS enters.)

THARBIS: I'm sorry to keep you waiting.

AARON: That's quite all right. We're waiting to see Moses.

THARBIS: I was the one that sent for you.

AARON: I see.

MIRIAM: Does Moses know that we're here?

THARBIS: Not yet. He should be here shortly though. I just thought that we ought to get to know one another. Won't you have a seat? Please.

> *(AARON sits. MIRIAM reluctantly follows suit. THARBIS joins them.)*

THARBIS: The fact of the matter is I'm rather concerned about him. That's one of the reasons I sent for you.

AARON: What's the matter with him?

THARBIS: Have you seen him recently?

AARON: No. No, we haven't.

THARBIS: He's changed quite a bit in the last couple of weeks.

AARON: In what way?

THARBIS: He's become withdrawn and sullen. He's not the same man. It's rather frightening.

AARON: And what do you think brought that about?

THARBIS: I know he feels very deeply about the plight of the Hebrews and, apparently he's very frustrated. The pharaoh isn't exactly sympathetic...

MIRIAM: But you are.

THARBIS: Yes. Yes, I am. I'm appalled at the way you people are being treated. Of course, I am a stranger here with not that much influence, but I am anxious to do what I can. I understand that there's been some sort of a misunderstanding between you and Moses.

AARON: It's nothing to be concerned about.

THARBIS: If I can be of any help...in any way...

MIRIAM: As a matter of fact...

AARON: It's just that we're strangers really and it will take some time for us to become acquainted. To get to know one another.

THARBIS: Yes, I know all that.

MIRIAM: If you really want to know...

AARON: Miriam, please.

THARBIS: No, please. I'd like to hear what she has to say.

MIRIAM: The fact of the matter is we can never accept a man as our leader who has married outside of our faith..

AARON: You must understand She does not speak for all of us.

MIRIAM: I speak for those of us who want to preserve our heritage, for those of us who observe our laws, for those of us who refuse to mix our blood with the blood of heathens.

THARBIS: Are you saying that he must give me up? Is that what you're saying?

MIRIAM: Either he's one of us or he is not.

AARON: You mustn't listen to her.

THARBIS: Suppose...

(MOSES enters.)

MOSES: W-what are these people doing here?

THARBIS: I invited them.

MIRIAM: Your wife seems to be a rather sensible woman.

MOSES: W-what have they been telling you?

THARBIS: Just a moment. Suppose I were to convert? Suppose I were to adopt this god of yours?

MOSES: There's no need for you to do anything of the sort.

THARBIS: But if it means that much...

MOSES: I said no.

THARBIS: But, darling...

> *(NICIAS enters.)*

MIRIAM: I think everything's been said that need be said. *(To NICIAS)* We're ready to leave.

NICIAS: Come along then. *(NICIAS starts toward the terrace.)*

THARBIS: Moses... Miriam...

> *(MIRIAM hesitates and goes off.)*

AARON: She'll come around. I'm sure of it. It's just a matter of time.

> *(AARON goes off followed by NICIAS.)*

MOSES: They're impossible.

THARBIS: But I do understand. I really do. When one is abused and mistreated it's only natural to cherish one's beliefs, to try to preserve one's uniqueness. That's all they have.

MOSES: They're an arrogant, stiff-necked people and I'm sick to death of them.

THARBIS: But...

MOSES: I don't want to talk about it. If they can't accept us as we are...

THARBIS: But, darling...

MOSES: It's just plain arrogance. That's what it is. *(HE goes to the interior of the apartment.)*

THARBIS: *(After a moment.)* You're quite right, my dear. That's exactly what it is.

(THARBIS sits, lost in thought. NICIAS reenters.)

THARBIS: Nicias?

NICIAS: Your grace?

THARBIS: *(SHE rises and paces about.)* I've been thinking...

NICIAS: What's that?

THARBIS: It's been quite some time since I've seen my father and he is getting on. I really ought to pay him a visit.

NICIAS: I see.

THARBIS: I'd like you to help me to pack.

NICIAS: Yes, of course. When where you thinking of leaving?

THARBIS: Tomorrow.

NICIAS: Tomorrow? Are you quite...? *(HE stops himself and sighs.)* How long will you be gone?

THARBIS: That all depends. You will look after him, won't you, while I'm gone?

NICIAS: I always have.

THARBIS: Thank you, Nicias.

> *(NICIAS goes off to the interior. THARBIS sits and sighs
> as the lights come down.)*

Scene Five

(The following afternoon. NICIAS enters from the interior with two large travelling bags which he carries off to the exterior and then reenters. THARBIS enters from the interior.)

NICIAS: That's it.

THARBIS: I keep thinking I've forgotten something.

NICIAS: Before you leave I think there's something you ought to know.

THARBIS: What's that?

NICIAS: The other day I was gathering some clothes for the wash and I saw these stains on one of his robes. They looked like blood and I asked him if he'd cut himself. He asked me why and I showed him the robe. He turned pale and told me to get rid of the garment. I said that the stains would probably come out and he shouted, "Get rid of it!"

THARBIS: What did you do with it?

NICIAS: I burned it.

THARBIS: You don't think...

NICIAS: He has been acting strangely ever since the day that overseer's body was found.

THARBIS: Why haven't you mentioned this before?

NICIAS: I wasn't sure and I didn't want to upset you.

THARBIS: I knew something like this was going to happen. I just knew it. Where are my bags?

NICIAS: In the hallway.

THARBIS: Bring them back in. And Nicias...?

NICIAS: Yes?

THARBIS: You haven't said anything about this to anyone, have you?

NICIAS: No, of course not.

> *(NICIAS goes off. THARBIS sits greatly disturbed. MOSES enters from the outside.)*

MOSES: Y-you're still here?

THARBIS: I wasn't planning to leave until this evening. You're back early.

MOSES: It's very hot out there.

> *(NICIAS reenters with the bags.)*

MOSES: Wh-where's he going with those bags?

THARBIS: I've changed my mind.

MOSES: Oh? Why?

THARBIS: I'm just not up to it.

MOSES: Wh-what about your father?

THARBIS: Moses...

MOSES: Yes?

THARBIS: Sit down.

MOSES: Wh-what is it?

THARBIS: That robe of yours...

MOSES: What robe is that?

THARBIS: The one with the spots. The one you asked Nicias to get rid of.

MOSES: What about it?

THARBIS: Nicias seemed to think there was blood on that robe.

MOSES: I cut myself.

THARBIS: Why did you ask him to destroy it?

MOSES: It was just an old robe.

THARBIS: I see.

MOSES: I wouldn't p-postpone that trip if I were you. Who knows? I might even join you.

THARBIS: And that will solve everything?

MOSES: I don't know w-what you're talking about.

THARBIS: Am I your enemy, too? How did it happen?

MOSES: What?

THARBIS: Don't play games with me, please. How did it happen?

MOSES: I came across this b-brute beating this helpless old Hebrew. I don't even remember what happened next. All I know is that when I came to my senses the overseer was lying d-dead at my feet, his head all b-bloody. I think I must have beaten his head against a rock. I looked about and there was no one in sight so I d-dragged the body behind a boulder and b-buried it in the sand.

THARBIS: Were you seen, do you think?

MOSES: I thought not at the time. The spot was so isolated. But then, just now I c-came across these two Hebrew slaves. They were quarreling and they were starting to come to b-blows. I tried to separate them when one of them turned on me and said, "W-what are you going to do? Kill me like you k-killed that overseer?" And then the other one laughed. "You'll get yours," he said. "You just wait and see."

THARBIS: You think they may give you away?

MOSES: They've recently posted a large reward.

THARBIS: But you were protecting one of their own.

MOSES: I don't think loyalty is a quality these people possess. And this is just what the pharaoh's been waiting for.

THARBIS: He used to be very fond of you.

MOSES: He's always looked upon me as a rival.

THARBIS: Perhaps if we explained to him...

MOSES: I don't think that's a good idea.

THARBIS: What will you do?

MOSES: I'll have t-to wait and see. I used to have these blackouts years ago. They only happened when I drank too much. But lately...

THARBIS: Yes, I know.

> *(MERNEPTAH enters from the outside.)*

MERNEPTAH: So there you are. I've been looking all over for you.

MOSES: I came back to change. It's very hot out there.

MERNEPTAH: Yes, isn't it?

THARBIS: Would you care for something to drink, your majesty? Some beer, perhaps.

MERNEPTAH: That might be nice.

(THARBIS rings and NICIAS enters.)

THARBIS: Some beer, Nicias.

(NICIAS nods and goes off.)

THARBIS: It has been unbearably hot these past few days.

MERNEPTAH: If you don't mind I'd like to speak to Moses privately.

THARBIS: Certainly. *(SHE hesitates and then goes off.)*

MERNEPTAH: Sit down, sit down.

(THEY sit.)

MERNEPTAH: She's a remarkable woman, that wife of yours. I didn't think so at first. But then I've been wrong about many things.

(NICIAS enters with a pitcher of beer and some goblets on a tray which he sets down, then leaves. MOSES pours the beer and THEY drink.)

MOSES: *(After a moment.)* Y-you said you were looking for me.

MERNEPTAH: What's that?

MOSES: I said...

MERNEPTAH: I miss her, you know. And the sad thing is I'm beginning to forget what she looked like. But then suddenly a woman walks by and there she is. But then close up the woman looks nothing like her at all. My sister's gone. Do you really think it exists? That other world we make such a fuss about?

MOSES: I don't know.

MERNEPTAH: What do you think?

MOSES: I haven't given the m-matter much thought.

MERNEPTAH: I never understood the pharaoh, my father that is. The burden he bore. The decisions he had to make. But now, to my astonishment, I find that I'm much more like him than I thought. Isn't that odd? He was very fond of you, you know. He kept throwing you up to me. "Why aren't you more like Moses?" he'd say. Not in those words exactly, but that was the gist of it. And you were my idol. Did you know that?

MOSES: I'm very flattered.

MERNEPTAH: The dreams of ones youth. Gone up in smoke. Fairy tales. Golden falsehoods. The promise of some glorious future. And now the taste of ashes in ones mouth. That's what the future's turned out to be. The taste of ashes. Where is one to look for guidance, can you tell me that, when the idols of ones youth have turned out to be false? I've learned my lesson though. Give your heart to no one unless you want it broken. Ironic, isn't it? Life. Death. Destiny. Fate. The dashing prince has turned into an ugly toad. That's not the way the story's supposed to end, is it? You murdered that overseer, didn't you? It's no use denying it. There were witnesses.

MOSES: I...

MERNEPTAH: Spare me the details. I don't want to hear them. I used to blind myself to what you were really like. But no longer, my dear Hebrew. For her sake, for the sake of my dear sister, and it's only because of her, I will not turn you over to the authorities. And believe me, they are clamoring for your life. However I've put my foot down. Aren't you proud of me, Moses? I'm a man after all. You have until sundown. *(HE rises, starts off then stops.)* Ah, Moses, Moses, what a monster I'm going to be! And aren't you the lucky one? You won't be around to witness the transformation. That beer is sour, by the way.

(MERNEPTAH goes off. THARBIS reenters.)

THARBIS: I'm sure that with time we can turn him around.

MOSES: You really think so?

(NICIAS enters with a backpack)

THARBIS: We've packed some things for you.

(A commotion of voices is heard from the terrace.)

THARBIS: What's that?

(NICIAS sets down the backpack and goes off through the terrace.)

THARBIS: Where will you go?

MOSES: I don't know.

THARBIS: I'll be here, waiting for you.

(NICIAS reenters from the terrace followed by MIRIAM and AARON. AARON rushes to embrace MOSES.)

AARON: We heard...

THARBIS: What?

AARON: About the overseer. The council of the elders have voted overwhelmingly to meet with you.

MOSES: Y-you're a little too late I'm afraid .

AARON: What's happened?

THARBIS: Someone's informed the authorities.

MOSES: A f-fellow Hebrew at that.

THARBIS: We can't be sure.

AARON: But you're royalty. The pharaoh's brother. Won't he protect you?

MOSES: He's given me until sundown.

AARON: What will you do?

MOSES: W-what can I do?

MIRIAM: We can hide you.

MOSES: *(HE shakes his head.)* It's too risky.

AARON: Where will you go?

MOSES: I don't know.

AARON: You will keep in touch.

MOSES: When I get settled.

AARON: And you will come back?

THARBIS: Yes, of course he will.

MIRIAM: If it was one of us we will find him and, whoever he is, you can rest assured he will be taken care of.

MOSES: I'd b-better get started.

> *(MOSES embraces THARBIS then NICIAS. AARON embraces MOSES then MOSES and MIRIAM embrace.)*

NICIAS: I'll come with you to the gate.

> *(MOSES goes off followed by NICIAS.)*

AARON: We'd better be getting back.

MIRIAM: *(To THARBIS)* I have nothing against you personally. It's just that...

THARBIS: I know, I know.

MIRIAM: And you will let us know when you hear from him.

AARON: If you hear from him.

MIRIAM: What do you mean "if"?

AARON: He's a fugitive now. How can we count on him?

MIRIAM: He's still young.

AARON: Exactly.

> *(AARON goes off. MIRIAM embraces THARBIS and follows AARON off. THARBIS sits with a sigh. After a moment NICIAS reenters.)*

THARBIS: Nicias...?

NICIAS: Your highness?

THARBIS: Will he come back, do you think?

NICIAS: If he does it will not be the young man that left here.

> *(The lights slowly fade.)*

LOST IN MIDIAN

A Play In One Act

CAST OF CHARACTERS

MOSES

ZIPPORAH . . . . His wife

JETHRO . . . . His father-in-law

GERSHOM . . . . His older son

ELEAZER . . . . His younger son

SCENE

The home of Moses in Midian

(The home of Moses in Midian. JETHRO and ZIPPORAH are discovered.)

JETHRO: So, what did you want to see me about?

ZIPPORAH: I'm leaving him.

JETHRO: You're leaving him?

ZIPPORAH: Didn't you hear what I said?

JETHRO: I heard you, I heard you.

ZIPPORAH: And you have nothing to say?

JETHRO: Why are you leaving him?

ZIPPORAH: You're going to take his side?

JETHRO: I'm not taking anyone's side.

ZIPPORAH: You don't know what it's like.

JETHRO: So tell me.

ZIPPORAH: You don't think I'm serious, do you?

JETHRO: Has he beaten you? Has he mistreated you?

ZIPPORAH: How can he mistreat me? He doesn't even know that I exist.

JETHRO: He ignores you? I'm trying to understand.

ZIPPORAH: I've lived with this man for how long now? And he doesn't even know who I am. I've borne him two sons and we're like strangers, the two of us.

JETHRO: If you've borne him two sons...

ZIPPORAH: Then what? What does that prove? That we make love? No, we don't make love. We cohabit, like two animals But there's got to be something more. A man and wife should be friends. They should talk to one another. They should confide in one another. They should be partners. I know nothing about this man, absolutely nothing.

JETHRO: What do you want to know?

ZIPPORAH: You think this is a joke? You don't care whom your daughter's married to?

JETHRO: I'm trying to understand.

ZIPPORAH: What do we know about him really? He came here, a perfect stranger. Do we know anything about him really? He came from Egypt. He was dressed like an Egyptian, at any rate. Do we know anything about his family, his friends, what he did in Egypt? If he actually came from there.

JETHRO: He's an intelligent man, a well educated man; and obviously from a good family.

ZIPPORAH: So why doesn't he talk about it?

JETHRO: It's part of the past.

ZIPPORAH: What has that got to do with it?

JETHRO: Maybe he doesn't want to talk about the past?

ZIPPORAH: Why? Why doesn't he want to talk about the past?

JETHRO: Maybe he wants to forget?

ZIPPORAH: Why?

JETHRO: Have you asked him?

ZIPPORAH: Have you? You have these long philosophical discussions. Do you know anything more about him than you did when he first came here?

JETHRO: I don't like to pry.

ZIPPORAH: You're not interested? He's your son-in-law.

JETHRO: I like him. He seems to be a fine man. A little troubled, perhaps...

ZIPPORAH: Aha! What is he troubled about? Why doesn't he want to talk about it? What is he hiding? You know what I think? I think he has another family back in Egypt. That's what I think. You don't think so? Yes or no?

JETHRO: Zipporah, I don't know what to think. If it bothers you why don't you ask him?

ZIPPORAH: You think I haven't tried? I ask him what's bothering him. Nothing. I try to talk about Egypt, about his life there. He changes the subject. I have nothing more to say to him and he has nothing to say to me. I can't live like this anymore.

JETHRO: I'll have a talk with him.

ZIPPORAH: You can do as you please, but after dinner I'm leaving him and I'm coming home with you.

JETHRO: All right, we'll see.

　　　(GERSHOM enters.)

ZIPPORAH: You're home early.

GERSHOM: On the contrary.

ZIPPORAH: I'll start dinner. *(SHE goes off.)*

GERSHOM: Grandfather. *(HE embraces him.)*

JETHRO: Well, stranger, it's good to see you.

GERSHOM: I've been pretty busy.

JETHRO: That's quite all right. I understand.

GERSHOM: No. No, really. I'll come by soon, I promise. I think about you all the time, I really do. When the rainy season starts I'm going to pay you a long visit.

JETHRO: You'll be choosing a wife soon. Have you started to look around?

GERSHOM: I'm not quite sure that I want a wife.

JETHRO: Oh?

GERSHOM: A woman, maybe, but not a wife.

JETHRO: I see. How are you and your brother getting along?

GERSHOM: We get along fine.

JETHRO: No more fighting?

GERSHOM: No more than usual.

JETHRO: Have you been saying the prayers I taught you?

GERSHOM: Occasionally.

JETHRO: You're supposed to say them every morning.

GERSHOM: I know, I know.

JETHRO: And your father? How is he these days?

GERSHOM: All right, I guess.

JETHRO: You guess?

GERSHOM: We don't have that much to say to each other. Grandfather...?

JETHRO: Yes? What is it?

GERSHOM: He doesn't believe in a god, or does he?

JETHRO: Your father? It's difficult to tell what your father believes in.

GERSHOM: I mean as far as the god of Abraham is concerned?

JETHRO: Your father seems to be reluctant to put his faith in anything or anyone, for that matter.

GERSHOM: He objected to having us circumcised.

JETHRO: He thinks it's a barbaric ritual. You've never asked him about it?

GERSHOM: No.

JETHRO: He doesn't discuss these things with you?

GERSHOM: Or anything else, for that matter.

JETHRO: You are on good terms with him?

GERSHOM: Let's just say we share the same space. If Eleazer and I misbehave, which is very rare, of course, Mother's the one that scolds us. But sometimes when we do get out of hand she turns to him for help and that's when we run for our lives.

JETHRO: He beats you?

GERSHOM: He doesn't have to. He just looks at us and that's enough. There's something about him that's really frightening.

JETHRO: Is there? That's a side of him I haven't seen.

GERSHOM: He does have a terrible temper, you know. He doesn't lose it often, but when he does... I don't think I'd like to have him for an enemy.

JETHRO: What about when the three of you are tending the sheep? Doesn't he ever talk to you then?

GERSHOM: Most of the time he's off by himself. Sometimes at dinner, you know, I sit watching him, studying him, trying to imagine what's going on inside of him. Once I woke up in the middle of the night and I could see him out there, sitting in the field, gazing up at the moon. He'll sit like that for hours at a time. I wanted to go up to him and ask him what he's thinking about.

JETHRO: But you never have.

GERSHOM: I did once.

JETHRO: And?

GERSHOM: He turned around and looked at me with those eyes like two burning coals. I got all confused and I forgot what I was going to say. I really worry about him though. Take this afternoon for example.

JETHRO: What happened this afternoon?

GERSHOM: He started talking to this tree?

JETHRO: He was talking to a tree? Are you quite sure?

GERSHOM: He was. I swear it.

JETHRO: Sometimes people think outloud.

GERSHOM: Grandfather, I know what I saw.

JETHRO: And what was he saying to this tree?

GERSHOM: I wasn't close enough to hear.

JETHRO: Then...

GERSHOM: I could see his lips. They were moving. I could see them clearly. You know how sometimes the sun can play all sorts of tricks? Well this acacia tree was caught up in the center of this whirlwind; and the rays of the sun shining through the wind made it look like the tree was on fire. Well, Father was sitting near this tree and I saw him get up. He took off his sandals. He knelt down and he started talking to this tree.

JETHRO: And then what happened?

GERSHOM: I don't know. Just then one of my sheep bolted and I had to run after it. When I got back I saw Father sitting on the ground. He looked like he was in a daze. I ran over to him and Eleazer joined us.

JETHRO: And what did he say, your father?

GERSHOM: Nothing. He just looked up at us and he asked us what was wrong.

JETHRO: You didn't ask him about it?

GERSHOM: I was too embarrassed.

(MOSES enters with ELEAZER. MOSES stammers occasionally. His speech is marked sometimes by involuntary stops and little explosive spurts.)

ELEAZER: Grandfather?!

(JETHRO and ELEAZER embrace.)

MOSES: J-Jethro?! What a pleasant surprise!

(MOSES and JETHRO embrace.)

JETHRO: So near and yet so far.

MOSES: It's been a busy time. *(To ELEAZER)* Go. Wash up. D-dinner will be ready soon.

(ELEAZER and GERSHOM go off.)

MOSES: To what do we owe this honor?

JETHRO: Your wife invited me to dinner.

MOSES: Oh, good.

JETHRO: They grow so quickly.

MOSES: So they do.

JETHRO: Have I come at a bad time?

MOSES: No, no, no. I'm always glad to see you.

JETHRO: Are you?

MOSES: Can I offer you something?

JETHRO: No, no. I'm fine.

MOSES: Zipporah knows you're here?

JETHRO: Yes. Yes, she knows.

MOSES: G-Good, good.

JETHRO: I've missed our little chats.

MOSES: So have I.

JETHRO: But you've been occupied.

MOSES: You might say that.

JETHRO: Preoccupied?

MOSES: What's that?

JETHRO: Sit down, sit down.

MOSES: Yes. Yes, of course.

(THEY sit.)

JETHRO: Moses, look at me.

MOSES: Yes? What is it?

JETHRO: Am I your friend?

MOSES: What a question!

JETHRO: Then if something's troubling you why can't you confide in me? No, let me finish, please. I've welcomed you into my home. I gave you my daughter. To me you're more than a son-in-law. You're more than a friend. You're like a brother. And I had hoped that you felt the same.

MOSES: I do, J-Jethro, I do.

JETHRO: We have these long discussions, these philosophical debates but you've never really opened up your heart to me. If something's bothering you why can't you confide in me?

MOSES: What makes you think...?

JETHRO: Moses, please!

MOSES: The less you know, the better.

JETHRO: Why? Why can't you trust me?

MOSES: You don't understand!

JETHRO: How can I unless you tell me? And your wife and your sons? Your own flesh and blood? Are they to remain in ignorance as well? How can you play games like this with yourself, with those that love you? For good or bad we are family. Are you so cynical that you can't put your faith in anyone?

MOSES: It isn't that?

JETHRO: What is it then?

MOSES: It's something I must work out for myself.

JETHRO: But don't you see? This problem that you have, this thing that you're struggling with...it affects us all.

MOSES: There's nothing anyone can do.

JETHRO: And what makes you so sure of that?

MOSES: *(After a moment)* It's been so peaceful here, so restful. This is where I would like to spend the rest of my days.

JETHRO: Is there any reason why you shouldn't?

MOSES: I k-killed a man. So there you are.

JETHRO: You must have had a good reason. Was it self defense?

MOSES: No.

JETHRO: How did it happen?

MOSES: This Egyptian overseer was beating a Hebrew slave. And I lost control. I have this terrible rage inside of me. I don't know where it comes from. It's not the first time I t-took a human life. I've seen battle as a soldier. But I was fighting for my country then. I was fighting for my life. But this... It was a rash, uncontrollable act and I've never forgiven myself.

JETHRO: You sympathize with the Hebrews.

MOSES: I suppose so. Even before I knew...

JETHRO: Knew what?

MOSES: I was born a Hebrew.

JETHRO: I see.

MOSES: I was raised as an Egyptian, an Egyptian prince, no less. I was adopted by the Princess Thermutis, you see.

JETHRO: You were royalty then.

MOSES: My position at the palace was a rather ambiguous one at best. I wasn't a Hebrew slave, and yet I wasn't truly an Egyptian, much less a prince.

JETHRO: And how did you see yourself?

MOSES: I was born a Hebrew.

JETHRO: And your loyalty lies...?

MOSES: That's the question I've been struggling with for all these years. Everything I am I owe to Egypt. I ate the best food. I wore the best clothes. I had the best teachers. I was brought up in the lap of luxury. And the Hebrews...the Hebrews are strangers to me. A race of slaves. They're treated like slaves, they act like slaves and they think like slaves.

JETHRO: And yet...?

MOSES: And yet these people are my flesh and blood. But their way of life...what they think, what they feel...is completely alien to me.

JETHRO: Moses?

MOSES: Yes? What is it?

JETHRO: What happened this afternoon?

MOSES: Gershom told you?

JETHRO: What little he knew.

MOSES: I had this... I don't know what it was. A visitation, an hallucination. I don't know. This voice. I don't know where it came from but it spoke to me. It said things...things I've been telling myself for years.

JETHRO: And what was that?

MOSES: That I must go back. I must go back to Egypt. The moment that I've always dreaded has finally come.

JETHRO: But why? And why now?

MOSES: You heard about the death of the pharaoh. He was my nemesis, you see. He found out about the murder. He could have forgiven me. He could have pardoned me. We were close at one time, but he was always a little envious. Why, I don't know. But as long as he was alive...

JETHRO: If you're happy here why must you go back?

MOSES: I gave my word.

JETHRO: To whom?

MOSES: To my brother, to my sister, to myself.

JETHRO: You have family back in Egypt then?

MOSES: A brother and a sister, that I know of. And probably some aunts and uncles and cousins as well.

JETHRO: And you think they're all waiting for you to return?

MOSES: I don't even know if they're still alive.

JETHRO: And what will you do if you do go back?

MOSES: The impossible.

JETHRO: And what might that be?

MOSES: Help the Hebrews.

JETHRO: In what way?

MOSES: Free them.

JETHRO: You mean a revolution?

(MOSES shakes his head.)

JETHRO: What then?

MOSES: A revolution would be impossible. The Hebrews are not prepared to fight nor are they equipped to fight. No, they've got to leave Egypt and start fresh in a new land, a land of their own.

JETHRO: And where might that be?

MOSES: Canaan. They believe it's been promised to them by their god, the god of Abraham.

JETHRO: Do you believe that?

MOSES: That's neither here nor there.

JETHRO: You're talking about an exodus?

(MOSES nods.)

JETHRO: And what makes you think they'd be willing to follow you if, as you say, you were raised as an Egyptian?

MOSES: My brother will support me and my sister as well. They do have considerable influence in the Hebrew community. As a matter of fact it was my sister who broached the subject of an exodus.

(ZIPPORAH enters.)

ZIPPORAH: Dinner will be ready soon. *(SHE hesitates then goes off.)*

JETHRO: And Zipporah?

MOSES: Zipporah?

JETHRO: Yes, Zipporah and your sons? What are you plans for them?

MOSES: Zipporah's my wife.

JETHRO: I'm glad you're aware of that.

MOSES: She'll come with me, of course, and the boys as well. You have no objection, have you? What I mean to say is she is still your daughter.

JETHRO: And suppose she refuses to go?

MOSES: Why would she refuse?

JETHRO: I brought up my daughters to think for themselves, to have minds of their own.

MOSES: But why would she refuse? She's my wife. You mean the danger. Yes, of course. I hadn't thought of that. What are you smiling at?

JETHRO: Nothing.

MOSES: What is it then?

JETHRO: Remember once we were discussing the honor system, in regard to government and taxes? And you said, "Yes, but what about human nature?"

MOSES: I don't follow you.

JETHRO: My dear boy, what do all of us crave? Man, woman and child?

MOSES: Love? Is that what you're talking about? She thinks I don't love her? Is that what she told you? That I don't love her? She has her moods, I know that, and I try not to upset her. I go out of my way not to upset her.

JETHRO: She wants to leave you.

MOSES: Leave me? Where does she want to go?

JETHRO: *(HE rises.)* I think you ought to have a talk with her.

MOSES: Yes, of course, I will. I'll talk to her.

JETHRO: Now.

MOSES: This minute? What's the rush? We can wait until after dinner. at least.

JETHRO: If you wait until after dinner, my son, she'll be gone. *(HE goes off.)*

MOSES: Jethro...

> *(MOSES sighs and walks about uneasily. ZIPPORAH enters.)*

ZIPPORAH: You wanted to talk to me? Yes? No?

MOSES: Yes.

ZIPPORAH: I'm listening.

MOSES: What's wrong with you?

ZIPPORAH: What's wrong with me? It's no use. *(SHE starts off.)*

MOSES: Where are you going?

ZIPPORAH: You want your dinner, don't you?

MOSES: The dinner can wait. You have nothing to say to me?

ZIPPORAH: I thought it was you that wanted to talk to me.

MOSES: We've been married for how long now?

ZIPPORAH: You don't know how long we've been married?

MOSES: The point is...

ZIPPORAH: Yes? I'm listening.

MOSES: If you had any complaints why didn't you come to me? Why do you have to drag your father into this? To shame me like this... You had no right.

ZIPPORAH: What is my right?

MOSES: I think I've been a good husband.

ZIPPORAH: What is my right?!

MOSES: What is your right?

ZIPPORAH: Yes. What is my right? What rights do I have?

MOSES: You have the same rights as anyone else. To tell your father that I don't love you!? How can you say that?

ZIPPORAH: What color are my eyes?

MOSES: Your eyes? They're brown.

ZIPPORAH: They're hazel.

MOSES: What difference does that make?

ZIPPORAH: Exactly.

MOSES: Because I don't know the color of your eyes?

ZIPPORAH: If another woman were here in my place would it make any difference? You wouldn't even notice.

MOSES: What do you want me to do?

ZIPPORAH: I don't want you to do anything. I'm leaving you.

MOSES: Where are you going?

ZIPPORAH: I'll move in with my father.

MOSES: You're going to leave your husband and move in with your father? How will it look?

ZIPPORAH: What do I care how it looks?

MOSES: And you think you'll be happier there with your father?

ZIPPORAH: At least I'll be treated with some respect.

MOSES: I don't respect you?

ZIPPORAH: I don't exist as far as you're concerned.

MOSES: What kind of talk is that? You want me to flatter you? Is that it? You want me to tell you how attractive you are? Is that it?

ZIPPORAH: No!

MOSES: What then?

ZIPPORAH: Though it certainly wouldn't hurt.

MOSES: What do you want?

ZIPPORAH: Is it because I'm a woman? You think I'm fragile? You think I'll break? After bearing you two sons?

MOSES: If you have no self respect is that my fault?

ZIPPORAH: I **have** self respect! That's why I'm leaving you.

MOSES: That makes sense.

ZIPPORAH: Do you know what it's like being treated like a servant? "Give me this. Give me that. The soup is cold. This robe needs mending."

MOSES: You have that girl to help you.

ZIPPORAH: What girl? I sent her away a long time ago.

MOSES: Why did you send her away?

ZIPPORAH: What difference does it make?

MOSES: So get someone else to help you.

ZIPPORAH: It's not the work. I don't mind the work.

MOSES: So what are you complaining about?

ZIPPORAH: Look at me.

MOSES: I'm looking.

ZIPPORAH: Because I asked you to. I look at you all the time and I ask myself, "What's going on inside that head of his? What is he thinking?"

MOSES: What difference does it make?

ZIPPORAH: None whatsoever.

> *(SHE turns to go as GERSHOM enters.)*

GERSHOM
I'm hungry.

> *(ZIPPORAH glares at the boy and goes off.)*

MOSES: Your mother's a very strange creature.

GERSHOM: Aren't we all?

MOSES: What is that supposed to mean?

GERSHOM: Nothing.

MOSES: Are you unhappy, too? Do you want to go and live with your grandfather too?

GERSHOM: Is that what she wants to do? Are you going to let her?

MOSES: I'm not her keeper.

GERSHOM: You're actually human. That's the first time I've ever seen you show any emotion. What happened this afternoon? I saw you talking to that tree.

MOSES: I had some sort of...visitation.

GERSHOM: What sort of a visitation?

MOSES: Don't tell your mother.

GERSHOM: Why not?

MOSES: She doesn't have to know.

GERSHOM: Why not?

MOSES: Why do you shake your head?

GERSHOM: Why must everything be kept a secret?

MOSES: Why upset her?

GERSHOM: Don't you think she has a right to know? Why do you have to keep things to yourself all the time?

MOSES: What things?

GERSHOM: Whatever's bothering you.

MOSES: She thinks I don't respect her.

GERSHOM: You don't want to talk about it.

MOSES: What?

GERSHOM: This afternoon. You and that tree.

MOSES: I heard this voice.

GERSHOM: Coming from the tree?

MOSES: It was like I was caught up in this dream. And this voice...It seemed to be coming from all over.

GERSHOM: What did it say?

MOSES: What?

GERSHOM: This voice. What did it say?

MOSES: *(After a moment)* I was born a Hebrew. I never told you that.

GERSHOM: No. No, you didn't.

MOSES: You don't feel ashamed? A race of slaves? The lowest of the low?

GERSHOM: I don't imagine the Hebrews are that much different from anyone else.

MOSES: You think not?

GERSHOM: They worship the god of Abraham just as we do. Mother, that is, and grandfather and Eleazer.

MOSES: Much good it does them. My parents died as slaves, worshipping this god of Abraham. My brother, Aaron, and my sister, Miriam, continue to live as slaves, worshipping this god of Abraham. And you? What about you? You believe in this god of Abraham. too. Don't you?

GERSHOM: I haven't quite decided yet. I suppose you believe in the gods of the Egyptians.

MOSES: No.

GERSHOM: What do you believe in?

MOSES: I believe in myself.

GERSHOM: Maybe that's where God really is, in oneself. This voice you heard? Could it have been your own?

MOSES: As you well know, when you're out in the sun too long anything is possible.

GERSHOM: And what did it say, this voice that you heard? What did it say?

MOSES: It said that my peaceful life here in Midian is over. It said that I must go back to Egypt.

GERSHOM: Why?

MOSES: To lead the Hebrews out of Egypt. To give them back their freedom. To give them back their dignity.

GERSHOM: That's quite an undertaking, to say the least. What makes you think you're capable of leading an entire nation out of Egypt?

MOSES: I led an army into battle. I don't think I'd have any trouble leading a ragtag bunch of slaves?

GERSHOM: You led an army into battle? What kind of an army?

MOSES: An Egyptian army.

GERSHOM: You led an Egyptian army into battle? When was this?

MOSES: I was not much older than you are now.

GERSHOM: And where was this battle?

MOSES: In Abyssinia.

GERSHOM: Really?!

MOSES: It was just a minor skirmish.

GERSHOM: Did you win?

MOSES: Oh, yes.

GERSHOM: Why haven't you ever told us any of this?

MOSES: War isn't something that you brag about.

GERSHOM: But you're a hero.

MOSES: I am not a hero. And war is not that glamorous, believe me.

GERSHOM: Amazing. Absolutely amazing. And what about us? I mean when you go back. What about us?

MOSES: I'm not leaving yet.

GERSHOM: Well what about this visitation of yours?

MOSES: You think this is something pleasant to look forward to? Some sort of romantic adventure? Something you can boast about to your friends?

GERSHOM: Well, yes.

MOSES: Yes, well I don't think your mother would feel that way.

GERSHOM: How do you know how she'd feel?

MOSES: Right now your mother's planning to move in with your grandfather.

GERSHOM: She hasn't as yet, has she? Don't you think you ought to discuss it with her? Or have you?

MOSES: No. Not yet.

GERSHOM: What are you waiting for?

MOSES: Watch your tongue. I'm still your father.

(ELEAZER enters.)

ELEAZER: Dinner's almost ready.

(MOSES goes off.)

ELEAZER: Well?

GERSHOM: Well what?

ELEAZER: Did you find out anything?

GERSHOM: Oh, yes.

ELEAZER: Well?

GERSHOM: He's a Hebrew.

ELEAZER: He's what? How do you know?

GERSHOM: He told me.

ELEAZER: He told you that he was a Hebrew?

GERSHOM: What are you, deaf?

ELEAZER: I thought he was Egyptian.

GERSHOM: I guess he's both.

ELEAZER: That means that we're Hebrews, too, doesn't it?

GERSHOM: Half, at any rate.

ELEAZER: That's what he told you?

GERSHOM: No, I'm making it all up. In addition to that he was a general.

ELEAZER: What kind of a general?

GERSHOM: An army general. What other kind of general is there?

ELEAZER: In the Hebrew army?

GERSHOM: There is no Hebrew army, dummy. The Egyptian army.

ELEAZER: He led an Egyptian army?

GERSHOM: To Abyssinia. And he's thinking of going back.

ELEAZER: To Abyssinia?

GERSHOM: No, idiot! To Egypt.

ELEAZER: When?

GERSHOM: I don't know. He's going to lead the Hebrews out of Egypt.

ELEAZER: Our father's going to lead the Hebrews out of Egypt?!

GERSHOM: I know, I know.

ELEAZER: And where's he going to lead them?

GERSHOM: He didn't say.

ELEAZER: What about us?

GERSHOM: That's a good question since Mother's planning to move in with grandfather.

ELEAZER: Oh? Well, if he's leaving for Egypt...

GERSHOM: I'd like to go with him.

ELEAZER: Did you ask him?

GERSHOM: No. Not yet.

ELEAZER. What about this afternoon?

GERSHOM: You mean about the tree? He had this visitation.

ELEAZER: What sort of a visitation?

GERSHOM: He heard this voice telling him that he had to go back to Egypt to help the Hebrews.

ELEAZER: Are you making this up?

GERSHOM: I know, I know.

ELEAZER: And if he was really a general in the Egyptian army why did he leave Egypt?

GERSHOM: Maybe he deserted.

ELEAZER: Generals don't desert.

GERSHOM: Maybe he was involved in some sort of a plot. An attempted assassination or something and maybe he had to get out of the country. The pharaoh died recently, didn't he? And maybe now it's safe for him to go back.

ELEAZER: He certainly carries himself like a general. But the Hebrews are slaves.

GERSHOM: They weren't always slaves. And they do worship the god of Abraham, don't they?

(ELEAZER nods. ZIPPORAH enters.)

ZIPPORAH: I need some more wood for the fire. Eleazer?

ELEAZER: Why does it always have to be me? Oh, all right, all right. *(HE sighs and goes off.)*

ZIPPORAH: What happened this afternoon?

GERSHOM: Who told you?

ZIPPORAH: Never mind who told me. What happened?

GERSHOM: He had some sort of a visitation.

ZIPPORAH: What sort of a visitation?

GERSHOM: Why don't you ask him?

ZIPPORAH: I'm asking you.

GERSHOM: Did you know that he was a Hebrew?

ZIPPORAH: How long have you known?

GERSHOM: He just told me. Why are you leaving him?

ZIPPORAH: That's between him and me.

GERSHOM: Mother, whatever you do affects everyone of us.

ZIPPORAH: You'll do fine.

GERSHOM: You think you can do better on your own?

ZIPPORAH: I can't talk to you.

GERSHOM: You can't talk to me. You can't talk to your husband. Who can you talk to?

ZIPPORAH: If you were a woman you would understand.

GERSHOM: Men are stupid and women are clever.

ZIPPORAH: Don't twist my words around. And why do you always take his side?

GERSHOM: What side? I didn't even know there was a side. He's going back to Egypt, you know. I'd like to go with him.

ZIPPORAH: So go! Who's stopping you?

GERSHOM: If he'll have me, that is.

ZIPPORAH: Did you ask him?

GERSHOM: No. Not yet. Wouldn't you like to go with him? I said...
Mother, are you listening to me?

(*MOSES enters. GERSHOM looks from MOSES to
ZIPPORAH and goes off.*)

ZIPPORAH: Why didn't you tell me?

MOSES: What?

ZIPPORAH: That you're a Hebrew, for one thing. After all these
years... I'm your wife!

MOSES: It's not something I care to discuss.

ZIPPORAH: Are you ashamed?

MOSES: You think that's something to be proud of? That I was the son
of slaves? That my entire life was a lie. I've never forgiven her.

ZIPPORAH: Who?

MOSES: My mother, the princess, the one who adopted me. She led me
to believe that I was an Egyptian, that I was really the son of one of her
maidservants. She concocted this whole story, this fairy tale about a
father that died in battle, leaving behind an unmarried pregnant lover.

ZIPPORAH: Maybe she was trying to protect you.

MOSES: All I know is I don't belong anywhere.

ZIPPORAH: After all these years? After all we've been through
together?

MOSES: I'm a stranger here as well.

ZIPPORAH: Whose fault is that?

MOSES: I'm not blaming anyone.

ZIPPORAH: Jethro loves you like a son.

MOSES: I know, I know. When I came here, I was your savior, your hero. And that's what I wanted to be. I wanted to be what all of you imagined me to be. When I rescued you and your sisters from those bullies at the well, when I was welcomed into your father's house it was as if I was given a new identity. And yet I knew that one day I would have to go back, that my destiny lay back there in Egypt. And now, now that the day has come... I'm not so sure.

ZIPPORAH: Then why go?

MOSES: Because that's what's expected of me.

ZIPPORAH: By whom?

MOSES: By everyone. My Hebrew brother, my Hebrew sister, even the princess, my Egyptian mother. I think that's what she really wanted for me. The life of the Hebrews is an unbearable one and, apparently, she sympathized with them. I see now that she felt that I was the one to help them. That that was to be my mission in life.

ZIPPORAH: Gershom is all excited. He wants to go with you.

MOSES: And you? How would you feel?

ZIPPORAH: About what?

MOSES: About coming to Egypt with me...if I should decide to go, that is?

ZIPPORAH: And if I didn't come with you, would it make any difference?

MOSES: Maybe I'm not as attentive as I should have been, but you're my wife...

ZIPPORAH: And what?

MOSES: What do you mean, and what? We're a family, aren't we? You're a part of my life.

ZIPPORAH: And?

MOSES: And I respect you.

ZIPPORAH: I see.

MOSES: What are you smiling at?

ZIPPORAH: Nothing.

MOSES: I must have said something.

ZIPPORAH: I'm not unintelligent, you know. I do have a mind of my own.

MOSES: I know that.

ZIPPORAH: But...

MOSES: But what?

ZIPPORAH: Nothing. So you were really an Egyptian prince?

MOSES: I had no real authority. Except, perhaps, as far as the army was concerned. I was made a general and I actually did conduct a campaign in Abyssinia.

ZIPPORAH: I see.

MOSES: Oh, yes. I cut quite a figure. I won the war and the hand of the Abyssinian princess.

ZIPPORAH: What princess? Moses?

MOSES: Yes?

ZIPPORAH: What princess?

MOSES: I married this Abyssinian princess.

ZIPPORAH: That's an interesting bit of news. And where is she now, this Abyssinian princess of yours?

MOSES: In Egypt, as far as I know

ZIPPORAH: And you saw no need to tell me this? You saw no need to tell me that you had another wife?

MOSES: It had nothing to do with you.

ZIPPORAH: You saw no need to tell me that some day I must share you with another woman?

MOSES: I never knew when and if that day would ever come. Besides I'm telling you now.

ZIPPORAH: You're not telling me anything. It just happened to slip out, by accident.

MOSES: I don't even know where she is right now. I don't even know if she's still alive.

ZIPPORAH: But you're going back to Egypt where you left her.

MOSES: I just told you...

ZIPPORAH: You must have had some feelings for her.

MOSES: Well, yes, of course.

ZIPPORAH: And she for you.

MOSES: Well, yes.

ZIPPORAH: Then why did you leave her behind?

MOSES: She was a princess. She had obligations.

ZIPPORAH: Such as?

MOSES: She represented her country at the Egyptian court.

ZIPPORAH: And that was more important than her marriage vows?

MOSES: Marriage is not the be-all and the end-all.

ZIPPORAH: Not for you, apparently, and your Abyssinian princess. And yet you're anxious to get back to her. You can't wait till you see her again.

MOSES: I'm not anxious to see her again. You make it sound more important than it is.

ZIPPORAH: You're not planning to get in touch with her?

MOSES: Well, of course, I'd get in touch with her, if she's still alive that is and if she's still in Egypt, and if I do decide to go back. She is my wife.

ZIPPORAH: And what about me?

> *(ELEAZER enters with an armful of wood. HE looks from one to the other then goes off.)*

MOSES: Look, my feeling for her has nothing to do with my feeling for you.

ZIPPORAH: Whatever that may be.

MOSES: This is ridiculous. If you don't want to come back with me, don't come. Go to your father! I don't care what you do. All this fuss and bother! All this pettiness! As if I didn't have enough on my mind...

> *(MOSES stalks off as JETHRO reenters.)*

JETHRO: I did come here for dinner, you know. At least, that's what you said when you invited me. *(HE looks towards the house.)* What happened?

ZIPPORAH: Did you know that he had another wife?

JETHRO: That doesn't surprise me.

ZIPPORAH: He told you? And you never even mentioned it?

JETHRO: Don't get excited. He never told me.

ZIPPORAH: Then how did you know?

JETHRO: There's something about a married man.

ZIPPORAH: And you think it was right for him to deceive me like that?

JETHRO: Perhaps he thought it wasn't very important.

ZIPPORAH: And what's important to him?

JETHRO: I think we know now.

ZIPPORAH: Oh yes, the Hebrews. The fact that he has a family here in Midian, I guess that's not important. *(After a moment)* It's ironic, you know. I thought that I was the lucky one. All the girls were so envious. This noble Egyptian, this shy giant was mine, all mine. Even his speech impediment was part of his charm. And I thought, at first, that maybe that was the reason for this wall that existed between us. He was embarrassed by this handicap. But no, I came to see that that was his nature. He was this walking statue, this enigma that no one must fathom. And then I thought that maybe when the children came he might change, that he might become human. And, for a while he actually did. At least when they were young. He would actually sit down and join in their childish games. Once I even heard him laugh. But then when they started to grow, when they started to think for themselves, when they began to have an identity of their own...

JETHRO: Maybe the blame lies with us as well. Maybe we didn't really want to know. Maybe we wanted to preserve that image we had of him. And maybe now that we do know...

ZIPPORAH: What? You think he can change? Is that what you think?

JETHRO: I don't know. He needs you now, now more than ever, I do know that. What he's hoping to do, what he would like to do would change the course of history. One man, burdened with a speech impediment, is planning to challenge the greatest power on earth.

ZIPPORAH: But why?

JETHRO: Perhaps he's convinced himself that he's some sort of a messiah.

ZIPPORAH: Then perhaps we ought to discourage him.

JETHRO: No. It's something he must decide for himself. As a matter of fact that may have been the reason he kept this all to himself. Insecure as he is, maybe he was afraid that he could easily be talked out of it.

ZIPPORAH: Then...

JETHRO: If he's to follow through it must be now, and whatever he decides we must give him our support.

(MOSES reenters.)

MOSES: Would dinner be an imposition?

(ZIPPORAH hesitates and goes off.)

MOSES: I cannot put up with all this pettiness. She's upset because I have another wife. Men have three, four wives. I haven't seen the woman in over twenty years.

JETHRO: I know, I know.

MOSES: If she had asked me I would have told her. The fact of the matter is I don't even know if this woman is alive or not.

JETHRO: That's a woman for you. And if you should decide to leave you wouldn't want to drag her along, I'm sure.

MOSES: Well...

JETHRO: Would you?

MOSES: The fact of the matter is...I'm not easy to live with. I know that, and I've been giving the matter a great deal of thought. This mission is ridiculous. I can't even speak properly. And returning to Egypt, to all that intrigue. I was so glad to get away from it. And the Hebrews themselves, are they any different really? Ignorant and bigoted, with a slave mentality. They cling to this one god of theirs as if he or she or it is their salvation.

JETHRO: Quite right.

MOSES: Because putting one's faith in a god, no matter which god it is, is not enough.

JETHRO: And why subject yourself to something that you really have no heart for?

MOSES: Exactly.

JETHRO: So it's settled then.

(*ZIPPORAH reenters.*)

ZIPPORAH: Dinner's ready.

JETHRO: It's about time. I am starved. (*HE nods to Zipporah, meaning for her to stay and settle things once and for all, and HE goes off.*)

ZIPPORAH: When are you leaving? I said...

MOSES: I heard you.

ZIPPORAH: So?

MOSES: I don't know.

ZIPPORAH: You've changed your mind?

MOSES: I never made it up, so how can I change it?

ZIPPORAH: So what's all the fuss about?

MOSES: You're the one that's making the fuss, not me. After all these years you're ready to walk out on me. I thought that I was your storybook hero, the dashing stranger who came from nowhere to rescue you, the man of your dreams.

ZIPPORAH: That's not who I fell in love with.

MOSES: I see. And who was it that you fell in love with?

ZIPPORAH: I fell in love with a vulnerable, sensitive man who was in need of love, in need of nurturing.

MOSES: I see.

ZIPPORAH: Are you ashamed of that?

MOSES: What? That you fell in love with me because you thought I was weak?

ZIPPORAH: Even my father sometimes asks for my advice and I think you respect my father.

MOSES: It's not that I don't want to confide in you.

ZIPPORAH: You want to spare me.

MOSES: You don't believe that, do you?

ZIPPORAH: I believe that you believe it.

MOSES: And what's the real reason, may I ask?

ZIPPORAH: Pride, perhaps?

MOSES: Pride!?

ZIPPORAH: Vanity? A man cannot reveal any weakness. He must be superhuman.

MOSES: You really think I'm that vain? You really think that I'm that foolish?

ZIPPORAH: Or did you think that we would despise you because of your Hebrew lineage?

MOSES: I just didn't see the need...

ZIPPORAH: Then you don't need a wife. You may need a woman, but you don't need a wife.

MOSES: Why must you know everything? Tell me that.

ZIPPORAH: Because that's what a marriage is. I want to be your friend. I want to be treated as an equal. Is that so difficult to understand? You might even enjoy sharing things. It might even make your life more pleasant. Did that ever occur to you?

(GERSHOM enters.)

GERSHOM: The food is getting cold

ZIPPORAH: Let it.

GERSHOM: I'm hungry and so is Eleazer.

ZIPPORAH: Then eat.

GERSHOM: All right, I will. *(HE goes off.)*

MOSES: Do you want to know how confused I am? How weak? How mistrustful I am of everyone and every thing, myself above all? My mother, the princess, adored me. She led me to believe that I was godlike, and then to find out that I was the son of slaves. That I had a sister and brother who were slaves.

ZIPPORAH: Was that so terrible?

MOSES: It was to me. My whole life has been a sham. In Egypt, I was popular. I went out of my way to be popular, to be well liked, but I never really knew if people accepted me for myself or because of my position, and even that was ill defined, to say the least. The only really happy times were the hours I spent with my troops. We were dependent on one another for our very lives, and there was this sense of brotherhood, this sense of trust.

ZIPPORAH: And your marriage, to this Abyssinian princess?

MOSES: Tharbis was a remarkable woman. Yes, it was a good marriage except, of course, that it created a problem.

ZIPPORAH: Oh?

MOSES: My sister, Miriam, refused to accept her. She felt I should have married a Hebrew or, at least, a woman who worshipped the god of the Hebrews. She wanted me to get rid of her.

ZIPPORAH: And did you?

MOSES: No.

ZIPPORAH: You've never really accepted the god of the Hebrews, have you?

MOSES: I haven't really rejected him...or her...or it.

ZIPPORAH: But how can you expect these people to accept you as their leader? You have nothing in common with them. You don't believe as they do. You don't observe their customs, their rituals. Your own sons aren't even circumcised?

MOSES: I will not subject my sons to that...primitive...

ZIPPORAH: All right, all right. But you yourself...

MOSES: I had nothing to say about it. I'm sure that you and Miriam would get on very well together. She'd welcome you with open arms.

ZIPPORAH: But if, as you say, she has a great deal of influence.

MOSES: So has my brother and he happens to be the spokesman for the Hebrew community. And besides...

ZIPPORAH: What?

MOSES: This is pointless, this entire discussion. How can I face them all, the Hebrews and the Egyptians with this crippled tongue of mine? I can't even speak properly.

ZIPPORAH: But if, as you say, your brother is their spokesman...?

MOSES: Then what?

ZIPPORAH: And if the two of you see eye to eye, he can be your spokesman as well.

   (JETHRO enters.)

JETHRO: You invite me to dinner and then you desert me.

ZIPPORAH: I'm sorry. You must be hungry.

JETHRO: Not anymore.

ZIPPORAH: You've eaten?

JETHRO: As much as I care to. I must be getting back. I really hadn't expected to stay this late. Are you ready?

ZIPPORAH: For what?

JETHRO: I thought you were coming back with me.

ZIPPORAH: I've changed my mind.

JETHRO: Yes, well, I suppose that is a woman's prerogative.

ZIPPORAH: As a matter of fact we'll be leaving for Egypt shortly.

JETHRO: I see. When is this?

ZIPPORAH: As soon as we get packed. *(SHE turns to Moses.)* Isn't that so?

MOSES: Yes. As soon as we get packed.

JETHRO: I see.

   (GERSHOM and ELEAZER enter.)

JETHRO: This is good-bye then.

GERSHOM: You're leaving, grandfather?

JETHRO: And so are you, apparently.

GERSHOM: Oh?

ZIPPORAH: We're leaving for Egypt.

GERSHOM: When?

MOSES: As soon as we get packed.

ELEAZER: We are?

GERSHOM: *(To MOSES)* Are we really?

MOSES: You heard your mother.

ELEAZER: All of us?

ZIPPORAH: All of us.

JETHRO: I won't be seeing you for a while then.

MOSES: I'll be in touch. I will need your advice. I will need your help. I will need all the help I can get.

JETHRO: If I can be of any use....

MOSES: You can, my friend, and you will be.

> *(MOSES and JETHRO embrace. JETHRO then embraces GERSHOM and ELEAZER then ZIPPORAH.)*

JETHRO: Take good care of him.

ZIPPORAH: I'll do my best.

> *(JETHRO embraces MOSES once more and goes off.)*

ZIPPORAH: I'll need your help with the packing, the both of you.

ELEAZER: Tonight?

ZIPPORAH: Tonight.

ELEAZER: May we finish our dinner first?

ZIPPORAH: Who's stopping you? *(To MOSES)* You must be hungry.

MOSES: I'm starved.

ELEAZER: Let's eat.

> *(MOSES places his arm around ELEAZER'S shoulder and THEY go off.)*

GERSHOM: So, you've made it up with him.

ZIPPORAH: Let's just say that he's on trial.

GERSHOM: Do you really think that he can do all that he proposes to do? That he can defy all of Egypt?

ZIPPORAH: That remains to be seen, does it not?

GERSHOM: And even if he does manage to get the Hebrews out of Egypt, what then?

ZIPPORAH: I know, I know.

GERSHOM: He may have commanded an army but he won't be dealing with soldiers, well trained men who are used to taking orders. These are civilians, ordinary people, people that have been slaves all their lives, and not only men but women and children as well.

ZIPPORAH: I know, I know.

GERSHOM: We'll be back here in Midian inside of a month.

ZIPPORAH: Don't be so sure.

GERSHOM: He'll be up against the entire Egyptian empire with an army of millions. Isn't he afraid? Aren't you afraid?

ZIPPORAH: Yes, my dear, I am, but not for your father.

GERSHOM: Who then?

ZIPPORAH: The Egyptians. Come, let's eat.

> *(ZIPPORAH and GERSHOM go off as the lights come down.)*

KING OF THE ISRAELITES

CAST OF CHARACTERS

SAUL . . . . The King

JONATHAN . . . . Saul's eldest son

ABNER . . . . A general, Saul's cousin

DAVID . . . . A shepherd

MICHAL . . . . Saul's younger daughter

SAMUEL . . . . The high priest

ABISHAI . . . . A follower of David

A WOMAN

(If so desired the actor playing MICHAL can double as the WOMAN.)

SCENE

Various parts of the kingdom of Israel

ACT ONE

Scene One

(The Israelite camp near Aijalon. Military drums are heard in the distance. JONATHAN, Saul's oldest son, enters followed by ABNER, Saul's cousin and general.)

ABNER: All right, all right. Now just calm down.

JONATHAN: I'm perfectly calm.

ABNER: You're going to have to apologize.

JONATHAN: Apologize?! For what?

ABNER: Now listen to me, son. You are in a lot of trouble.

JONATHAN: I'm listening.

ABNER: *(After a moment, a twinkle in his eye)* Why don't you spend more time with your wife? Give him another grandson.

JONATHAN: You think this is a joke? He really wants to have me executed.

ABNER: I'm just trying to figure you out.

JONATHAN: Figure me out? How about trying to figure out the king? One minute he's playing high priest, issuing these holy mandates. The next he's sitting in his tent, plunged into gloom.

ABNER: Let's not exaggerate.

143

JONATHAN: No wonder the men are insecure. They don't know what to expect from one minute to the next.

ABNER: You want him to abdicate? Is that it? You want him to turn the kingdom over to you?

JONATHAN: No.

ABNER: But if they should happen to come to you and offer you the crown...

JONATHAN: Abner, I swear to you, I've never even thought about it.

ABNER: What do you think about? What goes on in that head of yours?

JONATHAN: I want to serve him. I want to serve our country the best I can.

ABNER: All right, now look. It was a foolish oath. I'm the first to admit it. He made a mistake.

JONATHAN: Asking the men to fast before going into battle.

ABNER: It was thoughtless.

JONATHAN: No man can fight on an empty stomach. Any idiot with an ounce of common sense...

ABNER: I said it was a mistake.

JONATHAN: Then why didn't you stop him?

ABNER: He never consulted me.

JONATHAN: He never consults anyone.

ABNER: Unfortunately it was a holy oath.

JONATHAN: I swear to you, Abner. My world of honor, I wasn't aware of the oath when I ate that honey.

ABNER: And afterwards?

JONATHAN: All right. Maybe that was wrong. Maybe I shouldn't have encouraged the men to eat. But, like you yourself said, sending a man into battle on an empty stomach was foolish, to say the least.

ABNER: Nevertheless you don't countermand an order given by your commander in chief.

JONATHAN: The man is completely irrational.

ABNER: The man happens to be your king, and your father.

JONATHAN: And I love him dearly.

ABNER: He was chosen by Samuel and he has the Lord's blessing.

> *(SAUL enters. SAUL and JONATHAN stand facing one another.)*

ABNER: *(To JONATHAN)* Go to your tent. I said...

> *(JONATHAN hesitates then strides off.)*

SAUL: Well?

ABNER: You paint yourself into a corner and then you turn to me.

SAUL: He keeps running off on his own. He never listens to me.

ABNER: It was a scouting expedition.

SAUL: And he ends up killing twenty Philistines? He ends up this big hero. What kind of a fool do you take me for?

ABNER: Fine. The boy's a threat. He must die.

SAUL: That is not the issue and you know it.

ABNER: What is?

SAUL: That so-called scouting expedition is just an example of what I have to put up with. He disobeyed a holy edict!

ABNER: Oh come on, Saul, talk sense.

SAUL: What?

ABNER: The Lord does not expect men to fight on an empty stomach.

SAUL: I took an oath. The men took an oath. And he defiled that oath.

ABNER: It's all settled then. Chop off his head.

SAUL: *(HE sits with a sigh.)* Abraham was faced with the same dilemma, you know.

ABNER: What are you talking about?

SAUL: He had to choose between his god and his son.

ABNER: Saul, listen to me. You are the king. You're commander in chief. Can't we just leave it at that?

SAUL: What is that supposed to mean?

ABNER: You cannot be high priest as well.

SAUL: All I'm trying to do is to serve the Lord the best that I can. What's wrong with that?

ABNER: Well, you try too hard.

SAUL: I can't go back on my word. How would it look?

ABNER: All right. All right. When you face his mother and she asks you "Why did you kill our son?" you just tell her, "I couldn't go back on my word?"

SAUL: I must maintain some sort of discipline. How can I keep the men's respect?

ABNER: Executing Jonathan, I can assure you, will not gain you the men's respect, if that's what you're really concerned about. Like you yourself said, he's a great hero now and you might well may have a rebellion on your hands. Oh look, you do what your conscience tells you to do. Leave me out of this.

SAUL: All right, all right. Send him in.

>*(ABNER sighs, shakes his head and goes off. SAUL paces nervously. JONATHAN reenters.)*

SAUL: You can't wait until I'm dead, can you?

JONATHAN: How is one to tell?

>*(SAUL starts off.)*

JONATHAN: No, no! Please! I'm sorry. Look, Father, I wasn't aware of that edict. I swear to you.

SAUL: And afterwards?

JONATHAN: All right, I was wrong. I'm sorry. What do you want me to do?

SAUL: I want you to behave. That's what I want you to do.

JONATHAN: I've just told you...

SAUL: You encouraged the men to eat against my orders!

JONATHAN: The men were hungry.

SAUL: It was my decision to make, not yours. Not only did the men break their oath, they ate meat with blood on it, and now what am I to do? Tell me that.

JONATHAN: The sin is mine, not yours.

SAUL: I'm trying to maintain some sort of authority. I'm trying to establish some sort of precedence. Do you know what it's like to be a king? Do you know what it's like to be the first? No one understands. No one. If you're a blacksmith, if you're a carpenter you serve an apprenticeship. A musician learns to play an instrument; he has instructions. How do you learn to be a king? Tell me that. I have no one, no one to turn to, no one teach me, no one to support me.

JONATHAN: You have Abner.

SAUL: Yes, I have Abner!

JONATHAN: What's wrong with Abner?

SAUL: I have never trusted Abner.

JONATHAN: What are you talking about? You grew up together. You're like brothers. How can you say that?

SAUL: He's always been envious of me.

JONATHAN: Envious of you? Why?

SAUL: I'm better looking, for one thing. You think that's funny, do you? Well, it just happens to be true. I'm taller than he is and stronger. In addition to that he's always had his eye on the throne.

JONATHAN: What nonsense!

SAUL: It isn't nonsense. And then there's Samuel, watching over me, waiting for me to make a fool of myself.

JONATHAN: Samuel anointed you.

SAUL: Why? Why do you think he anointed me?

JONATHAN: All right. Why?

SAUL: I'm his revenge.

JONATHAN: Revenge? For what?

SAUL: The people rejected him and they rejected his sons and he chose me because he thought that I would fail. Samuel's a bitter man, and he's just sitting there waiting, waiting for me to fall on my face.

JONATHAN: Samuel is old and senile.

SAUL: He may be old, but he's far from senile, and he is still our spiritual leader. He still speaks for the Lord.

JONATHAN: Well, you're not going to fail.

SAUL: I didn't say I was going to fail. I said he's waiting for me to fail.

JONATHAN: Well you're not going to fail.

SAUL: Not if I have your support. You're the only one, the only one I can turn to. With you by my side I can be the king the people want me to be, but I need your help. All right, all right. You made a mistake but, from here on in, come to me first. Whatever you have to say I will listen and I will try to understand. Promise me. Promise me this will never happen again.

JONATHAN: I promise.

SAUL: And you will never run off on your own. No more scouting expeditions. Give me your word.

JONATHAN: I just said so, didn't I?

SAUL: All right, all right. You'll do some sort of penance. I'll think of something. *(HE kisses him on both cheeks.)* You're a good boy, Jonathan, a good boy. And you're going to give me another grandson, aren't you? That lame little boy of yours just won't do. Now go to your tent.

JONATHAN: Yes, Father.

> *(JONATHAN heaves a sigh and goes off. After a moment ABNER reenters.)*

ABNER: So?

SAUL: What's that?

ABNER: When does the execution take place?

SAUL: He promised to behave.

ABNER: He's a good boy, Saul, and you have every reason to be proud of him.

SAUL: We keep calling him a boy, but he's not, is he? He's a grown man with a boy of his own, and a mind of his own. That's the trouble with children. They grow up.

ABNER: He's young and full of energy.

SAUL: And ambition.

ABNER: I wish my sons were that devoted.

SAUL: You think he's devoted, do you?

ABNER: Poor Saul! Everyone's against him.

SAUL: Who can I trust? Tell me that.

ABNER: No one.

SAUL: You can tell the men that I've pardoned the boy and that he's going to do penance.

ABNER: Your word is my command.

> *(ABNER salutes him and strides off. After a moment cheers are heard. SAUL stands listening, perplexed and concerned, as the lights come down.)*

Scene Two

(The house of Saul at Gibeah. DAVID, a young shepherd, enters with MICHAL, Saul's younger daughter.)

MICHAL: Did you really kill a lion with your bare hands?

DAVID: Guilty as charged.

MICHAL: That must have taken a great deal of courage.

DAVID: It was a foolish thing to do.

MICHAL: Then why did you do it?

DAVID: Because I was foolish.

MICHAL: You must have had a reason.

DAVID: He was attacking my father's sheep. If I'd had any sense I would have used my slingshot.

MICHAL: Well, I think you were very brave.

DAVID: Bravery is a form of madness.

MICHAL: Abner thinks you're arrogant.

DAVID: Why?

MICHAL: I don't know. Maybe it's the way you carry yourself.

DAVID: How do I carry myself?

MICHAL: Like a prince...or a king.

DAVID: Because I stand up straight and look people in the eye?

MICHAL: Well, you are just a shepherd boy.

DAVID: So was your father, before he became king. Do you think I'm arrogant?

MICHAL: I haven't made up my mind.

DAVID: Let me know when you do.

MICHAL Would it make any difference?

DAVID: Has your father always been subject to these moods of his?

MICHAL: As far as I can remember. You must have magic in those fingers of yours. No one's been able to help him, until now. What's your secret?

DAVID: I don't have any secret. He just seems to like my music.

MICHAL: Do you believe in witches?

DAVID: I never thought about it. Why do you ask?

MICHAL: That's who my father blames for his illness.

DAVID: Is that why he had them banished?

MICHAL: Do you?

DAVID: What?

MICHAL: Believe in witches?

DAVID: Don't worry. I won't give you away

MICHAL: *(SHE giggles.)* You think I'm a witch?

DAVID: Well, you do have cat's eyes. And sometimes witches turn themselves into cats, or vice versa.

MICHAL: You're making fun of me.

DAVID: Now why would I do a thing like that?

MICHAL: Do you believe in destiny?

DAVID: I don't know what you mean by destiny.

MICHAL: I mean that our whole life is laid out before hand? That we have nothing to say about it?

DAVID: I certainly hope not.

(ABNER enters.)

ABNER: Where's your harp?

DAVID: It's in my room.

ABNER: Go fetch it.

DAVID: Yes, sir. *(HE goes off.)*

ABNER: You seem to be very fond of our young harp player.

MICHAL: I think I'm going to marry him.

ABNER: Does he know that? What's more to the point, does your father?

MICHAL: I'm worried about him, Uncle Abner. He's gotten worse ever since that run in with Samuel. What happened between him and Saul? Do you know?

ABNER: No.

MICHAL: You don't know or you won't say?

ABNER: I wasn't there.

MICHAL: I thought you were in his confidence.

ABNER: No one's in your father's confidence, not even your father

> (DAVID reenters with his harp.)

DAVID: I'm ready.

ABNER: So I see.

MICHAL: Good luck! (SHE hesitates, kisses DAVID quickly on the cheek and runs off.)

DAVID: Shall we go? (HE starts off then stops.) What's the matter?

ABNER: What's that?

DAVID: You were staring at me.

ABNER: I was under the impression that you liked to be stared at.

DAVID: You don't like me, do you?

ABNER: Don't flatter yourself.

DAVID: Have I done something to offend you?

ABNER: No, my boy, you're much too clever for that.

DAVID: I'm not a thief, you know. I'm not going to steal anything?

ABNER: Nothing small, perhaps. Come along.

> (ABNER starts off. DAVID follows him off as the lights
> come down.)

Scene Three

(The Valley of Elah between Palestine and Philistia. Saul's tent. A taunting voice is heard in the distance. "Is there no man among you? Come out and fight, you cowards." SAUL and JONATHAN enter.)

JONATHAN: It's humiliating. An entire army cowed by this one man!

SAUL: It's not a man. It's a monster.

JONATHAN: Let me go.

SAUL: No!

JONATHAN: It's expected of me.

SAUL: And suppose you're killed?

JONATHAN: Then I'll die a hero. He's weighed down with all that armor. I'm light on my feet. He won't touch me.

SAUL: And once he does?

JONATHAN: He won't.

SAUL: I said no.

VOICE: Lily-livered cowards! All of you.

(ABNER enters.)

SAUL: What's he doing now?

ABNER: Parading up and down and waving his sword. He makes us look like fools.

JONATHAN: Why don't we just move in on them?

ABNER: I'd like nothing better.

JONATHAN: Then why don't we?

ABNER: Because the men won't budge.

JONATHAN: If you ordered them to?

ABNER: I don't want to risk it.

JONATHAN: Why not?

ABNER: Because they might just refuse to obey, that's why. And I can't blame them. Why should they risk their lives if one man can settle this so-called battle?

JONATHAN: And you really think they'll throw down their arms if this Goliath is defeated.

ABNER: It's not what I think. It's what the men think that matters.

JONATHAN: It's getting close to harvest time. How much longer can we wait?

ABNER: *(HE sighs.)* I know, I know.

    (Raised voices are heard outside the tent.)

SAUL: What's going on out there?

VOICE: Where are your soldiers, Israelites? Where are your men?

    (ABNER goes off and reenters a moment later with DAVID.)

ABNER: We have a visitor

SAUL: David?! What are you doing here? I thought you were needed at home.

DAVID: I was. I am. I just came here to bring my brothers some food.

SAUL: You came at a bad time, my boy.

DAVID: Your majesty...?

SAUL: Yes? What is it?

DAVID: I'd like to volunteer.

SAUL: For what?

ABNER: To give us a song.

DAVID: I want to fight the monster.

ABNER: Now there's a brilliant thought. Let's put the fate of our nation into the hands of this little harp player.

SAUL: He'd make mincemeat of you, son.

DAVID: Not if I wound him and still stay out of his reach.

ABNER: And how are you going to manage that?

DAVID: With my slingshot.

ABNER: He's covered with armor.

DAVID: Not his forehead and I've never missed yet. And once he's on the ground he'd be so weighed down with armor he'd be helpless.

ABNER: *(To JONATHAN)* What are you laughing at?

JONATHAN: Why didn't someone think of that before?

ABNER: Actually it's not a bad idea. And just think, a legendary Philistine felled by a Hebrew child. I beg your pardon, our young harp playing warrior.

SAUL: I don't know.

ABNER: Actually we have nothing to lose.

JONATHAN: And actually we don't have much of a choice, do we? We're not exactly flooded with volunteers.

ABNER: And the men are getting restless.

SAUL: All right. All right, but you've got to wear some armor.

DAVID: I don't have any armor.

SAUL: You can wear mine.

DAVID: It would only weigh me down.

ABNER: He's right.

DAVID: I'll need some stones. Some nice sharp stones. *(HE runs off.)*

VOICE: I'm waiting for you. Can't you see? I'm trembling in my boots.

SAUL: So, you've changed your mind about the boy.

ABNER: Not really, no.

JONATHAN: What have you got against him?

ABNER: I just don't trust him.

JONATHAN: He's young.

ABNER: No, it's more than that. There's something about him that makes me very uneasy. *(To SAUL)* And it was a great mistake to offer your daughter as an incentive to fight that monster.

JONATHAN: Why? You think he fancies Merab?

ABNER: I don't know about that. But I do know Michal is smitten.

SAUL: Well, you're the one that convinced me to send him out there.

ABNER: I know, I know.

SAUL: I'm going to make the announcement.

ABNER: Go ahead.

   (SAUL goes off.)

ABNER: You're not concerned about him apparently.

JONATHAN: Who? David? Why should I be?

ABNER: He's got you fooled too.

JONATHAN: What are you talking about?

ABNER: He's got his eye on the throne.

JONATHAN: What nonsense!

ABNER: It isn't nonsense. I've seen that look in his eye. It's as if he were practicing to balance the crown on those wavy locks of his. He's a clever, ambitious boy.

JONATHAN: *(HE laughs.)* Thank you, Abner.

ABNER: For what?

JONATHAN: For caring.

ABNER: Everything seems to amuse you these days.

JONATHAN: Apparently you haven't heard.

ABNER: Heard what?

JONATHAN: I will not be succeeding my father.

ABNER: What are you talking about?

JONATHAN: I'm talking about that little run in with Samuel. I'm talking about the bargain my father struck with him.

ABNER: What bargain? I know nothing about a bargain.

(Cheers are heard in the distance.)

JONATHAN: Listen to them cheer. The word's gotten out. There's a new hero waiting in the wings.

ABNER: Jonathan, what happened at Gilgal? Do you know?

JONATHAN: Oh, yes, I know.

ABNER: Well?

JONATHAN: Samuel was due to make a burnt offering and give his blessing to the troops. He was delayed. Saul got tired of waiting and took it upon himself to make the burnt offering. In addition to that we were not supposed to take any trophies and no one was to be spared. It was a holy battle, you see. Well, Saul let the men take the best of the cattle. In addition to that, against explicit instructions from Samuel, he decided to spare the king as well.

ABNER: And?

JONATHAN: Samuel was beside himself. He insisted that Saul abdicate. My father pleaded with him. Got down on his hands and knees. He wept and he begged.

ABNER: Not in front of the troops?

JONATHAN: No, no, no. This all took place in private.

ABNER: Then...?

JONATHAN: I have it on good authority.

ABNER: And what was the outcome?

JONATHAN: Saul will be allowed to finish out his reign, but none of his sons will succeed him.

ABNER: I see.

(Loud cheers and shouting is heard.)

JONATHAN: The show's about to begin.

ABNER: I'll have a talk with your father.

JONATHAN: I'm afraid, dear uncle, there's nothing much to talk about. It's out of his hands.

ABNER: With Samuel then.

JONATHAN: *(HE smiles and pats ABNER on the shoulder.)* It's pointless, but thank you, Abner.

(A loud shout is heard.)

JONATHAN: We'd better get out there. We're missing all the fun.

(JONATHAN goes off. The cheering grows louder. ABNER stands thoughtfully as the lights come down.)

Scene Four

*(The house of Saul at Gibeah. Cheering is heard. SAUL
enters followed by ABNER. A loud cheer goes up.)*

SAUL: Listen to them out there.

ABNER: He's a hero now.

SAUL: Mindless animals. They'll cheer for anyone.

ABNER: He is responsible for our victory.

SAUL: You know what I think?

ABNER: Not unless you tell me.

SAUL: I think this is Samuel's doing.

ABNER: Will you forget about Samuel!? He's not responsible for
everything that goes on in this country.

SAUL: I wouldn't be too sure about that. *(HE gazes out the window.)*
Look at him. Look at the way the people adore him, slobbering over him
as if he were some sort of a god. And look at the way he drinks it in,
smiling and waving. And the women. They're hysterical. Even Jonathan,
my own flesh and blood, tagging after him like some handmaiden. I'm
worried about him, Abner. I really am. He used to be so full of energy,
so lively.

ABNER: He volunteered to fight the monster.

SAUL: The old Jonathan wouldn't have bothered to volunteer. He would
have gone out and done it.

162

ABNER: And that would have pleased you, wouldn't it?

(A loud cheer is heard.)

SAUL: Listen to them will you?

ABNER: There's something about that boy. It's as if he had some glorious secret.

SAUL: So you've been smitten too.

ABNER: I told you that, the first time I laid eyes on him. I warned you. Didn't I?

SAUL: Yes. Yes, you warned me. And you were the one that talked me into letting him fight that monster.

ABNER: It was a risk worth taking.

SAUL: No, it's true. There is something special about him. When he plays for me, when he sings, those dark clouds seem to disappear.

ABNER: You're not still troubled, are you?

SAUL: I don't want to talk about it. The fact of the matter is I am cursed. Let's leave it at that. You really think he has his eye on the throne?

ABNER: I don't doubt it for a minute.

SAUL: What would you suggest?

ABNER: Give him enough rope and he'll hang himself.

SAUL: What makes you so sure?

ABNER: He's ambitious, he's inexperienced and he's human.

(A loud cheer is heard.)

ABNER: A promotion, of course, is unavoidable.

SAUL: And then what?

ABNER: Send him off somewhere, into the thick of things. He's not a soldier. I doubt if he knows how to handle a sword. He'll never come back.

SAUL: There is that trouble in the north.

ABNER: Exactly.

SAUL: What about Merab? I did give my word.

ABNER: There's no rush, is there? And if he doesn't come back how can he claim her?

SAUL: That's true. Bring him in.

> (ABNER goes off. Cheering is heard. SAUL paces about. ABNER reenters followed by DAVID accompanied by JONATHAN.)

ABNER: May I present the hero of the day?

DAVID: I'm hardly that.

ABNER: And modest, too.

DAVID: Not really, General. It was the army, led by yourself and the king that won the day.

SAUL: Come, come, David. You're already a legend. I hope, however, that doesn't mean you're going to give up your music.

DAVID: I would never do that, your majesty.

SAUL: I'm glad to hear it.

ABNER: It's obvious, however, that the road to fame and fortune lies in your career as a warrior.

DAVID: I've never aspired to fame and fortune.

ABNER: Oh? And what have you aspired to?

DAVID: To serve his majesty.

ABNER: The diplomatic corps. That's the place for you.

SAUL: Actually...

ABNER: Your majesty? You were saying?

SAUL: I was thinking. We have all that trouble up north. We could use someone capable up there. How would you like that, David?

ABNER: Excellent idea. What do you say?

DAVID: I'm here to serve.

SAUL: That's what I like to hear. We're going to put you in charge of a thousand men.

ABNER: Which means a promotion, of course.

SAUL: Yes. Yes, of course. You'll be a captain now.

DAVID: I'm greatly honored.

SAUL: And we'd like you to dine with us this evening. You've met Merab, I believe, my older daughter.

DAVID: I've had the privilege of meeting Michal, and she's very charming, but not Merab.

SAUL: Then you'll want to get acquainted. You can bring along that friend of yours over there, if he can spare the time.

DAVID: Thank you.

SAUL: Till this evening then. *(HE goes off.)*

ABNER: Congratulations.

DAVID: Thank you.

(ABNER goes off.)

JONATHAN: So, how does it feel to be the hero of the day?

DAVID: It's overwhelming.

JONATHAN: Don't get too used to it. Fame is rather fickle, my friend. It can also be insidious.

DAVID: In what way?

JONATHAN: It can delude you into thinking that anything is possible.

DAVID: Isn't it?

JONATHAN: No, indeed, it is not. There's a pecking order, my boy, and it has to be carefully observed.

DAVID: For example?

JONATHAN: There's the rooster who rules the roost. That's Samuel, of course. And then there's the second in command, that's Saul and so on and so on.

DAVID: And where do you stand in this pecking order?

JONATHAN: I don't.

DAVID: What do you mean?

JONATHAN: It was Samuel's decision that I'm not to succeed my father.

DAVID: Doesn't your father have anything to say about that?

JONATHAN: My father sold my birthright, not for a pot of lentils. Oh no. He sold it for something much more precious than that.

DAVID: And what might that be?

JONATHAN: Power, my boy. It's an aphrodisiac.

DAVID: Didn't you put up a fight?

JONATHAN: You don't fight God. And Samuel speaks for God, I'm afraid. Oh, I was furious at first.

DAVID: And now?

JONATHAN: It's as if a great weight has been lifted from my shoulders. For the first time in my life I can smell the fresh air, look at the trees and the grass and actually see them. You look skeptical.

DAVID: No, no. It isn't that. Jonathan, I...

JONATHAN: Yes? What is it?

DAVID: There's something I think you ought to know. I hope this won't affect our friendship.

JONATHAN: Go on.

DAVID: Before I was summoned to play for your father, before I even met him, before I met any of you...Samuel paid us a visit.

JONATHAN: By us you mean...?

DAVID: My family.

JONATHAN: Go on.

DAVID: He asked to see all my brothers and myself.

JONATHAN: And?

DAVID: He anointed me and said that I was to succeed your father.

JONATHAN: *(HE studies David for a moment.)* Why did you tell me this?

DAVID: If we're to be friends I think you ought to know.

JONATHAN: Have you told this to anyone else?

DAVID: No one knows, except for my family, and Samuel, of course.

JONATHAN: You're sure?

DAVID: As far as I know.

JONATHAN: Keep it that way, if you value your life,

DAVID: Perhaps some day we can share the throne, you and I.

(JONATHAN shakes his head.)

DAVID: Why not? We will be brothers soon, when I marry your sister, that is.

JONATHAN: When and if you marry my sister. He's sending you up north where the fighting is the thickest. If you're not around, dear boy, how can you collect your prize? David, David, don't you realize, you're his rival now?

DAVID: You don't have a very high opinion of your father, do you?

JONATHAN: I love him dearly. However, in addition to his other malady, my father has caught a very common disease?

DAVID: And what disease is that?

JONATHAN: Ambition.

DAVID: You think it's catching?

JONATHAN: If I see any symptoms I'll let you know.

DAVID: Would you?

JONATHAN: Tell me something. Have you ever been on a battlefield before?

DAVID: Not really, no.

JONATHAN: Suppose I were to accompany you up north? You'd have to share the authority, of course. How would you feel about that?

DAVID: I'd be honored.

JONATHAN: Come along then. You can't always fight with a sling shot, my friend. You're going to have to learn how to handle a sword.

> *(JONATHAN throws his arm around DAVID's shoulder and THEY go off. Cheering is heard, then the sound of battle.)*

Scene Five

(The scene is the same. Two months later. SAUL enters with ABNER.)

SAUL: Stop a minute and think. Just think. Someone whispers in my ear, "There's this boy. He plays like an angel. He can drive away those evil spirits of yours."

ABNER: Who was it?

SAUL: What?

ABNER: Who whispered in your ear?

SAUL: What difference does it make? The point is this. This young man shows up out of nowhere. This golden boy and he proceeds to charm everyone in sight. He plays and he sings and, as if by magic...

ABNER: Witchcraft!

SAUL: What's that?

ABNER: I'm sorry. Go on.

SAUL: Yes. Yes, witchcraft. As if by witchcraft my malady is cured, temporarily, that is. And then there's this business with Goliath, this ogre that has intimidated an entire army. The boy reappears just at the crucial moment. He steps up, destroys the monster and he's a national hero. And then look at the way my son follows him about like some pet dog. And now even Michal...Michal who's turned up her nose at every prospective suitor...even Michal is enchanted with him.

ABNER: Like I said, it's witchcraft. There's no doubt about it.

170

SAUL: You can laugh all you want to, but here we send him up north where the fighting is the fiercest. The boy has never even handled a sword before and he returns more triumphant than ever. And you don't think that's odd?

ABNER: Not really, no. He had Jonathan to help him.

SAUL: There you are. That proves my point. And here he is, back again, to claim his bride.

ABNER: I told you to not to marry her off.

SAUL: The question is what are we going to do about it?

ABNER: Send him back out, and offer him Michal.

SAUL: Oh, fine!

ABNER: Look at it this way. Even if he comes back again, as your son-in-law he'd be part of the family and, as part of the family, all his triumphs will reflect upon you. In addition to that a man with a wife has less time to spend with friends. And there's one more important plus.

SAUL: And what might that be?

ABNER: You're going to make Michal a very happy young lady.

SAUL: All right all right. Bring him in.

> (ABNER goes off. SAUL sits, deep in thought. ABNER reenters followed by DAVID who's accompanied by JONATHAN. SAUL rises quickly.)

SAUL: Welcome, David, welcome. (HE embraces HIM.) You've done nobly.

ABNER: And Jonathan as well.

SAUL: Yes. Yes, of course. And a promotion is in order. What do you say to the title of general? You'll be second in command now to Abner and Prince Jonathan.

DAVID: I'm overwhelmed.

SAUL: In regard to Merab you must forgive me. I'm a father, you see, a father first and foremost. My little girl was smitten with this young man and, I just couldn't bring myself to break her heart. All is not lost, however. I understand my younger daughter, Michal, seems to please you. Bring me the foreskins of one hundred Philistines and Michal is yours. *(HE kisses DAVID on both cheeks and goes off.)*

ABNER: You're a lucky man.

JONATHAN: It took a little more than luck.

ABNER: We've missed you, Jonathan, your father and I. We never see you anymore.

JONATHAN: I've been busy fighting a war.

ABNER: Now that you're back, don't you think you ought to spend some time with your father?

JONATHAN: I've got another war to fight and a bride to be won...for my friend here.

   (ABNER hesitates and goes off.)

DAVID: Abner doesn't like me, you know. And somehow or other I've got the feeling that the king resents our friendship.

JONATHAN: My father resents anyone or anything that threatens his popularity.

DAVID: You think he suspects something...about my anointment?

DAVID: For your sake, I sincerely hope not. One hundred Philistines!?

JONATHAN: Fifty! What are brothers for?

   (THEY go off, arms about each others shoulder. The sound of battle is heard)

Scene Six

(Soft music is heard. The scene is the same. Several months later. SAUL enters with MICHAL.)

MICHAL: You don't want me to marry him, do you?

SAUL: Now, now, now. I never said that.

MICHAL: But that's what you're hinting at.

SAUL: I just want you to be sure that this is the man you want to spend the rest of your life with.

MICHAL: How can anyone be sure of that?

SAUL: Then you do have doubts.

MICHAL: I'd be a fool if I didn't have any doubts.

SAUL: It's not too late, you know.

MICHAL: Now, Father, you've given your word. You went back on it once. How would it look?

SAUL: What do I care how it looks?!

MICHAL: You used to be fond of him.

SAUL: That was before, before I saw his true colors. Look at the way he's wormed himself into everyone's affections. It's...unnatural.

MICHAL: You think he's a witch?

SAUL: Your brother seems to be bewitched by him.

MICHAL: They're friends.

SAUL: Why? Tell me that. Why has that young man gone out of his way to cultivate your brother's friendship? And what are the two of them always whispering about to one another?

MICHAL: You think they're up to some mischief?

SAUL: You said it, not I.

MICHAL: You're not serious?

SAUL: There's no use talking to you. You're under his spell as well.

MICHAL: Father, please...

> *(SAUL starts off, almost running into DAVID who's just entered. SAUL turns and goes off in the opposite direction.)*

DAVID: He can't stand the sight of me.

MICHAL: He suspects you have your eye on the throne.

DAVID: Why would he think that?

MICHAL: Do you?

DAVID: Jonathan's his rightful heir.

MICHAL: You haven't answered my question.

DAVID: What difference does it make what I think? What difference does it make what any of us think? Your father's the king and Samuel's still the power behind the throne.

MICHAL: Why are you marrying me?

DAVID: You're my prize. I've won you fair and square.

MICHAL: Is that the only reason?

DAVID: Why are you marrying me? You don't have to if you don't want to. As a matter of fact, if the wedding never took place that would please your father no end.

MICHAL: It's just that he feels left out. Look at him out there pouting like a child. Why don't you go and talk to him? For my sake, David. Please.

DAVID: If you think it'll do any good.

MICHAL: Thank you.

> *(MICHAL kisses HIM. DAVID hesitates, sighs and goes off. MICHAL stands apprehensively watching the two of them offstage. Wedding music is heard as the lights come down.)*

Scene Seven

(The following week. Early morning. The wedding music slowly fades. The house of Jonathan. The room is dark. SAUL enters unsteadily and staggers about.)

SAUL: Wake up! Wake up! Where is everybody? Jonathaaan!

(SAUL plops onto a stool. JONATHAN enters hurriedly in the process of donning a robe.)

JONATHAN: What's the matter? What's wrong?

SAUL: Where is everyone?

JONATHAN: Everyone's gone to bed.

SAUL: Gone to bed? On a night like this?

JONATHAN: It's almost morning.

SAUL: Then why is it so dark?

JONATHAN: Shhhh.

SAUL: Shhhhh.

JONATHAN: What's the matter? Is there anything wrong?

SAUL: Wrong? What could be wrong? Everything's right. Except for the fact that it's so dark in here. Let there be light!!

JONATHAN: All right, all right. You'll wake up everyone. *(HE lights a lamp.)*

176

SAUL: That would be an achievement, wouldn't it? There! That's better. Now I can see you. I need a drink. Where's the wine?

JONATHAN: Don't you think you've had enough? All right, all right. *(HE pours a cup of wine and hands it to SAUL.)*

SAUL: Thank you. Aren't you joining me?

(JONATHAN pours a second cup.)

SAUL: Now let's make a toast. Let me see. Whom shall we toast? I have it. Let's drink to the bride and the groom. Long may they reign. Did I say reign? A slip of the tongue. Long may they love. Live, whatever. Did I hear an amen?

JONATHAN: Amen.

SAUL: That's better. *(HE drinks.)* You're not drinking. Don't you approve of the marriage?

JONATHAN: Look, Father, it's been a long night.

SAUL: But what a glorious one! I did well by her, didn't I? I did well by your little sister, didn't I? What a magnificent wedding. What a triumph! Not for you, perhaps. Your sister's gained a husband. I've gained a son, but you, dear boy, you've lost a friend. But then again maybe your friendship's served its purpose. What a handsome groom he made! It's not often that the groom is prettier than the bride.

JONATHAN: It's very late, Father. What do you want?

SAUL: I want my son back. That's what I want. I want my Jonathan.

JONATHAN: I'm right here.

SAUL: But you're not, dear boy. You're not. You're fast asleep. Wake up! Don't you see what he's after?

JONATHAN: By he I assume you mean David.

SAUL: No, the man in the moon.

JONATHAN: And what is he after?

SAUL: What is he after?! Your inheritance, you fool!

JONATHAN: You're drunk.

SAUL: I may be drunk, but you are bewitched, bewitched by that boy otherwise you'd realize how he's used you.

JONATHAN: And how has he used me?

SAUL: To worm his way into the family.

JONATHAN: He wants my inheritance, you say.

SAUL: Exactly.

JONATHAN: And what inheritance might you be referring to?

SAUL: What inheritance? Are you joking? The throne, my son, the throne.

JONATHAN: Oh, come on, Father!

SAUL: What? What?

JONATHAN: Let's not play games.

SAUL: What are you talking about?

JONATHAN: You know perfectly well what I'm talking about.

SAUL: Don't believe everything you hear.

JONATHAN: Are you denying that you bargained away my succession?

SAUL: Samuel will be dead inside of a year.

JONATHAN: And if he's not?

SAUL: He's a foolish old man.

JONATHAN: Foolish or not, he still speaks for God.

SAUL: I'm the one who speaks for God. I'm the one that was chosen. And I've chosen you, dear boy. I've chosen you as my successor. Now listen to me. Whatever passed between that old man and myself is nothing. Nothing, you understand? When I am gone you are the king, and that's what he's after. That's why he befriended you. That's why he wormed his way into your heart just as he wormed his way into mine. Oh, I admit it. He had me fooled as well. But I've escaped from his spell. I've come to see him for what he really is, a scheming little mongrel, faithless and deceitful. Oh, I know how charming he can be. I know how he can wrap you around his finger, how he can make himself indispensable. And that's why he's so dangerous. That's why he's got to be stopped.

JONATHAN: And how are we going to manage that?

SAUL: Let me ask you this.

JONATHAN: I'm listening.

SAUL: How does one deal with a traitor?

JONATHAN: You want me to kill him? Is that it?

SAUL: Don't be a fool!

JONATHAN: What then?

SAUL: People meet with accidents. Along the road. At home. A robbery gone astray. A fatal stabbing. A young man with a great future comes to an untimely end. How unfortunate! What a tragedy! But that's life, is it not? These things happen! Don't they? Don't they?!

JONATHAN: Let me think about it.

SAUL: That's all I ask. *(HE rises and staggers.)*

JONATHAN: I'll see you home.

SAUL: No, no. I'm fine, I'm perfectly fine. You're my favorite, Jonathan, my first born and my favorite. You know that, don't you? I love you, son.

JONATHAN: I love you too. Now get some sleep.

SAUL: You're right. That's what I need. A good night's sleep. You won't disappoint me, will you?

JONATHAN: I'll try not to.

SAUL: You're a good boy, Jonathan. A good boy. You always have been.

> *(SAUL kisses him on both cheeks, embraces him then staggers off. JONATHAN sighs and sits thinking. HE rises and puts away the jug of wine and the cups. HE's about to blow out the lamp when he hears a noise.)*

JONATHAN: Who's there?

> *(DAVID enters.)*

JONATHAN: David?

DAVID: Was that your father?

JONATHAN: The great man himself. What are you doing here? It's your wedding night.

DAVID: So it is.

JONATHAN: You haven't had a quarrel already?

DAVID: I made the mistake of telling her.

JONATHAN: Telling her what?

DAVID: About Samuel. About his anointing me.

JONATHAN: On your wedding night? What on earth possessed you?!

DAVID: I hadn't meant to. We got to talking and somehow or other it just slipped out.

JONATHAN: How did she take it?

DAVID: She wouldn't let me near her. It was as if I was suddenly the enemy. I tried to reason with her. I tried to tell her it was not my choice, that I had no say in the matter. And then I got angry and we started to quarrel...and finally I left.

JONATHAN: She'll get over it. Give her time. She'll come round.

DAVID: She has to choose between me and her father, and she adores him. What did he want?

JONATHAN: What's that? He wants me to kill you. I beg your pardon. He wants me to arrange for someone to kill you.

DAVID: Are you serious?

JONATHAN: I don't know. It may have just been the wine.

DAVID: I'm sure it was. He'll feel differently in the morning.

JONATHAN: Look outside, my friend. It's morning now.

DAVID: What are you going to do?

JONATHAN: I'm going to invite him to dinner. I want to talk to him when he's sober. I want you to listen in. I've become so suspicious I don't trust myself anymore.

DAVID: All right.

JONATHAN: Would you like some breakfast?

DAVID: I'm not very hungry.

JONATHAN: Neither am I. I'm going back to bed.

DAVID: Go ahead.

JONATHAN: What will you do?

DAVID: I'll just sit here for a while.

JONATHAN: Be patient with her, David. She loves you.

DAVID: I know, I know. Go to bed. Go on. I'll be all right.

> *(JONATHAN sighs, pats DAVID on the shoulder and goes off. DAVID sits thinking and then leaves as the lights come down.)*

Scene Eight

(The scene is the same. The following evening. SAUL enters from the interior of the house followed by JONATHAN.)

SAUL: You seem preoccupied.

JONATHAN: Do I?

SAUL: We used to be able to confide in one another.

JONATHAN: May I ask you a personal question? Promise you won't get angry or upset. When you get these spells, when you're sitting there in the dark clutching that javelin of yours what goes through your mind?

SAUL: Why do you ask?

JONATHAN: I was just wondering?

SAUL: Have you been...?

JONATHAN: No, no.

SAUL: It's a curse, and I hope you never know what it's like.

JONATHAN: I just don't understand why you're so unhappy. Look at all you've accomplished. You've united all the tribes. You've had victory after victory. You're loved and respected by everyone.

SAUL: Everyone?

JONATHAN: Is that the problem? You've got to please everyone? You've got to be all things to all the people? I'm just trying to understand.

183

SAUL: Don't.

JONATHAN: Would you care for some more wine?

SAUL: No, thank you. My head's still woozy from last night.

JONATHAN: You were certainly feeling no pain. You don't usually drink that much.

SAUL: How often does one marry off a daughter?

JONATHAN: Do you remember anything about last night?

SAUL: My own daughter's wedding?!

JONATHAN: I meant afterwards. Do you remember coming here in the early hours of the morning?

SAUL: You'll have to refresh my memory.

JONATHAN: You insisted that David was plotting against you.

SAUL: Did I?

JONATHAN: And that...

SAUL: Go on, go on.

JONATHAN: You don't really think he is. Or do you?

SAUL: If he were I should think you'd be the first to know.

JONATHAN: You're one of his idols, Father. And you've always been mine.

SAUL: David's a fine young man. As a matter of fact, I owe him my life. He brought me back from the brink. Would I have made him a general if I thought he was plotting against me? Would I have given him your sister? To be quite frank, however, there are times when I envy that young man. So young to climb so quickly. I was forced to wait years. And I envy him his friendship with you. I've never had a friend I could trust completely. You're lucky to have found a friend like that. I think maybe I will have a little more wine after all.

JONATHAN: Yes. Yes, of course.

> *(JONATHAN pours two cups of wine and hands one to SAUL.)*

SAUL: To friendship.

JONATHAN: To friendship.

> *(THEY drink.)*

JONATHAN: That was quite a wedding. Michal looked so happy.

SAUL: She's in love apparently, like everyone else.

> *(There's a knock at the door.)*

SAUL: Are you expecting anyone?

JONATHAN: Not really, no. Excuse me.

> *(JONATHAN goes off and reenters a moment later with DAVID.)*

SAUL: Well, well, well! Speak of the devil.

> *(DAVID and JONATHAN exchange glances.)*

SAUL: *(HE laughs.)* It's just an expression, boys. It's just an expression.

DAVID: *(To JONATHAN)* I'm sorry. I didn't know you had a guest.

SAUL: Guest?

JONATHAN: Of course, you're a guest. A most honored guest. *(To DAVID)* Would you care for some wine?

DAVID: Thank you.

*(JONATHAN pours a cup of wine which HE hands to
DAVID.)*

SAUL: To the bride and groom. To David and Michal. May they be
fruitful and multiply.

JONATHAN: Amen.

DAVID: Thank you.

(THEY drink.)

SAUL: So, how does it feel to be a married man?

DAVID: I'll let you know in a month or so.

SAUL: It takes some getting used to. Soon, however, you'll wonder how
you ever managed. And then when the children come... Philosophers
often argue about what gives one the greatest pleasure. For me it's
fatherhood. To see one's sons grow straight and tall. To realize that
when you're gone a part of you will still live on. You can write all your
songs and your poems but your sons, David, your sons...they're your
immortality. And with those words of wisdom I shall take my leave.
Now where did I put my cloak?

JONATHAN: I'll get it.

SAUL: That's all right. Sit, sit. *(HE goes off to the interior of the
house.)*

JONATHAN: I thought you were just going to listen.

DAVID: I did, and obviously you were mistaken. Sometimes people say
things they don't mean.

JONATHAN: And sometimes we mean things we don't say.

DAVID: You still have doubts?

(SAUL reenters with his cloak.)

SAUL: *(To JONATHAN)* Thank you, my boy. Thank you for a very pleasant evening.

JONATHAN: Thank you, Father.

> *(SAUL and JONATHAN embrace.)*

SAUL: David...

DAVID: Your majesty?

SAUL: Your majesty? I'm your father now. Walk a ways with me. *(To JONATHAN)* You don't mind, do you?

JONATHAN: No. of course not.

SAUL: *(HE throws his arm around DAVID's shoulder.)* I want you to play for me. It's been so long. Those fingers of yours must be rusty by now. You're an artist as well as a warrior. You mustn't give up your music, son. Anyone can wield a sword.

> *(SAUL and DAVID go off together. JONATHAN sits thoughtfully sipping his wine. Harp music is heard as the lights come down.)*

Scene Nine

*(The music continues. A room in the house of Saul.
Through a curtain we can see SAUL, in silhouette,
sitting on his throne, clutching his javelin and brooding.
DAVID, in silhouette, sits on the other side of the room
playing and singing. ABNER is pacing nervously outside
the room toward the side of the stage. Suddenly SAUL
whirls about and hurls his javelin at DAVID barely
missing him. DAVID jumps up then walks out quickly,
almost colliding with ABNER, as the curtain becomes
opaque.)*

ABNER: What's the matter? What happened?

DAVID: He tried to kill me.

ABNER: What are you talking about?

DAVID: He tried to kill me I'm telling you.

ABNER: You must be mistaken.

DAVID: The man is demented.

ABNER: All right, all right. Calm down. I'll have a talk with him.

DAVID: You do that little thing. *(HE starts off.)*

ABNER: Where are you going?

DAVID: I'm getting out of here. He might decide to try it again.

ABNER: I'll have a talk with him. There's no reason for you to run off
like this.

DAVID: The man is stark raving mad. Don't you understand? He sits there, staring into space, clutching that javelin of his. I sit there, trying to concentrate on my music, one eye on those itchy fingers of his. It's like being in a room with some wild animal.

ABNER: I'm sure it's all a misunderstanding.

DAVID: Abner, let's face it. The man is unbalanced.

ABNER: It's an illness.

DAVID: A deadly one, I'm afraid.

ABNER: I don't blame you for being upset.

DAVID: One inch more and I'd be lying dead on the floor.

ABNER: Oh, come come.

DAVID: Ever since the first day I came here I've had this uneasy feeling. I tried not to think about it, but every time I entered that room it was like going into the lion's den. It's been an absolute nightmare. But never again. It's over and done with.

ABNER: Where are you going?

DAVID: I don't know.

> (DAVID goes off. ABNER is about to follow him when SAUL enters holding his javelin.)

SAUL: Where is he?

ABNER: What happened in there?

ABNER: He says you tried to kill him.

SAUL: I tried to kill him? Is that what he said?

ABNER: He said you threw your javelin at him.

SAUL: And you believe him?

ABNER: Why would he lie about a thing like that?

SAUL: Abner, he was sitting right there across the room from me. If I wanted to kill him would he still be walking around?

ABNER: But why would he make up a story like that?

SAUL: You believe him, don't you? And if you believe him so will everyone else. Don't you see what he's up to? He's going to go around spreading this story and everyone will think that I've gone mad. Can't you see? He wants the people to think that I'm incompetent, that I'm incapable of ruling a kingdom. Where is he? He's got to be stopped. *(HE starts off.)*

ABNER: Saul!

(SAUL strides off.)

ABNER: Saul!

(ABNER follows SAUL off as the lights come down.)

Scene Ten

(A room in the house of David. DAVID and MICHAL are discovered.)

DAVID: You didn't happen to say anything to him, did you?

MICHAL: About what?

DAVID: About Samuel anointing me.

MICHAL: David, I gave you my word.

DAVID: He's jealous of me. Ever since I slew Goliath he's been trying to get rid of me, sending me out to the most dangerous trouble spots. The night of the wedding he tried to persuade Jonathan to have me killed. Did you know that?

MICHAL: You must be mistaken.

DAVID: Ask Jonathan.

MICHAL: It just doesn't make sense. He knows how close you and Jonathan are.

DAVID: He was drunk.

MICHAL: Well, there you are.

DAVID: And that's when we say what we really think.

MICHAL: He's insecure. I know that.

DAVID: That's no excuse.

191

MICHAL: He's united the country. He's led us into victory after victory. I know he has this sickness.

DAVID: And it's getting worse. He's a menace. I'm sorry, Michal. I know how you feel about him, but you haven't seen him the way I have, sitting there in that room, staring into space like some demented... He's not fit to rule.

MICHAL: All right!

DAVID: You love him, I know. He's our king. But for the sake of the country he should be persuaded to abdicate.

MICHAL: And name you his successor?

DAVID: That's not the way I wanted it and you know it.

MICHAL: He needs our support. He needs our help.

DAVID: And what about me? Don't you understand? He's made up his mind. He's going to get rid of me one way or another.

MICHAL: You were sitting right across the room from him...?

DAVID: You don't believe me, do you?

MICHAL: Maybe he was just trying to frighten you.

DAVID: Well, he sure has succeeded.

MICHAL: What do you intend to do?

DAVID: Maybe I ought to talk to Samuel. He's the one that's really running the country.

MICHAL: Shh.

DAVID: What is it?

MICHAL: There's someone coming. *(SHE looks out the window.)* It's Abner.

(There's a knock at the door.)

DAVID: I'm not here.

(There's another knock at the door.)

DAVID: Answer it. You haven't seen me. Please! Do as I say.

(MICHAL goes off to answer the door.)

MICHAL: *(Offstage)* Abner?! What a pleasant surprise! Come in, come in.

(DAVID goes off to another room. ABNER enters followed by MICHAL.)

MICHAL: Sit down. Have you had your lunch? What can I offer you?

ABNER: Where's David?

MICHAL: He's with the king, isn't he?

ABNER: There's been some sort of a misunderstanding.

MICHAL: What sort of a misunderstanding?

ABNER: It's nothing really. So, my dear, how is married life?

MICHAL: Abner, please. What happened?

ABNER: Has he been here?

MICHAL: What happened? Did he try to kill him?

ABNER: Is that what he told you?

MICHAL: Did he?

ABNER: According to David.

MICHAL: Were you there?

ABNER: I wasn't in the room.

MICHAL: What did Saul say?

ABNER: He denies it, of course.

MICHAL: What do you think happened?

ABNER: I don't know. *(HE sighs and looks about.)* Is he here? Where is he, Michal?

     (SAUL enters.)

MICHAL: Father? What a pleasant surprise!

     (MICHAL approaches SAUL and attempts to kiss him. HE pushes her away.)

ABNER: I asked you to wait.

SAUL: *(To MICHAL)* Where's David? I want to have a talk with him.

MICHAL: What happened? Tell me, please.

SAUL: Your husband's been acting very strangely, to say the least.

MICHAL: You didn't try to harm him, did you?

SAUL: Is that what he told you?

MICHAL: He said you tried to kill him.

SAUL: And you believe him?

MICHAL: I don't know what to believe.

SAUL: Why would I try to kill him? He's your husband. He's my son-in-law.

ABNER: It was just a misunderstanding.

MICHAL: And did Jonathan misunderstand as well?

SAUL: What has Jonathan got to do with this?

MICHAL Did you or did you not try to persuade Jonathan to kill him?

SAUL: *(HE turns to ABNER.)* You see? You see what kind of stories he's spreading.

MICHAL: Then he was lying.

SAUL: Where is he? I just want to talk to him.

ABNER: We're all upset. Why don't we wait until everyone calms down?

SAUL: He's a traitor. That's what he is.

ABNER: Come on, Saul.

SAUL: I want him to stand right here in front of me. I want him to tell me to my face that I tried to kill him. He's the one that's crazy, not me. He's turned my son against me. He's turned my daughter against me. And now he wants to turn the people against me.

ABNER: He's turned no one against you.

SAUL: He wants to take my throne away from me. Don't you understand? Where is he, Michal? *(HE looks about.)* David?

ABNER: Saul, please.

SAUL: *(HE looks into the next room.)* David? *(HE reenters and goes from room to room. HE looks about grabs MICHAL by the shoulders and shakes her.)* Where is he? Where is he, you ungrateful bitch? *(HE starts to throttle her.)*

ABNER: Saul!

(ABNER grabs hold of SAUL and pulls him off her.)

SAUL: So you're against me, too. You're all against me.

MICHAL: Father, please...

SAUL: I'll find him. I'll find him, if it's the last thing I do. *(HE rushes off.)*

ABNER: The moment I laid eyes on him I knew that boy was trouble. If you value his life keep him out of sight.

> *(ABNER follows SAUL off. MICHAL goes quickly into the room that David took refuge in.)*

MICHAL: *(Offstage)* David? David?

> *(After a moment MICHAL reenters slowly and sits with a sigh as the lights come down.)*

ACT TWO

Scene One

(The house of SAMUEL at Naioth in Ramah. The room is dark. The sound of rain and wind is heard. There's a knocking at the door. The knocking grows louder and turns into hammering. SAMUEL, the high priest, enters from the interior carrying a lighted lamp.)

SAMUEL: All right, all right. *(HE goes off and is heard offstage.)* What do you want? Do you know what time it is? Come in, come in, whoever you are.

(SAMUEL reenters followed by SAUL, his face hidden by the hood of his cloak.)

SAMUEL: Well, what do you want? Who are you?

(SAUL removes his hood.)

SAMUEL: Well, well, well! What an honor! What brings you out on a night like this?

SAUL: We never see you anymore.

SAMUEL: What can I do for you?

SAUL: Things are not going well. I don't know who to turn to. Those I love the most, those that are closest to me seem to be turning away from me. Nobody seems to understand. Nobody seems to realize the pressure I'm under, the burden I carry. And then there's this dark cloud hanging over me, this curse that keeps coming back to haunt me. There are days when I feel I can't go on.

197

SAMUEL: We all have a burden to carry.

SAUL: The only thing that seemed to help was when David sang for me. And now, for some reason or other he's turned against me too.

SAMUEL: And why do you think that is?

SAUL: I don't know. I love him like a son. Even before he became my son-in-law. Sometimes I'm abrupt. I know that. And there are times, perhaps, when I lose my temper. I get impatient and maybe I've offended him somehow.

SAMUEL: What makes you think that?

SAUL: He's been making up all these terrible stories about me.

SAMUEL: What sort of stories?

SAUL: They're too ridiculous. I don't even want to repeat them.

SAMUEL: What do you want me to do?

SAUL: If I could only sit down and talk to him. To find out what he has against me. I've been told that he's here. May I see him, please?

SAMUEL: You're drenched to the skin. Let me get you some dry clothes.

SAUL: I won't stay long. I just want to talk to him. I mean him no harm.

SAMUEL: Let me get you some hot soup.

SAUL: Nothing, please.

SAMUEL: May I offer you a seat?

　　　(SAUL sits.)

SAMUEL: The fire's out. I'll call one of the servants.

SAUL: Don't bother, please.

SAMUEL: Take off your cloak.

SAUL: *(HE removes his cloak and throws it aside.)* What has he told you?

SAMUEL: I've done you a great disservice, Saul. But how is one to know? How is one to predict? When I first laid eyes on you I said to myself, "Yes, he will do. He will do very nicely. He's a good man, a kind man. Not brilliant perhaps, but sensible. Simple and down to earth He looks like a king. He carries himself like a king." I thought surely you would succeed, if not memorably, at least you would prove serviceable. But somewhere deep inside of you there's this little flaw, this little maggot...

SAUL: Where is he, Samuel, please? I just want to talk to him.

SAMUEL: Well, maybe the people get what they deserve. They wanted a king, just like all the other nations. So now they've got a king. A priest wasn't good enough. Oh, no! They turned away from God. They've lost respect for the church. They worship mammon.

SAUL: I've always had the greatest respect for you.

SAMUEL: Yes, I'm sure you have. Listen, my friend, with all your problems you're still a lucky man. At least you've got sons you needn't be ashamed of. Things don't always go as planned, you know. Life has been a disappointment to me as well.

SAUL: I'm sure it has.

SAMUEL: But there's one thing I've learned.

SAUL: And what might that be?

SAMUEL: One cannot be all things to all people.

SAUL: May I see him, please? I don't mean him any harm. I swear to you.

SAMUEL: Then why do you pursue him?

SAUL: I'm not pursuing him.

SAMUEL: Then what are you doing here?

SAUL: I want him to take his rightful place.

SAMUEL: And where might that be?

SAUL: By my side. I need him. The country needs him. We want him back.

SAMUEL: You're chasing a phantom, Saul. Go home. Forget about David.

SAUL: If I could just talk to him, explain to him.

SAMUEL: Why should he trust you? You tried to kill him once. You tried to persuade your son to have him killed. Why should he trust you? I've given you my word that you'll complete your reign. Don't make me regret it.

SAUL: *(Bitterly)* Your word! What does that mean, your word? You gave me your word that I'd establish a dynasty, that my sons and my sons' sons would carry on my work. You came to me. I didn't come to you. And now that I sit on the throne, now that I've done my best to rule this country I'm entitled to fulfill my destiny.

SAMUEL: Your destiny is decided by God. Go home, Saul. And since you're so fond of David you'll be happy to know that he's been chosen to succeed you.

SAUL: What are you saying?

SAMUEL: I've anointed David as your successor.

(*SAUL sways and sinks to the floor in a faint.*)

SAMUEL: Saul? (*SAMUEL pulls him up and seats him in a chair. HE pats SAUL's face.*) Saul?

*(SAUL opens his eyes and looks about. SAMUEL pours
a cup of wine and puts it to SAUL's lips.)*

SAMUEL: Here. Drink this.

*(SAUL takes a sip of the wine then pushes the cup
away.)*

SAMUEL: Are you starving yourself again? When did you eat last?

SAUL: When did you anoint him?

SAMUEL: What difference does it make?

SAUL: How could you do this to me? If I acted hastily, if I offended
you I never meant to. I swear it. I never meant to show you any
disrespect.

SAMUEL: Saul, Saul, you've been king for how long now? Is it such a
great honor? Is it so rewarding?

SAUL: To castrate me like this.

SAMUEL: Oh, come, come!

SAUL: What sort of a spiteful monster are you?

SAMUEL: You watch your tongue, you!

SAUL: I hope you die a long, lingering death. I hope you suffer every
second like I do in my darkest hours, and then may you rot in hell!

*(SAUL rises unsteadily and staggers off, out into the
night. The sounds of the wind and the rain grow louder.)*

SAMUEL: Saul? *(SAMUEL picks up SAUL's cloak and runs off after
him.)* Saul?!

*(After a moment SAMUEL reenters still holding Saul's
cloak. HE throws the cloak onto a chair. DAVID enters
from the interior of the house.)*

DAVID: You've signed my death warrant. You know that, don't you?

SAMUEL: What are you talking about?

DAVID: Why did you tell him?

SAMUEL: Tell him what?

DAVID: That I'm to succeed him. I told you he knew nothing about it. You know what a madman he is. What kind of a crazy game are you playing?

SAMUEL: I've been very patient with you, young man.

DAVID: Now that he knows he'll never leave me alone.

SAMUEL: Stay out of his way.

DAVID: He'll never rest until he buries me. Don't you understand?

SAMUEL: All right. Don't get so excited.

DAVID: What do I do now? I'm a marked man.

SAMUEL: I'm sure he'll come to his senses.

DAVID: And what am I supposed to do in the meantime?

SAMUEL: You're young, my son. You'll manage.

DAVID: And supposes he doesn't come to his senses? The man is obsessive. Don't you understand? He'll never give up on me now. Am I to spend the rest of my life on the run? I came to you for help and all you've done is make things worse.

SAMUEL: You watch your tongue!

DAVID: He's right. You are a monster! *(HE strides off to the interior of the house.)*

SAMUEL: You come back here, you, and apologize! You hear me? Who do you think you are?

> *(SAMUEL sighs, shakes his head, sits and pours himself a glass of wine. HE sits sipping the wine, sighs, shakes his head and smiles ironically as the lights come down.)*

Scene Two

(The house of Saul at Gibeah. ABNER enters with JONATHAN.)

JONATHAN: How long has he been back?

ABNER: Almost a week now.

JONATHAN: And? What happened?

ABNER: I don't know.

JONATHAN: Have you asked him?

ABNER: He doesn't want to talk about it. As a matter of fact he doesn't want to talk at all these days.

JONATHAN: The old affliction?

ABNER: I don't know what's going on with him. There's a look in his eye I've never seen before, a wild sort of haunted look. I'm really worried about him. Have you been in touch with David?

JONATHAN: Why do you ask?

ABNER: He is your friend, isn't he? The two of you are as thick as thieves.

JONATHAN: You think we're plotting to steal something? Is that it?

ABNER: Jonathan, listen to me. No matter what passed between Samuel and your father, you can rest assured he plans to see to it that you succeed him. He loves you, son.

JONATHAN: In his own twisted way I'm sure that he does .

ABNER: He behaves erratically at times, it's true. But he is our king, anointed by the church. And David's had his eye on the throne ever since he came here. You must be aware of that.

JONATHAN: And what if he has?

ABNER: That doesn't bother you?

JONATHAN: Frankly no.

> *(SAUL enters. Ignoring both of them HE goes straight to his chair, sits and takes hold of his javelin propped against the wall.)*

ABNER: Jonathan's here. He's come to pay you a visit. Saul?

JONATHAN: How are you, Father?

SAUL: Where's your friend? I sent word inviting him to join us for the new moon festival.

JONATHAN: He's in Bethlehem with his family. He asked me to give you his apologies.

SAUL: You're his messenger now in addition...?

ABNER: He's delivering a message. What's wrong with that?

SAUL: I'm talking to my son here. My son and heir who's the minion to this...this upstart, to the shame of his friends, to the shame of his family. And you ask me what's wrong? I've decided to put a price on his head.

ABNER: That is not a good idea.

SAUL: As a matter of fact I should have done it sooner.

JONATHAN: What has he done?

SAUL: He's a thief and a traitor.

JONATHAN: What has he stolen?

SAUL: Your inheritance, for one thing. He's persuaded Samuel to anoint him. Did you know that? Did your bosom companion tell you that? That behind your back he's betrayed you?

JONATHAN: That's ancient history.

SAUL: What are you talking about?

JONATHAN: David was anointed before we even met him. Before you ever sent for him.

SAUL: You knew this? You knew this all along? I'm asking you!

JONATHAN: You needn't shout.

SAUL: How long have you known?

JONATHAN: What difference does it make?

SAUL: You hear him? You hear what a fool I have for a son? His best friend betrays him and it makes no difference? What kind of an idiot have I spawned?

JONATHAN: Why don't you face facts? David stole nothing. I will not succeed you and the fault is yours.

(SAUL turns away from JONATHAN.)

JONATHAN: I'm talking to you, old man. Don't you turn away from me. I've been disinherited, and if there's anyone to blame it's you. You sold my birthright. You're the one and don't you try and deny it. But I don't care anymore. I am quite content to sit on the sidelines and watch the world go by. David's going to be the next king of Israel and the sooner you get that through your thick skull the better it will be for all of us.

*(JONATHAN hesitates. Seeing there is no response. HE
starts off. SAUL whirls about and hurls his javelin at the
spot where JONATHAN had been standing. JONATHAN
turns and sees the javelin quivering in the wall.)*

JONATHAN: You will never see me again. *(HE strides off.)*

ABNER: Call him back. Call him back!

SAUL: Let him go. I don't need him. I don't need you. I don't need
anyone.

ABNER: *(HE hesitates then goes off.)* Jonathan?

SAUL: *(Shouting)* Let him go. He can't even give me proper grandson.
Let him go! I want nothing to do with him. He's a poor excuse for a
man.

(SAUL stands defiantly as the lights come down.)

Scene Three

(A field, toward sunset. DAVID is discovered, waiting impatiently. JONATHAN enters. DAVID looks at him inquiringly. JONATHAN shakes his head.)

DAVID: What did he say?

JONATHAN: There's no talking to him.

DAVID: I told you. It's pointless.

JONATHAN: He tried to kill me.

DAVID: Now will you listen to me?

JONATHAN: And he's put a price on your head.

DAVID: Well, at least it's out in the open now. Join me.

JONATHAN: I just can't.

DAVID: I'm willing to share the throne with you.

JONATHAN: I know, I know.

DAVID: Between the two of us...

JONATHAN: He's our king, anointed by Samuel.

DAVID: So am I.

JONATHAN: Not while he's alive. It would mean a civil war. You know that.

208

DAVID: It needn't be that way. Not if Abner joins us. Why don't you speak to him? He respects you. He likes you. He's a sensible man and he is in control of the army.

JONATHAN: If you think that Abner will turn against him then you don't know Abner.

DAVID: He is out of control. He's not fit to rule.

JONATHAN: He's my father.

DAVID: Father or not he tried to kill you. He tried to kill me, and that was before he even knew about my being anointed. Who's going to be next? Who and when? If we could just put him away somewhere, somewhere where he won't do anyone any harm. Abner has got to listen to reason. For the sake of the country. *(HE sighs. After a moment)* Have you spoken to Michal?

JONATHAN: Not recently, no. Do you want me to speak to her?

DAVID: What would be that point, now that I'm a fugitive, now that there's a price on my head?

JONATHAN: She loves you, David.

DAVID: And she also loves her father, and you love him and he loves you and everyone loves everyone. *(After a moment)* I can't believe it. I'm a criminal now, a fugitive. Just yesterday I was the hero of the hour.

JONATHAN: He's getting old. Who knows how long he will last? Don't look at me like that. You've got your whole life ahead of you. One of these days the throne will be yours and you're going to make a magnificent king.

DAVID: If I live that long.

JONATHAN: You'll outlive us all.

DAVID: That's a cheerful thought.

JONATHAN: I'll miss you.

DAVID: As you sleep in your comfortable bed, in your comfortable house surrounded by your family and your friends?

JONATHAN: You're the only real friend I have. The only true friend.

DAVID: You say that so glibly.

JONATHAN: Ask me anything. Anything but that. And when you're the king...

DAVID: What then?

JONATHAN: I hope to be here to serve you. But if not I want you to promise me...

DAVID: Anything.

JONATHAN: I want you to promise me that you'll look after my family. Especially my son. He's helpless.

DAVID: You have my word. What are you smiling at?

JONATHAN: I'm remembering the first time we met. What an arrogant young snob you were!

DAVID: Me?! Your nose was so high in the air. "I suppose I do smell of sheep and manure," I thought to myself "but at least he could be civil." When did you change your mind about me?

JONATHAN: What makes you think I've changed my mind?

DAVID: I'm serious.

JONATHAN: The first time I heard you play. I decided that perhaps you did have something to be arrogant about.

DAVID: You've always been one of my idols, you know. The legendary Prince Jonathan. I never tired of hearing about you and the great King Saul. And then to meet the both of you in the flesh. What an awesome moment that was for me!

JONATHAN: And how disappointing!

DAVID: Your father, of course, was a terrible shock. To discover that he was just a man, beset with more than his share of human frailties.

JONATHAN: And the great Prince Jonathan, that faded star?

DAVID: Not faded. Reluctant.

JONATHAN: *(Ironically)* Honor thy father and thy mother! Why am I burdened with these empty lessons I was taught as a child?

DAVID: And you really think he appreciates your loyalty.

JONATHAN: Maybe not. And maybe it's not him I'm being loyal to.

> *(DAVID puts his arm around JONATHAN'S shoulder and THEY stand watching the setting sun.)*

JONATHAN: It's getting dark. I'd better be getting back. If you need anything, anything at all, just send word. In case I should want to reach you, where will you be?

DAVID: I wish I knew, my friend. I wish I knew.

> *(THEY embrace. DAVID runs off. JONATHAN stands watching him depart as the stage darkens.)*

Scene Four

(Just before sunrise outside a cave in the Wilderness of En-Gedi. SAUL is discovered sitting on a rock in front of the cave. ABNER enters a moment later and sits beside him.)

ABNER: Was that you walking about during the night?

SAUL: What's that?

ABNER: I heard someone creeping about during the night. Was that you?

SAUL: No.

ABNER: Saul, there were only the two of us in that cave.

SAUL: Well, it wasn't me.

ABNER: All right, all right. Saul, listen to me. We can't go on like this. We're going to have a rebellion on our hands. The men are tired of chasing around the country. This obsession of yours is turning the kingdom upside down.

SAUL: He was sighted in the area.

ABNER: So you said. But he's nowhere in sight.

SAUL: This time we've got him. I'm sure of it.

ABNER: Saul, you've got to listen to reason.

SAUL: You said yourself he's turning the people against me.

ABNER: It's you, Saul, you! You're the one that's turning the people against you.

SAUL: He's got to be stopped.

ABNER: Butchering all those priests.

SAUL: They were traitors.

ABNER: Saul, the sword that priest gave David was the one that belonged to Goliath. It was rightfully his.

SAUL: They gave him food. They gave him arms.

ABNER: He has a right to protect himself. And as far as food is concerned, you made him an outcast. How do you expect him to live? Butchering innocent women and children. I still can't believe that you did such a terrible thing. Killing our own people.

SAUL: And the battle he waged at Keilah? What about that?

ABNER: He saved that city from the Philistines.

SAUL: With that army that he's raised.

ABNER: I'm the first one to speak against him. But he's never raised a finger against you. The men are getting impatient. I'd better talk to them. I don't know how long I can keep them together.

> *(SAUL sits motionless and stone-faced. ABNER sighs, shakes his head and goes off. After a moment DAVID appears at a distance with ABISHAI, a follower. DAVID holds a piece of cloth in his hand.)*

DAVID: Saul?

SAUL: Who's that? David, is that you?

DAVID: It's me, Saul. It's David.

SAUL: David? Is that really you?

DAVID: In the flesh.

SAUL: Come closer. I can't see you.

DAVID: Thank you, but no thanks.

SAUL: Come back to us, David. You should be here by my side.

DAVID: That's a dangerous place to be these days.

SAUL: I miss your music, David. I want you to play for me.

DAVID: Why? Have you run out of objects for target practice?

SAUL: Jonathan keeps asking for you. And your wife, Michal. You should be with your wife, with your family.

DAVID: I am with my family, Saul. They've joined me now since you've never stopped hounding them. But I miss Michal. I want you to send her to me.

SAUL: To live like a fugitive with all those rebels you've surrounded yourself with?

DAVID: Those rebels, as you call them, are your own people, Saul, honorable men, and loyal supporters that were persecuted by you. And Michal is my wife. She should be with me.

SAUL: Then come back and take your rightful place.

DAVID: I wish I could, but I prefer to stay alive. I could have taken your life last night and believe me, Saul, I was sorely tempted. But I couldn't bring myself to do you any harm. Not for your sake but for the sake of those who love you, who still love you in spite of everything. *(HE holds up a piece of cloth.)* You see this piece of cloth? It's part of your robe, a piece of your robe that I cut off while you lay sleeping. You were at my mercy last night. I could have cut your throat, but I didn't. I spared your life.

SAUL: David, please, I mean you no harm.

DAVID: Then why have you brought your army with you? Three thousand men who could be defending the country against the Philistines. Go home, Saul. I'm no threat to anyone. Go home and leave me alone and you'll never hear from me again.

(DAVID goes off followed by ABISHAI. After a moment ABNER reenters.)

ABNER: Whom were you talking to?

SAUL: What's that?

ABNER: I heard you talking to someone.

SAUL: I must have been dreaming.

ABNER: We're going back home. The men refuse to go on. Did you hear what I said?

SAUL: Yes. Yes, you're right. Let's go. *(HE starts off.)*

ABNER: Be careful. That path is steep. Saul, watch your step!

SAUL: No, no. You're right. This is nonsense. *(HE goes off.)* No more, no more.

(ABNER follows SAUL off as the lights come down.)

Scene Five

(The house of Jonathan. Early afternoon. JONATHAN is discovered reading. MICHAL enters from the outside and stands watching him. After a moment HE looks up.)

JONATHAN: Michal? Come in, come in.

MICHAL: I didn't want to disturb you.

JONATHAN: I need some disturbing these days.

MICHAL: We never see you anymore.

JONATHAN: My door is always open. Sit down, sit down.

MICHAL: The family's well?

JONATHAN: Quite well, thank you. And you?

MICHAL: You've heard about Samuel, I suppose. The funeral's tomorrow.

JONATHAN: Yes. Yes, I know.

MICHAL: Will you be attending?

JONATHAN: Yes, of course.

MICHAL: Do you think that he might be there?

JONATHAN: David? Not if he values his life.

MICHAL: He has an army now. And there's a rumor going about that he's planning to storm the capital. That's what they're saying at any rate.

216

JONATHAN: Are they?

MICHAL: You don't believe it?

JONATHAN: Do you?

MICHAL: Father's had my marriage annulled. He's giving me to someone else. Did you hear what I said?

JONATHAN: I heard you.

MICHAL: I don't know what to do. Jonathan...

JONATHAN: Yes? What is it?

MICHAL: What should I do?

JONATHAN: You do have a choice.

MICHAL: Do I?

JONATHAN: You could join David.

MICHAL: So could you.

JONATHAN: He's not my husband.

MICHAL: Nor is he mine any longer.

JONATHAN: Then that settles that.

MICHAL: Don't you miss him?

JONATHAN: Yes, I do.

MICHAL: Why haven't you joined him?

JONATHAN: For the same reason that you're not joining him. *(After a moment)* Is Saul attending the funeral?

MICHAL: I don't know. Right now he's on his way to Ziph?

JONATHAN: Ziph? What for?

MICHAL: David was sighted there.

JONATHAN: I thought that was over and done with.

MICHAL: It will never be over and done with. Not as long as they're both alive. He's getting old and forgetful, you know.

JONATHAN: Not forgetful enough apparently.

>   *(JONATHAN sits lost in thought. MICHAL rises, stands*
>   *indecisively then runs off. JONATHAN turns.)*

JONATHAN: Michal? Michal?

>   *(JONATHAN goes to the doorway and stands looking out*
>   *as the lights come down.)*

Scene Six

(The hill of Hakilah in the Wilderness of Ziph. A foggy morning. DAVID and ABISHAI appear on a rise a short distance from the hill. DAVID carries a javelin and a water jug.)

DAVID: Saul? Wake up! Saul! Wake up, wake up!

(After a moment SAUL emerges sleepily from his tent and looks about.)

SAUL: Who is it? Who's out there?

DAVID: Don't you recognize my voice?

SAUL: David? Is that you? *(Lovingly)* David. David, my boy. Is that really you?

DAVID: It's me, your majesty, but a boy no longer.

SAUL: What are you doing out there?

DAVID: Trying to survive, your majesty.

SAUL: I've been waiting for you. Come play for me.

(ABNER enters from the tent.)

ABNER: What's happening? What's going on?

DAVID: It's me, Abner. It's David.

ABNER: David?

DAVID: Abner, Abner, you ought to be ashamed of yourself. Is that the way you guard your king? It's only out of the goodness of my heart that Saul is still alive. It's getting to be a habit, isn't it? These nightly visits of mine. And there you were, the both of you, dead to the world. Almost, at any rate. "He's a tyrant and a murderer." my cohort said, my good friend, Abishai, here. "Let's finish them off." "The king was anointed by God." I said. "I could never do him any harm." So we decided to spare your lives. We just took your javelin, Saul, and your water jug.

ABNER: What do you want?

DAVID: No, Abner, the question is what do you want, you and your army?

ABNER: Give yourself up.

SAUL: Yes, David, give yourself up. You're heir to the throne, are you not? Why are you running about the country like some fugitive? You're a great warrior now. You're no longer the shepherd boy who came to play for me. The boy with the magical fingers, the boy with the voice that charmed my heart.

DAVID: Where's Michal?

SAUL: I gave her to someone else.

DAVID: You had no right.

SAUL: You deserted her. What was I to do?

DAVID: Michal is my wife.

SAUL: Not any longer. I had the marriage annulled. Now don't be angry. Come home with me, David. Come home where you belong. Stop running around the country creatii ɔ all sorts of mischief.

DAVID: Incidentally, Saul, my men have you surrounded. If you don't believe me take a look.

SAUL: *(To ABNER)* Is that true?

DAVID: Oh, it's true all right.

SAUL: *(To ABNER)* What do we do now?

DAVID: I suggest you pack up your things, go home and forget about me.

ABNER: I suggest we do as he says.

DAVID: Good thinking, Abner.

> *(SAUL and ABNER start to leave.)*

DAVID: Abner?

ABNER: Yes? What is it?

DAVID: Haven't you forgotten something? The king's weapon and his water jug. He may need them both.

> *(ABNER hesitates then starts toward DAVID.)*

DAVID: Right this way, Abner. Right this way.

> *(DAVID holds up the javelin and the water jug. ABNER approaches DAVID and ABISHAI.)*

DAVID: I'd like you to meet Abishai here. A brave young man and an honorable one.

ABNER: The javelin, please.

DAVID: He's a lucky man, Abner, to have you at his side.

ABNER: May I have the javelin?

DAVID: He's getting old, isn't he, and senile, perhaps?

ABNER: The javelin, please.

DAVID: How's Michal?

ABNER: As well as could be expected.

DAVID: And Jonathan?

ABNER: I don't know. He keeps to himself.

(DAVID hands him the javelin.)

ABNER: And the water jug?

(DAVID hands him the water jug.)

ABNER: Get out of the country. He'll never give up on you. He doesn't even remember why, but he'll never give up on you.

SAUL: Abner?

DAVID: The master's voice.

ABNER: If you have any sense, if you care about what's happening to our people you'll take my advice and leave. *(HE returns to SAUL.)* Come along, come along.

(SAUL and ABNER go off together.)

ABISHAI: We should have finished him off when we had the chance. You heard him. He'll never give up on you.

DAVID: Maybe he's right.

ABISHAI: About what?

DAVID: About leaving the country.

ABISHAI: Where would we go?

DAVID: We could always join the Philistines. *(HE goes off.)*

ABISHAI: You're not serious, are you? *(HE follows DAVID off.)*

Scene Seven

(The house of Jonathan. A stormy night. There's a knock at the door. The knock is repeated again and again. JONATHAN enters from the interior of the house and goes off to answer the door.)

JONATHAN: *(Offstage)* Abner?! Come in, come in.

(ABNER enters followed by JONATHAN.)

ABNER: I'm sorry to disturb you at this late hour.

JONATHAN: Is he...?

ABNER: No, he's still alive. Barely.

JONATHAN: Is he ill?

ABNER: He's been starving himself.

JONATHAN: Not again?

ABNER: He's getting ready to go into battle and he can hardly walk. You know how he feels about witchcraft. He's heard about this woman at Endor. She's supposed to have supernatural powers. He's on his way there now.

JONATHAN: What do you want me to do?

ABNER: You're still his son.

JONATHAN: Did he send you?

ABNER: No.

223

JONATHAN: Does he know that you're here?

ABNER: No.

JONATHAN: Does he ever mention my name?

(ABNER shakes his head.)

JONATHAN: Then what makes you think...?

ABNER: You're his favorite, Jonathan. You always have been and you always will be. That ring you gave him for his birthday, it never leaves his finger.

JONATHAN: In all these years he's never made any attempt to get in touch with me.

ABNER: He's afraid you'll refuse to see him. It's true. He thinks about you all the time. I know that man. I can read him like a book. There are times when I'm appalled, when I'm disgusted but I have no choice. And neither have you.

JONATHAN: That's where you're wrong.

ABNER: Jonathan...son, if you ever had any feeling for him at all you won't desert him now.

JONATHAN: I used to worship that man.

ABNER: He's still your father. No matter what he's done he's still the same man.

JONATHAN: No! No, he's not the same man. I could forgive him for what he's done to me. I could forgive him for what he's done to Michal and even for what he's done to David. But what he's done to our country, what he's done to our people...

ABNER: And you think that you're in a position to judge him?

JONATHAN: I'm not judging anyone.

ABNER: What is it then?

JONATHAN: I'm empty, Abner. I have nothing to give. Don't you understand?

ABNER: You may regret this one day.

JONATHAN: Quite possibly.

ABNER: For my sake, Jonathan. You owe me.

JONATHAN: Ask me anything...

ABNER: All right. Forget that he's your father. Forget that you're his own flesh and blood. You're still an Israelite. He's still your king and he needs you. It's your duty to support him. I'll say no more. *(HE starts off then stops.)* Incidentally, I suppose you've heard about David.

JONATHAN: What about him?

ABNER: He's gone over to the Philistines.

JONATHAN: Poor David.

ABNER: Poor David has gone over to the enemy.

JONATHAN: What choice did he have?

ABNER: You'll defend him to the end, won't you?

JONATHAN: He'll be our king one day.

ABNER: Not if I have anything to say.

> *(ABNER goes off. JONATHAN stands thoughtfully, torn by conflicting emotions. The sound of the storm increases as the lights fade.)*

Scene Eight

(That evening. A dimly lit room in a house at Endor. The storm rages outside. A WOMAN enters followed by SAUL, his face hidden by the hood of his cloak.)

WOMAN: What can I do for you, sir?

SAUL: I want you to conjure up a spirit for me.

WOMAN: A spirit. I'm afraid you're mistaken. You've come to the wrong place.

SAUL: I don't think so.

WOMAN: That's strictly forbidden, you know.

SAUL: Is it really? *(HE takes a coin from his purse and places it in her hand.)*

WOMAN: Well, I...

SAUL: *(HE gives her another coin.)* I was told that you have special powers. Unless, of course, I was misinformed.

WOMAN: I've given up that sort of thing.

SAUL: I'm sorry to hear that. *(HE places a third and fourth coin in her hand.)*

WOMAN: I could make an exception, I suppose. But it's to go no further, you understand. I'll do it for you strictly as a favor, you understand. Whom do you wish to contact?

SAUL: Samuel.

226

WOMAN: Samuel? The high priest? He's a very important man. That may not be too easy.

(*SAUL slips her another coin.*)

WOMAN: I'll do my best. I'm not promising anything, mind you. Sit down. Sit down, please. What's your name, sir?

SAUL: What difference does it make?

WOMAN: Whom shall I say is asking for Samuel?

SAUL: (*HE removes his hood.*) Saul.

WOMAN: (*SHE falls to her knees.*) Your majesty?!

SAUL: Get up, get up. Nothing's going to happen to you, unless you try to hoodwink me.

WOMAN: No, no, your majesty. I'll do my best. I promise. Sit down. Sit down, please.

(*SAUL sits. The WOMAN puts out the lamp and the room is lit by moonlight only.*)

SAUL: What are you doing?

WOMAN: The spirits have an aversion to light.

SAUL: All right. Let's get on with it.

WOMAN: You must be patient, your majesty. This may take time.

SAUL: I don't have much time, I'm afraid.

WOMAN: (*SHE sits beside SAUL.*) You must close your eyes.

(*SAUL closes his eyes.*)

WOMAN: (*Calling out.*) Samuel! Oh mighty Samuel, can you hear me?

SAUL: Well? Can you see him?

WOMAN: You must be patient, your majesty.

SAUL: Tell him it's me. Tell him it's Saul.

WOMAN: King Saul wants to talk to you, oh mighty Samuel.

(SAUL opens his eyes.)

WOMAN: No, no, your majesty. You must close your eyes.

SAUL: I'm getting dizzy. *(HE sways.)*

WOMAN: Are you all right?

SAUL: Yes, yes, I'm fine. Let's get on with it. *(HE closes his eyes.)*

WOMAN: Oh mighty Samuel, it's King Saul. He's here with me now. He wants to talk to you. *(To SAUL)* He's here now. I'll leave the two of you alone. *(SHE backs out of the room.)*

SAUL: Samuel? It's me, Saul. Can you hear me? Can you see me?

(A light glimmers in the darkness.)

SAUL: Samuel, it's me. It's Saul.

(We hear the voice of SAMUEL.)

SAMUEL: What do you want?

SAUL: Can you hear me?

SAMUEL: I may be dead but I'm not deaf. Come, come, come. I don't have all day. What do you want?

SAUL: I'm going into battle and I want your blessing.

SAMUEL: You what? You have the nerve...?

SAUL: Samuel, please.

SAMUEL: After the way you've behaved?

SAUL: I've tried to walk in the ways of the Lord. I really have. If I've strayed at times...

SAMUEL: If?!

SAUL: It's this affliction of mine. It's this curse.

SAMUEL: Spare me your pitiful excuses, you miserable creature. You're talking to your priest, you black-hearted villain. I can see right through you into that evil heart of yours.

SAUL: I made a mistake.

SAMUEL: Mistake? Mistake?! Your whole life has been one big mistake.

SAUL: I've tried. I've really tried. And now my daughter's turned against me. She's a bitter old woman.

SAMUEL: Your daughter had a husband she loved. You took her away from him.

SAUL: He deserted her.

SAMUEL: You took her away from him and you gave her to another.

SAUL: David's a traitor. He's gone over to the Philistines.

SAMUEL: What choice did he have?

SAUL: He tried to take my throne away from me.

SAMUEL: David's your rightful heir. I anointed him.

SAUL: You anointed me as well.

SAMUEL: We all make mistakes and you, my son, are the biggest mistake I ever made. You are a disaster, Saul. A disaster as a man, a disaster as a father, a disaster as a king. You butchered my priests. You butchered innocent women and children.

SAUL: They were traitors.

SAMUEL: You are the traitor.

SAUL: And now my son won't come near me, my own Jonathan, my favorite.

SAMUEL: You tried to kill him, you madman. You tried to kill David. In addition to that you disobeyed the instructions of the Lord.

SAUL: I'm so weak.

SAMUEL: Of course, you are. You keep starving yourself. It's not enough that you're the king. You want to be high priest as well..

SAUL: Bless me, Samuel. Bless me, please. I beg of you. On my hands and knees. Bless me for I have sinned.

> *(SAUL falls to his knees and begins to weep, as the light fades. JONATHAN enters and kneels beside him.)*

JONATHAN: Father?

SAUL: Jonathan? Is that you?

JONATHAN: It's me, Father.

SAUL: Are you dead too?

JONATHAN: No, no. I'm right here, by your side. Open your eyes. Look at me.

SAUL: You won't disappear?

JONATHAN: No, Father, I won't disappear.

SAUL: *(HE opens his eyes.)* Oh, Jonathan, my dear, dear boy. *(HE embraces him.)* You've come back to me. I knew you would. You're a good boy, Son. A good boy. But it was wrong of you to defy my edict. You know that, don't you?

JONATHAN: Yes, Father, I know.

SAUL: But I forgive you, Son. And now you're going to be my heir. You mustn't pay any attention to that vicious old man. And that nasty little boy, that David. You see now what he was up to, don't you? You see now how he tried to steal my throne. How he tried to steal you away from me. But you were loyal to me, weren't you? Weren't you, Son?

JONATHAN: Yes, Father, I was.

SAUL: You're going to be the next king of the Israelites and I'm going to attend your coronation. And what a coronation that's going to be. All crimson and gold. Not like mine. An ignominious little affair. He poured that smelly oil on my head, and then, after that, I had to sneak back home like a criminal, like some common thief, and wait. Ten years I had to wait. But there's not going to be any waiting for you, my boy. No indeed. Everyone will be there to watch you receive the crown. Everyone will be there.

JONATHAN: Yes, Father.

SAUL: And now we're together again. Just like in the old days. Two warriors, side by side. But you won't go sneaking off on your own, will you, Son?

JONATHAN: No, Father.

SAUL: No more scouting expeditions. You hear me?

JONATHAN: I hear you, Father.

SAUL: That's a good boy. Now help me up.

(JONATHAN helps SAUL to his feet.)

SAUL: Your father's not as young as he used to be.

JONATHAN: And you've been fasting again.

SAUL: Guilty as charged. You were right. You were right, Son. A man cannot fight on an empty stomach.

JONATHAN: I've asked the woman to prepare some food.

SAUL: Good, good. I could use a good meal. It's just like the old days, isn't it? You and I. Two warriors, side by side. And you will give me another grandson, won't you? That crippled boy of yours, he just won't due.

JONATHAN: Yes, father.

SAUL: He won't do at all.

>   *(THEY go off together, JONATHAN supporting SAUL.*
>   *The sound of the storm fades and we hear the clash of*
>   *battle.)*

Scene Nine

(The house of DAVID in Hebron. Noon. DAVID is discovered sitting thoughtfully. ABISHAI enters.)

ABISHAI: He's here.

DAVID: Send him in.

ABISHAI: David...

DAVID: Yes? What is it?

ABISHAI: He won't accept you.

DAVID: That remains to be seen.

ABISHAI: And if he doesn't?

DAVID: I'll cross that bridge when I come to it.

ABISHAI: You'll let him leave here alive?

DAVID: Now look here, Abishai. The man came here in good faith. He's an honorable man and I intend to deal with him honorably.

ABISHAI: He's your sworn enemy. You've said so yourself.

DAVID: He was loyal to Saul.

ABISHAI: And now that Saul is dead he's loyal to himself.

DAVID: Abner has always been a sensible man.

233

ABISHAI: Oh, come on, David! Those last few years it was Abner who led Saul around by the nose. And now that you've got him here you can't let him go. Look, the death of this one man can save the lives of thousands. It would put an end to the threat of a civil war. Kill him I say and save us all a lot of trouble.

DAVID: You and Joab, the two of you; you just love the taste of blood, don't you?

ABISHAI: Luckily for you. If not for me and my brother, where would you be? After all we've been through...the humiliation, the squalor, the deceit, living in exile, kowtowing to our enemies... What else do we have to endure before you come to your senses, before you stand up and put up a fight?

DAVID: And kill our own people, the way that Saul did?

ABISHAI: Saul was a madman.

DAVID: That's a path I will never take.

ABISHAI: Never's a long, long time.

DAVID: Send him in.

ABISHAI: All I ask is that you think about it, that's all.

DAVID: All right, I'll think about it. Send him in.

> *(ABISHAI goes off. DAVID paces about. ABNER enters. The TWO MEN stand facing one another.)*

DAVID: It's good to see you, Abner. You're looking well. Sit down, sit down.

ABNER: I prefer to stand.

DAVID: I was hoping we might come to an understanding.

ABNER: In regard to what?

DAVID: I've been accepted by the men of Judah.

ABNER: That's fine. That's just fine. We're back now where we started from, a country divided. All that Saul accomplished just thrown away.

DAVID: It needn't be that way.

ABNER: That's true.

DAVID: You've never liked me. Why?

ABNER: That's not true. It's impossible not to like you, David. You work so hard at it. I've just never trusted you, that's all. And, apparently, I was right.

DAVID: I was anointed by Samuel. He came to me. I never sought him out.

ABNER: Samuel was in his dotage. Jonathan was Saul's rightful heir. Unfortunately Jonathan's no longer with us. His son's not fit to rule so Ish-Bosheth, as Saul's only living heir, is next in line.

DAVID: All right. I'd like you to arrange a meeting between the two of us.

ABNER: That won't be necessary since I speak for Ish-Bosheth.

DAVID: I see.

ABNER: Is there anything else you'd care to discuss?

DAVID: I'd like you to send me Michal.

ABNER: You've got two wives already. How many do you need?

DAVID: Michal is my wife.

ABNER: The marriage was annulled. She belongs to another. If there's nothing else...

(DAVID doesn't respond. ABNER starts off.)

DAVID: Abner?

ABNER: *(HE turns back.)* Yes? What is it?

DAVID: Were you with them at the end?

ABNER: I took part in the battle. They fought bravely and they died bravely.

DAVID: Together?

ABNER: Yes, together. No thanks to you.

DAVID: It might interest you to know that I had the man executed, the man that killed Saul.

ABNER: Saul took his own life. He fell on his sword.

DAVID: The man brought me Saul's arm band and his headgear.

ABNER: He was mortally wounded but still alive when this man came by. Saul asked the man to finish him off. The man did him a kindness.

DAVID: And Jonathan?

ABNER: He died sword in hand.

DAVID: He supported my claim.

ABNER: He joined his father in the end. I've had nothing but admiration for you, David. Starting with Saul I've watched you climb step by step, using your wiles, exuding your irresistible charm, breaking heart after heart. You're a clever man and a good soldier. I wish I thought your claim was legitimate. If you change your mind, however, let me know. We'd make a great team, you and I.

DAVID: That's true. We would.

>   *(ABNER hesitates and then goes off. After a moment ABISHAI reenters.)*

ABISHAI: Well?

(DAVID shakes his head. ABISHAI sighs.)

DAVID: I know, I know.

(Soft harp music is heard.)

DAVID: Michal once asked me if I thought that our lives were all laid out before us.

ABISHAI: And what did you say?

DAVID: I don't remember. I miss them Abishai. Not a day goes by that I don't think about them both, Saul...and Jonathan. Especially Jonathan. A friendship like ours comes once in a lifetime.

ABISHAI: What sort of a man was he?

DAVID: He was unique, loyal and brave. Too loyal, perhaps, with a soul too fragile, too vulnerable, too loving for this world. It broke his spirit and it broke his heart.

ABISHAI: And Saul?

DAVID: He wanted so to do the right thing. The trouble was he was never quite sure what the right thing was. There were times, when he came to his senses, and he would tell me stories about his childhood, about his hopes and his dreams...for himself and for our people. He just wasn't equipped to rule and he knew it. His greatest fear was that his mind would go before the end and, of course, it did. I think I understood him better than anyone else. Odd, isn't it? There is one consolation however.

ABISHAI: And what might that be?

DAVID: We are, after all, the sum total of those we love, are we not? They may be gone, Saul and Jonathan, but their spirit lives on in us.

ABISHAI: I'm not so sure that's a consolation. At any rate we'd better start preparing for war.

*(ABISHAI goes off. DAVID sits, lost in dreams of the
past, as the lights slowly fade.)*

LOOKING AT THE STARS

"We are all in the gutter
but some of us are looking at the stars."
Oscar Wilde

CAST OF CHARACTERS

DAVID . . . . King of Judah

ABNER . . . . A General

MICHAL . . . . David's Wife

JOAB . . . . David's General

NATHAN . . . . The High Priest

BATHSHEBA . . . . Uriah's Wife

URIAH . . . . A Captain

SCENE

The house of David in Hebron and the palace in Jerusalem

ACT ONE

Scene One

(The house of David in Hebron. DAVID, king of Judah, is discovered seated, deep in thought. ABNER, a general, enters. DAVID rises.)

DAVID: Abner.

ABNER: I come in peace.

DAVID: You're here alone?

ABNER: I speak for Ishbosheth.

DAVID: I see.

ABNER: I'm prepared to urge the elders of Israel to join with the people of Judah and accept you as their king.

DAVID: And what are your terms?

ABNER: There are no terms. The kingdom is yours for the taking.

DAVID: And what, may I ask, brought about this change of heart?

ABNER: I've come to realize that Ish-bosheth, though he is Saul's son, does not have the stuff that kings are made of. If you're not interested however...

DAVID: Of course, I'm interested. We're all of us sick of this war.

ABNER: What about Joab?

DAVID: What about him?

ABNER: Is he aware of this meeting?

DAVID: No.

ABNER: Where is he?

DAVID: He's off on a mission.

ABNER: I thought we could settle this thing today.

DAVID: What has Joab got to do with it?

ABNER: He is in charge of the army.

DAVID: I'm in charge of the army.

ABNER: I know how he felt about the boy.

DAVID: Abner, it's been almost a decade.

ABNER: In addition to that I'm sure he still believes that the meeting by the pool was a trap. The fact of the matter is we did not come prepared to fight. We were the ones that suffered all the losses that day.

DAVID: Things got out of hand. If I'd been there it would have turned out differently. At any rate, nine years of war is enough. Even Joab will agree.

ABNER: And you don't think that he still holds a grudge?

DAVID: Leave Joab to me.

ABNER: It's settled then. The kingdom is yours. *(Ironically)* A dream come true at last.

DAVID: I swear to you, Abner...

ABNER: Yes, yes. I know.

DAVID: Samuel came to me. I would have been quite content to write my songs and look after my father's sheep. And afterwards, when I met Saul, and saw how lonely and how miserable he was the prospect of being king was not one I looked forward to. You may not be aware of it but, it just so happens, that I offered to share the throne with Jonathan.

ABNER: No, no, no. You're right.

DAVID: I would never have taken anything from him that was rightfully his.

ABNER: I was wrong. I misjudged you.

DAVID: Our friendship was very precious to me.

ABNER: Yes, yes, I know.

DAVID: I promised him I would look after his son.

ABNER: Mephibosheth is a cripple, you know. He has to be carried about.

DAVID: I know. I'd like him to come and live with me.

ABNER: I'll see to it. So, what are your plans, now that the kingdom is yours?

DAVID: The first thing I'm going to do is to move the capital to Jerusalem. It's more central.

ABNER: You'll have the Jebusites to contend with.

DAVID: What's one more obstacle?

ABNER: And then?

DAVID: I'm going to bring the Holy Ark into the city and build a temple to house it, a magnificent temple.

ABNER: Oh?

DAVID: I swore that, when I was able, I would show my gratitude to the Lord, not only in verse, not only in music but with a glorious edifice that would house his holy words forever.

ABNER: Is Nathan aware of these plans of yours?

DAVID: I'll consult him, of course.

ABNER: If you'll remember Saul and Samuel had this running battle.

DAVID: Samuel was a bitter man. He resented turning the power of the church over to a monarch. I think Nathan is a little more reasonable.

ABNER: I hope so, for your sake. So, it's settled then. I'd better be getting back. The elders are eagerly waiting to hear from me.

DAVID: What about Michal?

ABNER: You asked for her and I've brought her with me. David...

DAVID: Yes? What is it?

ABNER: I have no right to say this but I must speak up. Saul was wrong to dissolve your marriage, but he did, and the man she's been living with, her new husband that is, whether you recognize the marriage or not...the man is very devoted to her. Forgive me for saying this. I don't want to offend you, especially on this historic occasion, but you do have other wives.

DAVID: And what difference does one more make?

ABNER: Please don't take offense. She's here. I recognize your claim.

DAVID: Our relationship was a very special one. And in a way, I suppose, it's my way of paying my respects to Saul. Since Jonathan refused my offer, it's only fitting that his daughter share the throne with me.

ABNER: At any rate, I think you ought to know. Her husband, the man she lives with...the man she's lived with for over ten years...came to me in tears. He followed us for miles, weeping openly.

DAVID: And what about Michal?

ABNER: Michal is not the eager young girl who fancied you years ago, if that's what you're hoping to find.

DAVID: Did she offer any resistance?

ABNER: Of course not. She knew it would have been pointless. But she's been living with this man for all these years. She's devoted to him And he's a good man, David.

DAVID: I'm sure she'll adjust.

ABNER: I've said my piece. It's your affair.

DAVID: Exactly.

ABNER: I'll be back within the week, and when I return we can arrange a proper coronation.

DAVID: And you'll bring the boy, Jonathan's son.

ABNER: Mephibosheth is no longer a boy.

DAVID: Yes, of course. Time has a way of creeping up on us, does it not?

ABNER: I'll send in Michal.

DAVID: Thank you, Abner.

> (THEY embrace and ABNER goes off. DAVID waits apprehensively. MICHAL enters. THEY stand staring at one another.)

DAVID: It's good to see you, Michal.

MICHAL: Have I changed that much? You were staring at me.

DAVID: We've all grown older.

MICHAL: You're better looking than ever.

DAVID: Oh, come now.

MICHAL: It's true. You were beautiful once, too beautiful perhaps.

DAVID: And now?

MICHAL: You're handsome. Distinguished. You look like a king.

DAVID: I've missed you.

MICHAL: Have you?

DAVID: I asked your father to send you to me, a number of times. He refused.

MICHAL: How many wives do you have now?

DAVID: Six.

MICHAL: And how many sons?

DAVID: Six.

MICHAL. Seems fair.

DAVID: You have no children?

MICHAL: No.

DAVID: You're still young. Perhaps we can present Saul with a grandson.

MICHAL: Wouldn't that be ironic, seeing how he felt about you?

DAVID: It must have been very difficult for you, living under the thumb of that madman.

MICHAL: And you, living in exile for all those years?

DAVID: It was a nightmare.

MICHAL: But they accepted you, the Philistines.

DAVID: Oddly enough.

MICHAL: It was to their advantage, of course. They could point to you and say, "This is the way the Israelites treat their heroes."

DAVID: What choice did I have? Saul was obsessed with getting rid of me. You saw what it was doing to the country.

MICHAL: But you're back now, and the kingdom is yours.

DAVID: And yours as well. We had so little time together. But I'll make it up to you. I promise. You'll have an honored place at my side.

MICHAL: And how will your other wives feel about that?

DAVID: You were the first. They'll understand. Did you see much of Jonathan?

MICHAL: Not really, no. Jonathan kept pretty much to himself. Do you still play and compose?

DAVID: It's the only time I find peace. Do you remember the first time we met?

MICHAL: Yes, of course. You called me a witch.

DAVID: I was teasing you.

MICHAL: You said I had cat's eyes.

DAVID: You still do.

MICHAL: Do I?

DAVID: Abner's about face was quite sudden. It came as a bit of a surprise. You're smiling. Is there something I ought to know?

MICHAL: It's not important.

DAVID: You've aroused my curiosity.

MICHAL: The war is over. That's what really matters.

DAVID: What changed his mind?

MICHAL: He's on the outs with Ishbosheth, if you must know.

DAVID: What happened?

MICHAL: Abner's been sleeping with one of Saul's mistresses. Ishbosheth found out and made a fuss about it, and one thing let to another.

DAVID: I see.

MICHAL: You're shocked.

DAVID: No, of course not. You must be tired.

> *(JOAB, David's general, enters then stops short.)*

JOAB: I'm interrupting.

DAVID: That's quite all right. *(To Michal)* Come along. I'll introduce you to the housekeeper. *(To Joab)* I'll be right back.

> *(DAVID goes off with MICHAL. JOAB paces about. DAVID reenters a moment later.)*

JOAB: Another concubine?

DAVID: That was Michal.

JOAB: Saul's daughter?

DAVID: The one and only.

JOAB: How did she get here?

DAVID: Abner brought her.

JOAB: Abner?

DAVID: I asked him to bring her with him, as part of our agreement.

JOAB: What agreement? What are you talking about?

DAVID: The war is over.

JOAB: Just like that?!

DAVID: He sent word that he wanted to meet with me. I didn't want to waste any time.

JOAB: Apparently.

DAVID: It came about very suddenly. There wasn't time to get in touch with you.

JOAB: So you agreed to his terms.

DAVID: There were no terms. The country is ours.

ABNER: And you believe him?!

DAVID: Now don't get upset.

JOAB: How dare you?! How dare you make peace without consulting me?

DAVID: I'm consulting you now.

ABNER: After the fact?

DAVID: The meeting was just a preliminary.

DAVID: We've got them on the run. They've been suffering tremendous losses.

DAVID: I'm aware of that.

JOAB: Are you also aware of the fact that Abner swore he'd never recognize your claim to the throne?

DAVID: Apparently he's changed his mind.

JOAB: It's a trick. Don't you understand? How could you be taken in by that lying, two-faced schemer?

DAVID: Joab, please. I know Abner. He's an honorable man.

JOAB: As long as he's alive...

DAVID: You're still brooding about that incident at the pool.

JOAB: Incident you call it?

DAVID: Misunderstanding.

JOAB: Incident he calls it!

DAVID: Joab, they were not prepared for battle. You know that as well as I. And, as far as your brother is concerned, it was most unfortunate.

JOAB: Unfortunate he calls it!

DAVID: I know how you felt about the boy. We all of us loved him. He was a sweet, gentle soul. Even Abner felt kindly towards him. He begged the boy to turn away but he refused, and he had no choice. He had to fight him.

JOAB: And you believe him?!

DAVID: Yes, I do. I've never known him to lie or cheat. Oh now look. How many men have died since this war began? How many more must die? Let's be sensible, Joab. There's got to be an end to this killing.

JOAB: And he wants nothing from us? He's going to retire to his farm? He's going to spend the rest of his days raising sheep?

DAVID: We haven't discussed all that.

JOAB: What have you discussed?

DAVID: Nothing really. This was just a preliminary meeting. Look, Joab, as far as you're concerned nothing is going to change. You're my right hand man. You always were and you always will be. On the other hand...

JOAB: On the other hand what?

DAVID: Abner is a magnificent general, a veteran of many wars. He'll be a great asset.

JOAB: To whom?

DAVID: To us. To you and me. To the country. And he's very much aware of protocol. I can assure you he's not going to ruffle any feathers. You're always complaining that I'm not aggressive enough, that I don't understand the military. I'm sure that Abner will prove to be a valuable ally for you.

JOAB: Exactly what position have you offered him?

DAVID: I haven't offered him anything.

JOAB: Do you take me for a fool? You and I both know that Abner is not going to fade into the night.

DAVID: Look, you are my commander in chief. Abner's aware of that. I am sorry you weren't here for the initial meeting, but there are all sorts of arrangements still to be ironed out and, I promise you, you will have your say. You have my word for it.

ABNER: *(Half under his breath)* Such as it is.

DAVID: What's that?

ABNER: Nothing.

DAVID: So, how did it go? The raid? How did it go?

JOAB: Fine, fine.

DAVID: Did we lose any men?

JOAB: There were no fatalities. Where is he now? I'd like to have a talk with him.

DAVID: Abner?

JOAB: Yes, Abner. I'd like to meet him face to face, unless you have some objection?

DAVID: No, of course not.

JOAB: Where is he?

DAVID: He's not here right now.

JOAB: Where is he?

DAVID: He left a few minutes ago to meet with the elders of Israel.

(JOAB strides off.)

DAVID: Joab? Joab?!

(DAVID sighs and sits apprehensively as the lights come down.)

Scene Two

(The palace of David in Jerusalem. Joyous music is heard through the window. NATHAN, the high priest, enters with MICHAL.)

NATHAN: What is it, now?

MICHAL: I'm frightened.

NATHAN: What are you afraid of?

MICHAL: You've heard about Ishbosheth.

NATHAN: It was most unfortunate. But that's all over and done with.

MICHAL: Is it?

NATHAN: What do you mean?

MICHAL: Isn't it obvious? First Abner, then my brother.

NATHAN: You think there's some sort of connection?

MICHAL: Abner was his general, wasn't he? Ishbosheth was his son. And I'm his daughter. Who do you think is going to be next?

NATHAN: Saul is dead and buried.

MICHAL: And so, apparently, is anyone that might challenge the king's legitimacy. Except for me, that is. For ten years he's neglected me and then suddenly he wants me by his side.

NATHAN: You're his wife, and that's where you belong.

MICHAL: Then why doesn't he come near me?

NATHAN: From what I gather...

MICHAL: Don't believe everything you hear.

NATHAN: And, as far as Abner's concerned...

MICHAL: Oh, I know, I know. The king's hands are clean. The man was murdered on his doorstep...

NATHAN: Let's not exaggerate.

MICHAL: I beg your pardon. The man was murdered within sight of the palace and yet the king had nothing to do with it. The fact that the assassin is David's right hand man, the fact that this assassin goes scot free...

NATHAN: David was very upset.

MICHAL: Oh, please! I was there. I attended the funeral. I watched with everyone else that amazing picture, the crocodile tears flooding down his cheeks as he followed the bier. What a glorious performance! What a great and noble king, to mourn the passing of his enemy.

NATHAN: Abner was no longer his enemy. There was, however, a private feud between Joab and Abner. And now that it's over and done with, it's pointless to perpetuate this trail of vengeance.

MICHAL: "Vengeance is mine, sayeth the lord."

NATHAN: For the first time in our history we're on good terms with our neighbors. Trade is flourishing.

MICHAL: Oh, yes, I know. Money's passing hands. The coffers are full Let's not ask too many questions. One murder, two. What difference does it make?

NATHAN: And as far as your brother is concerned he was murdered by his own men. David had them executed, didn't he?

MICHAL: And quickly too, before any questions could be asked. But then who wants to ask any questions when trade is flourishing and we're on good terms with our neighbors.

NATHAN: Are you accusing the king...?

MICHAL: I'm not accusing anybody of anything. How can I? There is no proof. There are no witnesses. Not anymore, that is. In addition to that the palace is getting rather crowded. We've got to make room for all the new wives, to say nothing of all the concubines. But then a king must live in style, I suppose. The question is, where is all this money coming from? Who's going to pay for this magnificent palace, this luxurious love nest for all these foreign princesses?

NATHAN: These foreign marriages are a matter of diplomacy.

MICHAL: Is that what they call it now? Diplomacy?

NATHAN: Unlike your father, David has always walked in the ways of the Lord.

MICHAL: Oh, I know, I know. His lovely songs, his immortal psalms. David is certainly devout. The entire world can testify to that.

> *(The music outside grows louder. MICHAL goes to the window.)*

MICHAL: Why just look at him out there! Have you ever seen such religious fervor? Have you ever seen such holy ecstasy?

NATHAN: Now look here, Michal, I'm getting sick and tired of all this whining. You're David's wife.

MICHAL: My marriage to David was annulled.

NATHAN: So you've said.

MICHAL: It was annulled by the king. The legitimate king.

NATHAN: Saul had no such authority. Your father had a very bad habit of infringing on the church's domain.

MICHAL: He consulted a priest as well.

NATHAN: Was it consummated, this marriage of yours?

MICHAL: Yes...

NATHAN: Then it cannot be annulled.

MICHAL: Desertion is a perfectly legitimate charge.

NATHAN: According to David you were the one who was derelict in your duties and he's been magnanimous enough to overlook that fact.

MICHAL: And what about my second marriage?

NATHAN: There was no second marriage.

MICHAL: I lived with this man for almost ten years. We lived as man and wife.

NATHAN: I beg to differ with you. You were not man and wife. You were living in sin. The church, however, is willing to overlook that sinful liaison. There were no children, were there?

MICHAL: No...

NATHAN: Let's just be thankful for that.

MICHAL: This man was devoted to me. I was all he had in the world. How can you say that a man like that simply doesn't exist? How can you say that a relationship like that, a loving one that lasted for almost a decade, was a sinful one?

NATHAN: I'm sorry, my dear, but according to the law...

MICHAL: What kind of law is that?

NATHAN: A holy law.

MICHAL: Laws are made by man and they can be changed, holy or not.

NATHAN: My dear Michal, you're the wife of a king...

MICHAL: A bogus king. And even if he is legitimate...

NATHAN: Now you listen to me. This has got to stop. You have a comfortable home. You're treated with respect and you have nothing to complain about. Why don't you find something to occupy your time.

MICHAL: Like what?

NATHAN: *(He sighs.)* I know it's difficult sometimes to accept the will of the Lord. But we must be humble. We must learn to accept our fate. You're still a young woman. You have many fruitful years ahead of you. And, from what I've been told, you were very much in love with David when you first married.

MICHAL: I was young and foolish when we first married.

NATHAN: But you loved him, didn't you?

MICHAL: I loved the image of him, the image that I'd built up in my mind. As a matter of fact we were all taken in by that glamorous facade of his...my father, my brother, all the people at court. He was so handsome, so talented, so charming. There was only one man, only one man that saw through David. That was Abner and look what happened to him.

(The music grows louder.)

MICHAL: He's going to throw his neck out of joint. Such naked passion! It's embarrassing.

(The music comes to a crescendo and then stops.)

MICHAL: What a relief! I'm exhausted just watching him.

NATHAN: This is a glorious day.

MICHAL: No doubt about that. If Samuel were alive, however, I just wonder what he'd have to say.

NATHAN: In regard to what?

MICHAL: The same thing, perhaps, that he said to my father. "Does the king want to be high priest as well?" But then you're so much more secure than Samuel ever was. Take David's plans for this temple of his.

NATHAN: What about them?

MICHAL: They don't cause you any concern?

NATHAN: Why should they cause me any concern? I'm sure you'll agree that it's unseemly for the Holy Ark to be housed in that shoddy tent.

MICHAL: Of quite, especially since the Lord's servant is housed in this magnificent palace. Why should the Lord himself be short changed?

NATHAN: Be careful now. I will not countenance any blasphemy.

MICHAL: You're absolutely right. The Lord can look after himself. What I'm concerned about is the people.

NATHAN: The people?

MICHAL: What if the people are groaning under an impossible financial burden, taxed till they bleed?! Let's import all sorts of exotic materials. Let's recruit more men to build this splendid temple of his. There must be men somewhere that aren't serving in the king's army. Let the crops rot. Let the animals tend to themselves. Let the countryside go to seed. The vanity of the king, his vaulted ambition, that's what must be served.

(DAVID enters looking flushed and jubilant.)

DAVID: *(To NATHAN)* So there you are!

NATHAN: What's that?

DAVID: I wondered where you'd disappeared to.

NATHAN: Yes, well, the sun was getting too much for me. Besides I have all sorts of things to attend to. *(HE starts off.)*

DAVID: Where are you off to? We were supposed to go over those plans.

NATHAN: What plans are those?

DAVID: The plans for the temple. I'm anxious to get your approval.

NATHAN: Yes, well, there's plenty of time for that.

DAVID: Not really.

NATHAN: Don't rush me, please. I don't like to be rushed. Especially on something as important as this.

DAVID: But...

NATHAN: I'll need more time to study the plans.

DAVID: You've had them for almost a month now. How much time do you need?

NATHAN: The plans for this temple of yours isn't the only item on my agenda. You'll have to excuse me. *(HE hurries off.)*

DAVID: What on earth's come over him?

MICHAL: It's all this excitement.

DAVID: I don't understand it. Just the other day he couldn't have been more enthusiastic.

MICHAL: That's a priest for you.

DAVID: It's very strange.

MICHAL: Life is so unpredictable.

DAVID: I didn't see you out there either.

MICHAL: I don't believe in overdoing it.

DAVID: How often is the Holy Ark brought into our new capital?

MICHAL: Besides I didn't think my poor measure of devotion would be missed. *(SHE starts off.)*

DAVID: Michal...?!

MICHAL: Yes? What is it?

DAVID: I'd like a word with you. Please. Sit down.

(SHE remains standing. DAVID sits.)

DAVID: I know that you're not happy here.

MICHAL: Now what makes you think that?

DAVID: I've been getting all sorts of complaints.

MICHAL: Have you now? What sort of complaints have you been getting?

DAVID: I've been told that you've been spreading nasty stories about me, making fun of me behind my back,

MICHAL: Nasty stories? What sort of nasty stories?

DAVID: Pitting one wife against the other. Poisoning my sons against me. I want you to stay away from those boys.

MICHAL: How could I possibly do that? Everywhere one goes they're always underfoot.

DAVID: You're determined to be unpleasant, aren't you?

MICHAL: I do my best.

DAVID: What do you hope to accomplish?

MICHAL: I don't know what you're talking about.

DAVID: I'm not going to send you back to that so-called husband of yours, so you might as well get forget about it. We are man and wife in the eyes of the Lord.

MICHAL: "The eyes of the Lord!" You're such a fraud, my dear. I've been watching you out there, prancing about like some demented demon. Who do you think you're fooling? You're no more devout than the sheep you used to attend on your father's farm. Shouting at the top of your lungs like some lovesick calf. People are laughing at you behind your back, if you really want to know.

DAVID: Are you quite finished?

MICHAL: I'm Saul's daughter. The daughter of a king, a real king. You can dance about to your heart's content but no matter how much you prance and howl you'll never be the man that he was. Cavorting around half naked in front of all those slave girls, making a vulgar fool of yourself.

DAVID: That's enough.

MICHAL: It's disgusting.

DAVID: I said, that's enough.

MICHAL: I'm not afraid of you, you shepherd boy. That's what you were and that's what you'll always be. Putting on those airs, but just you wait...

(HE raises his hand as if to strike her then stops himself.)

MICHAL: Go ahead. Hit me. Abuse me. Humiliate me. That's why you brought me here, isn't it. The memory of Saul still sticks in your craw. But you'll regret the day you ever laid eyes on me. I promise you.

(JOAB enters. MICHAL turns, notices Joab and goes off.)

JOAB: Why don't you get rid of her?

DAVID: When I want your advice I'll ask for it.

JOAB: She's a trouble-maker and she'll only get worse as the years go by.

DAVID: *(HE sighs.)* I know, I know. It's just that...

JOAB: Just that what?

DAVID: I keep hoping.

JOAB: She is Saul's daughter, however, and he still does have his followers. If you could just shut her up.

JOAB: Have you ever found a way to shut a woman up?

JOAB: One woman, yes. But a harem like yours? I take my hat off to you.

DAVID: *(After a moment)* Did you find out who she was?

JOAB: She? Who? *(Feigning forgetfulness)* Oh, yes. The woman on the terrace

DAVID: Well?

JOAB: You're interested.

DAVID: Let's just say curious. Well?

JOAB: She's the wife of one of my captains, Uriah, a Hittite.

DAVID: She's married?

JOAB: Isn't that what I said? Sorry.

DAVID: There's nothing to be sorry about.

JOAB: No, no, of course not.

DAVID: I'm just surprised, that's all. The way she makes a point of displaying herself.

JOAB: Perhaps you're misreading the message.

DAVID: Oh, come on. Bathing in full view like that.

JOAB: If you have wares, display them.

DAVID: Are they for sale, do you think?

JOAB: She's a respectable woman, as far as I can gather.

DAVID: You've met her?

JOAB: Briefly.

DAVID: What does she look like up close?

JOAB: She's very beautiful.

DAVID: Anything up here?

JOAB: You didn't ask for a report on her intelligence.

DAVID: I can't abide a stupid woman.

JOAB: You want to meet her?

DAVID: What would be the point? Like you say, she's married.

JOAB: Her husband's out of town right now. On duty.

DAVID: He's alive and well?

JOAB: As of last week.

DAVID: Then that's the end of that. So, you'll be leaving shortly.

JOAB: As soon as the weather improves.

DAVID: *(After a moment)* Do they have any children?

JOAB: Who? *(HE smiles.)* I thought you weren't interested.

DAVID: What's her name?

JOAB: Bathsheba.

DAVID: Bathsheba.

JOAB: If you'd like me to arrange an introduction say so now, or forever hold your peace.

> *(DAVID and JOAB go off together as the lights come down.)*

Scene Three

(David's chambers. Evening a week later. BATHSHEBA, a beautiful young woman, is discovered waiting uneasily. SHE rises, walks about then stands gazing out the window. DAVID enters.)

DAVID: The view's even better from the roof.

BATHSHEBA: *(SHE whirls about.)* Your majesty?! *(SHE kneels.)*

DAVID: Get up, get up.

(SHE rises.)

DAVID: Aren't you ashamed of yourself?

BATHSHEBA: I beg your pardon?

DAVID: You know perfectly well what I'm talking about. Making a spectacle of yourself like that. Or do you make it a habit of displaying your naked body in public?

BATHSHEBA: You must be mistaken.

DAVID: That is your apartment just across the way, is it not?

BATHSHEBA: Why yes.

DAVID: And you mean to tell me that you weren't aware that you could be seen from here?

BATHSHEBA: It never occurred to me.

DAVID: Oh come now.

267

BATHSHEBA: You're perfectly free to believe what you like.

DAVID: All right, all right. There's no need to get upset.

BATHSHEBA: I'm not upset. I'm angry. Is that why I've been summoned here? Am I being accused of indecent exposure?

DAVID: I'm not accusing you of anything.

BATHSHEBA: Then why am I here?

DAVID: You seem to be a respectable woman, and perhaps you're not aware...

BATHSHEBA: Of what?

DAVID: That when you bathe on your terrace you're exposing yourself to the world?

BATHSHEBA: The world, your majesty?

DAVID: Well, not the world, perhaps.

BATHSHEBA: For one thing the terrace is high above the city, surrounded by walls and plants. I never thought to look up to see who was spying on me.

DAVID: I wasn't spying on you.

BATHSHEBA: And besides it was late at night. Most people are in their beds.

DAVID: Except for you.

BATHSHEBA: The heat's been so unbearable, I couldn't sleep. And your majesty?

DAVID: I've been very restless of late. This time of year I'm usually in a tent somewhere, sword in hand.

BATHSHEBA: In your tent?

DAVID: No. Unfortunately when I'm in my tent my sword is usually in its sheath. You're blushing.

BATHSHEBA: I'm sorry.

DAVID: That was naughty of me. I was walking in the garden and I just happened to look down. I noticed this vision in the moonlight and I was intrigued.

BATHSHEBA: I see.

DAVID: Would you care for some wine? It is permitted.

BATHSHEBA: Since it is permitted...

  (DAVID pours two glasses of wine and hands her one.)

BATHSHEBA: Thank you.

DAVID: What shall we drink to?

BATHSHEBA: To the kingdom of Israel?

DAVID: And its beautiful women.

  (THEY drink. DAVID gazes intently at her.)

BATHSHEBA: You're embarrassing me.

DAVID: I'm sorry. You have the most beautiful skin. Do you take special care?

BATHSHEBA: Not really, no.

DAVID: Have we met before?

BATHSHEBA: No.

DAVID: Are you quite sure?

BATHSHEBA: I would have remembered.

DAVID: In another life, perhaps.

BATHSHEBA: Have we had another life, do you think?

DAVID: I've often wondered.

BATHSHEBA: So have I. Where do we come from, do you think? Did we exist before this present life or do we first come into existence at conception?

DAVID: Are you often plagued with such deep philosophical thoughts?

BATHSHEBA: I don't know where that came from.

DAVID: You have no children.

BATHSHEBA: No.

DAVID: Yes, I have been enquiring about you.

BATHSHEBA: I see. And what else did you find out about me?

DAVID: Your husband's a soldier.

BATHSHEBA: He's a captain in your army and he's very patriotic.

DAVID: Is he now?

BATHSHEBA: He loves nothing better than soldiering, facing the enemy, his comrades at his side.

DAVID: It must be very lonely for you then.

BATHSHEBA: I find things to do.

DAVID: Such as?

BATHSHEBA: It wouldn't interest you.

DAVID: Let me be the judge of that.

BATHSHEBA: Women's work.

DAVID: And what might that be? When I was a fugitive, which was not that long ago, we all of us shared in the household chores, the cooking, the washing, the cleaning up. Even now, after a meal, I sometimes find myself getting up automatically to help with the dishes. Or when I toss aside a dirty robe I still have the urge to wash it myself.

BATHSHEBA: Those must have been difficult years.

DAVID: They left their mark.

BATHSHEBA: In what way?

DAVID: It keeps me humble, the memory of those years. When I think of the depths to which I sank in order to keep alive. I've never talked about this to anyone before, but in order to escape from Saul...he pursued me relentlessly, you know...I had to leave the country. I once fled to Gath. The servants of the king there tried to persuade him to kill me. They said that I was a spy. In order to prevent losing my head I pretended to be mad. I rolled in the dirt and howled like a dog. I let the saliva drool from my mouth. Everyone laughed. They teased and tormented me, and decided I was harmless. How I hated myself! How ashamed I was!

BATHSHEBA: Yes, the price one must pay sometimes just in order to survive.

DAVID: Where was I?

BATHSHEBA: You said those years left a mark.

DAVID: Ah, yes. I know what it's like to be the lowest of the low.

BATHSHEBA: What kept you going?

DAVID: The dream I had of sitting on the throne, of building a temple to house the Holy Ark, the most magnificent temple ever built; the vision of myself ruling in peace with my wife by my side.

BATHSHEBA: Which wife was that?

DAVID: Michal, the daughter of Saul. She was the first, you know. We were separated by Saul and I looked forward to the day that she would join me.

BATHSHEBA: And now the dream's complete.

DAVID: So it is.

BATHSHEBA: Or is it?

DAVID: Sometimes wine turns to vinegar.

BATHSHEBA: Oh, dear! How sad!

DAVID: There are greater tragedies in life.

BATHSHEBA: At any rate you have other women to console you.

DAVID: What makes you think that I need consolation?

BATHSHEBA: I'm sorry. I didn't mean...

DAVID: No, you're right. I've never forgiven her.

BATHSHEBA: For what?

DAVID: She should have come back to me of her own free will.

BATHSHEBA: But she didn't.

DAVID: No, she didn't. I'm like an elephant, you know. I never forget. So beware! And you? What sort of person are you?

BATHSHEBA: I never thought about it.

DAVID: Aren't you jealous of the army that deprives you of your husband?

BATHSHEBA: I'm a soldier's wife. That's my fate.

DAVID: And you've become accustomed to lonely nights? Taking baths on your terrace in the early hours of the morning? Or perhaps...

BATHSHEBA: What?

DAVID: You've taken a lover.

BATHSHEBA: Is that why I'm here? Because you think I'm an adulteress?

DAVID: Don't get excited. I'm not accusing you of anything.

BATHSHEBA: But that's what you think.

DAVID: You can read peoples' minds?

BATHSHEBA: Why am I here, your majesty?

DAVID: I was curious...to see what you looked like up close.

BATHSHEBA: And do I pass inspection?

DAVID: Why are there no children?

BATHSHEBA: We haven't been blessed.

DAVID: Do you want children?

BATHSHEBA: More than anything in the world. And you, your majesty? If you could have anything in the world what would you ask for?

DAVID: My glorious temple. My greatest fear is that I won't live long enough to see it's completion.

BATHSHEBA: You're still a young man.

DAVID: A project like that isn't built in a day.

BATHSHEBA: When do you plan to start?

DAVID: As soon as I get Nathan's approval.

BATHSHEBA: An enterprise like that must take a lot of planning.

DAVID: Oh, the planning's all done. I've been in touch with the most talented architects in the country. They've drawn up all the floor plans. I've commissioned craftsmen to design all the furnishings. I've begun to import all sorts of exotic woods, all sorts of stone, marble and onyx. It's my temple is what I want to be remembered by. Not as a warrior, not as a poet. I'm boring you.

BATHSHEBA: On the contrary.

DAVID: I'm beginning to repeat myself. A sign of age, I suppose. It is getting late. I should send you home.

BATHSHEBA: Yes. Yes, of course.

DAVID: You must be sleepy.

BATHSHEBA: As a matter of fact I'm wide awake.

DAVID: So am I.

BATHSHEBA: What do you do when you can't fall asleep?

DAVID: I walk about in the garden. It's so quiet and beautiful at night. Sometimes I look up at the stars and I get lost in them...searching, searching, searching.

BATHSHEBA: With no one at your side?

DAVID: Would you like to see the garden?

BATHSHEBA: I'd love to.

DAVID: Come along then.

(HE holds out his hand to her. SHE takes it and HE pulls her close to him.)

DAVID: You're very beautiful.

> *(HE kisses her. HE kisses her a second time and SHE responds. THEY fall into a passionate embrace as the lights slowly fade.)*

Scene Four

(The scene is the same. Morning. Three months later. NATHAN is discovered, waiting impatiently. DAVID enters hurriedly from his bedchamber.)

DAVID: You're up bright and early.

NATHAN: It's not that early.

DAVID: What time is it?

NATHAN: It's almost time for lunch. We missed you at the morning prayer.

DAVID: I didn't get to sleep until late last night.

NATHAN: Your conjugal duties will be the death of you yet.

DAVID: What can I do for you?

NATHAN: You were the one that sent for me.

DAVID: Yes. Yes, of course.

NATHAN: What did you want to see me about?

DAVID: It's been months since I sent you those plans.

NATHAN: What plans are those?

DAVID: The plans for the temple.

NATHAN: Yes. Yes, of course.

276

DAVID: Have you had a chance to look them over?

NATHAN: Not really, no.

DAVID: I don't understand...

NATHAN: That is to say I did look them over briefly as soon as you sent them to me.

DAVID: And?

NATHAN: Let me ask you this. Where is all this money going to come from? This is going to cost a fortune.

DAVID: I have some money set aside.

NATHAN: Enough to cover a project like this?

DAVID: Enough to get it started.

NATHAN: And then what?

DAVID: Private donations, to begin with.

NATHAN: And then what?

DAVID: And, if necessary, we'll have to institute a special tax.

NATHAN: Don't you think the people are taxed enough as it is?

DAVID: It'll be a modest one.

NATHAN: Even so...

DAVID: I'm sure there are going to be complaints, if that's what you're concerned about. When it comes to money there are always complaints. However once the temple is built, once the people start coming here to worship they'll be asking "Why wasn't it built sooner?".

NATHAN: And it's not only the money.

DAVID: What else?

NATHAN: This is an enormous undertaking. Where is all this manpower going to come from?

DAVID: Oh now look, this is a project of national importance. One that's going to benefit the church as well as the state.

NATHAN: I am aware of that.

DAVID: So let's just take it one step at a time. The important thing is to get it started.

NATHAN: And another thing. I understand you've begun to import all sorts of expensive materials. Exotic woods and precious metals.

DAVID: What about it?

NATHAN: We are a simple people, David...

DAVID: We were a simple people. We are now a world power. Oh, now look here, Nathan, we're no longer a ragtag bunch of tribes wandering about the wilderness. We're a nation among nations and we've got a position to maintain. How can we hold our heads up when we treat our God so shabbily?

NATHAN: What on earth are you talking about?

DAVID: I'm talking about that miserable tent that houses the Holy Ark. How can the world respect a nation that has no respect for its God? How can we respect ourselves?! As head of the church you should be anxious for this building to get underway instead of dillydallying.

NATHAN: I'm not disagreeing with you.

DAVID: I have your approval then?

NATHAN: I need a little more time.

DAVID: For what?

NATHAN: To study the plans, your highness. If you had consulted me before you drew them up....

DAVID: I'm consulting you now and I welcome your input. I want your input. I'm anxiously awaiting your input.

NATHAN: And you shall have it.

DAVID: When?

NATHAN: I have one more circuit to make this month and, as soon as I return, I shall give the matter my full attention.

DAVID: I'd like to be around to see it's completion.

NATHAN: You will be, my son. Unless, of course, you kill yourself servicing all those wives of yours. *(HE starts off, then looks back.)* To say nothing of your concubines. *(HE goes off.)*

DAVID: Pompous ass!

(BATHSHEBA enters from the bedchamber.)

DAVID: He needs more time.

BATHSHEBA: He'll come around.

DAVID: Saul had his Samuel. I have my Nathan.

BATHSHEBA: You mustn't pressure him.

DAVID: He keeps putting me off.

BATHSHEBA: The thing to do is to make him think the idea was his.

DAVID: Yes, of course. And I suppose I should have consulted him to begin with. What would I do without you? *(HE kisses her.)* The day's just begun and I'm exhausted.

BATHSHEBA: No wonder. You were up half the night.

DAVID: Life was so simple when I had nothing to worry about but my father's sheep.

BATHSHEBA: Was it?

DAVID: I'd just lie in the grass and watch the clouds float by and dream.

BATHSHEBA: And what did you dream about?

DAVID: I'd be rich and famous with a beautiful woman at my side.

BATHSHEBA: And now that you're rich and famous?

DAVID: With a beautiful woman at my side.

BATHSHEBA: With a bevy of beautiful women.

DAVID: No. Only one.

BATHSHEBA: And yet you lie awake...dreaming?

DAVID: Worrying.

BATHSHEBA: About what?

DAVID: Life is so short. I want to be here to see the completion of my temple. I want to be here for the inaugural ceremonies.

BATHSHEBA: What's to prevent you?

DAVID: I have this terrible premonition. It's nonsense, of course, but there's so much I want to accomplish and so little time. All those wasted years...

BATHSHEBA: You've accomplished so much already. We're a nation to be reckoned with.

DAVID: No, you're right. I must be patient. I'm one man and I can only do so much. And then there's the future, after I'm gone. Who can I count on to fulfill my dreams? There's Absalom, of course. He's the brightest of the lot. Of course, they're all still young. What a bore I must be. All I can talk about, all I can think about are affairs of state. You've been so quiet these past few days. I saw you sitting by the window, looking so sad, as if you'd lost your best friend. What were you thinking of?

BATHSHEBA: Uriah's due home on leave this week.

DAVID: We'll postpone it. I'll to speak to Joab. Is there anything else? All you have to do is ask?

BATHSHEBA: I haven't seen my parents in quite a while and my mother hasn't been well lately.

DAVID: You said the other day that she was in the best of health.

BATHSHEBA: Yes well, she is getting on. I'm thinking that perhaps I ought to pay her a visit.

DAVID: Is it you or your mother?

BATHSHEBA: What do you mean?

DAVID: You haven't been well yourself lately.

BATHSHEBA: It's just an upset stomach.

DAVID: Are you pregnant? I want the truth. Bathsheba...?

BATHSHEBA: I don't want to add to your troubles.

DAVID: Are you or are you not?

BATHSHEBA: Yes. I'll go away somewhere.

DAVID: And what? Get rid of the child?

BATHSHEBA: Isn't that what you want?

DAVID: No.

BATHSHEBA: But if someone should find out...

DAVID: I want you here, by my side. That's what I want. Is that what were you planning, without even telling me?

BATHSHEBA: I'm afraid.

DAVID: Nothing is going to happen to you.

BATHSHEBA: Do you really want the child?

DAVID: Yes.

BATHSHEBA: Are you sure?

DAVID: I want a child from you.

BATHSHEBA: But someone's bound to find out.

DAVID: *(After a moment)* Suppose your husband did come home on leave?

BATHSHEBA: Go on.

DAVID: And suppose you spent the night with him? It was just a suggestion, mind you. Would you mind?

BATHSHEBA: I'll do whatever you say.

DAVID: Would you?

BATHSHEBA: If that's what you want.

DAVID: I want that child. And I promise you no harm will come to you. You have my word.

   (SHE clings to him.)

DAVID: *(HE comforts her.)* Shh, shh. You'd better get dressed. It's getting late.

BATHSHEBA: Yes.

DAVID: Don't worry.

BATHSHEBA: Oh, David! I do love you so.

DAVID: Go on, go.

> *(HE kisses her and SHE goes off to the bedchamber. DAVID paces thoughtfully. JOAB enters.)*

DAVID: You're back.

JOAB: Apparently.

DAVID: How's it going?

JOAB: The rain has stopped and we're making preparations to storm the city.

DAVID: Good, good. Uriah's due for leave this week.

JOAB: I'm postponing all leaves.

DAVID: I want him here.

JOAB: Tired of her already?

DAVID: As soon as possible.

JOAB: You are incorrigible.

DAVID: As soon as possible.

JOAB: You just said that.

DAVID: It's not what you think.

JOAB: Of course not.

DAVID: I am not trying to get rid of her.

JOAB: Of course not.

DAVID: You think you know everything.

JOAB: What is it then?

DAVID: What difference does it make?

JOAB: None whatsoever.

DAVID: If you must know...

JOAB: What?

DAVID: Never mind.

JOAB: You and your little secrets.

DAVID: So now you're offended.

JOAB: Why should I be offended? I'm just an errand boy. Your personal pimp.

DAVID: Oh, now really!

JOAB: Yes, really. Ever since Abner things haven't been the same between us.

DAVID: If you have a guilty conscience...

JOAB: I do not have a guilty conscience.

DAVID: Then what are you all worked up about?

JOAB: Because you've been treating me like a pariah unless, of course, you have a favor to ask. Then everything is fine between us. But don't you forget, my friend, I know where all the bodies are buried.

DAVID: As far as Abner is concerned, I couldn't possibly condone what you did.

JOAB: No, of course, not.

DAVID: As a matter of fact, I was furious with you and I told you so.

JOAB: The fact that he killed my brother...

DAVID: Look, I don't want to go into all of that. It's ancient history.

JOAB: Oh, I know what you think of me. I'm your brute. I'm your bulldog, good enough to do your dirty work for you.

DAVID: That's not true.

JOAB: Isn't it?

DAVID: No, it is not.

JOAB: I've served you faithfully for all these years. My brother gave his life for you.

DAVID: Look, I'm sorry you're so upset.

JOAB: No you're not, not really. You're an arrogant man. You always have been and you always will be. You think you're above it all. You and your poetry and your music.

DAVID: This is all very interesting. I didn't know you were nursing all these grievances.

JOAB: Well, now you know.

DAVID: The fact of the matter is you're a hot-headed oaf, and you love the taste of blood.

JOAB: Lucky for you.

DAVID: Yes, well you're right, I suppose. We happen to live in a brutal world.

JOAB: You're finally owning up to it. If you hadn't been so finicky we wouldn't have had to spend all those years on the run, groveling to the

Philistines. We should have gotten rid of Saul when we had the chance, but no, you wouldn't listen to me. You make treaties behind my back...

DAVID: If you're referring to Abner...

JOAB: There wasn't time. I know, I know. But it just so happens that I'm your second in command but the last to know. The fact of the matter is you cannot rule this country all by yourself. You need me and you need your army. But no, you think you can do it all by yourself. Take that temple of yours.

DAVID: What about it?

JOAB: If you'd consulted Nathan before you drew up all those plans, that precious temple of yours would have been underway by now.

DAVID: You're right. You're absolutely right.

JOAB: Why are you sending for the captain?

DAVID: If you must know, his wife is pregnant.

JOAB: (HE laughs.) Congratulations.

DAVID: It isn't funny.

JOAB: At this rate you're going to raise your own private army.

DAVID: It's no joking matter. If it should happen to come out, king or not, you know perfectly what might happen. You know what Nathan's like.

JOAB: Too bad you didn't think of that before.

DAVID: She's agreed to spend the night with him.

JOAB: (HE sneers and shakes his head.) And you think that I'm the brute.

DAVID: You're the one that used that term, not I.

JOAB: Well, it's true. I am not refined. I don't write psalms. I don't sing, I don't play an instrument, nor do I hop from bed to bed.

DAVID: I'm not particularly proud of it.

JOAB: Then why do you do it?

DAVID: It's something I need, like food and drink. It's something I can't do without.

JOAB: Neither can I but there is such a thing as moderation.

DAVID: And so endeth lesson number one.

JOAB: I'm just trying to show you that, strangely enough, in spite of all your airs, you're no better than I am.

DAVID: I never said that I was.

JOAB: And I don't pretend to be what I'm not. I'll have the captain back here for you before the end of the week.

DAVID: Thank you.

JOAB: Is there anything else?

DAVID: Not at the moment, no.

(JOAB starts off.)

DAVID: And Joab...

JOAB: *(HE stops and turns.)* Yes? What is it?

DAVID: It's to go no further. What I've just told you.

JOAB: Really? And here I was planning to make an announcement to the troops.

(JOAB goes off. DAVID stands looking troubled then goes off to his bedchamber. MICHAL appears from

*behind a pair of drapes. SHE looks in the direction that
DAVID went off, snorts, shakes her head and glides out
of the room as the lights come down.)*

ACT TWO

Scene One

(David's chambers. Early evening two days later. URIAH, a pleasant looking young man, is discovered waiting nervously. DAVID enters. URIAH jumps to attention and salutes.)

URIAH: Your majesty!

DAVID: At ease, Captain, at ease. And welcome home.

URIAH: Thank you, your majesty. I was told to report directly to you.

DAVID: Yes. Yes, I've been hearing great things about you and I wanted to meet you.

URIAH: I'm greatly honored, your majesty.

DAVID: No, no, no. I'm the one that's honored. *(HE stares at the soldier.)*

URIAH: Your majesty?

DAVID: *(HE catches himself.)* I'm sorry. You reminded me of someone.

URIAH: Someone worthy, I hope.

DAVID: Oh, yes indeed. A good friend and an honorable soldier. Won't you join me in a glass of wine?

URIAH: I hope you won't be offended, your majesty...

DAVID: Why should I be offended?

289

URIAH: I drink nothing but water.

DAVID: Oh?

URIAH: I made a vow. The siege is about to get underway and until the victory is ours...

DAVID: Yes, of course. I understand. I hope it won't be a long, drawn out affair.

URIAH: We are at a disadvantage, of course, since the city is well fortified.

DAVID: Yes. Yes, I know. Tell me about yourself, Uriah.

URIAH: There's nothing much to tell, Sire. I'm an ordinary soldier who lives to serve his country and his king.

DAVID: Where are you from?

URIAH: I was born in a little village outside the city. Right now I live nearby, in the shadow of the palace so to speak.

DAVID: And what are your interests?

URIAH: The army, your majesty. I have no other interest but the army. It's means everything to me.

DAVID: I see. And have you always been interested in a military career?

URIAH: Oh, yes. Even as a boy. I had these toy soldiers and I'd conduct these imaginary battles. I dreamt that one day I would grow up to be a great warrior like King Saul and Prince Jonathan, and I hoped that, one day, I would share the field with your majesty. It's presumptuous of me, I know, to think of myself in such exalted terms, but I've been preparing all my life to make my self worthy.

DAVID: In what way may I ask?

URIAH: For one thing I've been exercising great discipline.

DAVID: Oh?

URIAH: I pay strict attention to the dietary laws, for example. Besides being a sacred duty I find that they benefit ones health as well. It's not the fashionable thing to do, I know, and it's certainly not the way to gain popularity but I have my standards and I refuse to compromise. I exercise moderation in everything. I find that a simple crust of bread and a cup of clear water is just as delicious as the richest of foods. I keep myself pure; pure in body, pure in heart and pure in mind. I'm talking too much.

DAVID: No, no, please. Go on.

URIAH: I have been told as much in no uncertain terms.

DAVID: Please. I'm fascinated.

URIAH: I've no use whatsoever for those people that abuse their bodies.

DAVID: Oh? And what do you mean by abuse?

URIAH: Over indulgence, your majesty.

DAVID: I see. Like...?

URIAH: Like food, for example.

DAVID: And sex?

URIAH: Especially sex.

DAVID: I don't mean to get personal but you are a married man, are you not?

URIAH: Oh yes, your majesty.

DAVID: Happily married?

URIAH: Very much so.

DAVID: And how does this...discipline affect your married life?

URIAH: In what way?

DAVID: Well, your conjugal duties, for example.

URIAH: When I'm at home, once a week. Except, of course, for the weeks when my wife is impure.

DAVID: What's that? Yes. Yes, of course.

URIAH: I set aside one day a week, the day after the Sabbath when I'm fully rested. Love making does drain the body of its strength, you see, so I try not to overdo it. Less than once a week would be remiss, and more than that would be self-indulgent. You think once a week's too much?

DAVID: I wouldn't say so, no. How many wives do you have, Captain?

URIAH: Just the one.

DAVID: You must love her very much.

URIAH: I do, your majesty, I do, but I try not to spoil her. Women can be very demanding and one must be careful not to give in too much, otherwise it gets to the point where they're the ones that give the orders.

DAVID: You have very high standards.

URIAH: Too high, perhaps?

DAVID: No, no, no.

URIAH: Some people think so. I know that. Some of the enlisted men, you see, are not of the highest calibre and their behavior is not, what one might call, exemplary, so I try to set an example. In addition to that I try to encourage my fellow officers to do the same. It's our responsibility, don't you think?

DAVID: Why, yes.

URIAH: Sad to say, not all my fellow officers share this feeling. I'm not one to carry tales but the fact of the matter is that not all of my fellow officers bear their rank with distinction. What offends me most is when they continually give into their lusts. In addition to that they continually indulge in unsuitable language. I see no need for it. Unfortunately my censure goes unheeded so I've learned to hold my tongue with regard to my fellow officers, that is. In regard to the men that serve under me, however, I do have some control and I've instituted a fine for every foul word spoken, a double fine for unsuitable references to women and a triple fine for using the Lords's name in vain.

DAVID: I see.

URIAH: I insist that my men say their morning prayers. In private, I know, they grumble, but in their hearts I know they're grateful to me.

DAVID: Tell me, Captain, are there any children?

URIAH: I beg your pardon?

DAVID: Do you have any children, you and your wife?

URIAH: No, not yet.

DAVID: Well, we have something to look forward to, do we not? You do want children, don't you?

URIAH: Of course, Sire. I want a son.

DAVID: Well, Captain, we must see what we can do about that, eh?

URIAH: Yes, your majesty.

DAVID: I won't keep you any longer. You'll want to be getting home to spend some time with your wife.

URIAH: Thank you, your majesty.

DAVID: However, I would like you to report to me tomorrow.

URIAH: At dawn?

URIAH: No, no, no. Spend the day with your wife. You have so little time together. Tomorrow evening, however, I'd like you to dine with me.

URIAH: I'd be honored, your majesty.

DAVID: It's been a pleasure meeting you, Captain. It's men like you that I rely on.

URIAH: I shall do my best your majesty.

DAVID: That's all one can ask. Run along now.

URIAH: *(HE salutes.)* Your majesty. Till tomorrow.

DAVID: *(HE returns the salute.)* Till tomorrow.

> *(URIAH salutes again and DAVID returns the salute. URIAH goes off.)*

DAVID: Poor Bathsheba!

> *(The lights slowly fade.)*

Scene Two

(The scene is the same. Early evening of the following day. BATHSHEBA is discovered seated. DAVID enters from the outside.)

DAVID: Are you all right?

BATHSHEBA: Yes. Yes, I'm fine.

DAVID: How did it go last night?

BATHSHEBA: That's what I came to ask you.

DAVID: What do you mean?

BATHSHEBA: He was due back yesterday, wasn't he?

DAVID: Yes, of course. He was here last night and I sent him home to you. Didn't he show up?

(BATHSHEBA shakes her head.)

DAVID: I don't understand.

BATHSHEBA: Typical.

DAVID: What do you mean?

BATHSHEBA: He has all these rules, all these principles, all these vows. It's hard to keep up with them.

DAVID: I know he's very precise about his love-making. Once a week, I gather. But he's been away for quite some time now.

295

BATHSHEBA: I know, I know.

DAVID: Maybe something happened to him. Or perhaps he ran into some friends or family.

BATHSHEBA: He has no family in the city and the few friends he does have are in the army.

DAVID: I'm expecting him for dinner any minute now. I'll make sure he goes directly home afterwards. Go home and don't fret. You hear? And don't do anything foolish. Promise me.

BATHSHEBA: I promise.

DAVID: I love you. *(HE kisses her.)*

> *(BATHSHEBA goes off. DAVID heaves a sigh, pours himself a goblet of wine and sits musing. After a moment URIAH enters.)*

URIAH: Your majesty... *(HE salutes.)*

DAVID: *(HE sets down the wine, rises and salutes.)* Captain.

URIAH: I'm late.

DAVID: No, no, no. You're just in time. Let me pour you... Sorry. Sit down, sit down.

URIAH: Thank you.

DAVID: So, how are you enjoying your leave?

URIAH: Very much, thank you.

DAVID: You don't sound very enthusiastic.

URIAH: Oh, no. I'm very grateful to you, Sire. I feel greatly privileged... that you thought to honor me in this way. It's just that...

DAVID: Just that what?

URIAH: I'm anxious to get back to my men.

DAVID: And so you shall, Captain, so you shall. But all work and no play...? It's important, you know, to take some time to relax so that when one does returns to one's duties one returns refreshed and invigorated.

URIAH: You're right, your majesty. You're absolutely right.

DAVID: So, how did you spend your day?

URIAH: I spent several hours at the gymnasium.

DAVID: I see. And after that?

URIAH: After that I walked about the city.

DAVID: All day?

URIAH: And I paid a visit to an old teacher of mine.

DAVID: And your lovely wife? How is she?

URIAH: I have a confession to make, your majesty.

DAVID: Oh?

URIAH: I did not go home last night.

DAVID: I see.

URIAH: I hope you're not angry with me.

DAVID: Now why should I be angry?

URIAH: It's just that the thought of pleasuring myself while my men lay sleeping on the cold, wet ground, preparing to risk their lives... I just couldn't.

DAVID: I understand.

URIAH: I knew you would, your majesty.

DAVID: What a world this would be if we had more men like you! Where, may I ask, did you spend the night?

URIAH: In your servants' quarters, Sire.

DAVID: You're a remarkable man, Uriah, a remarkable man. Yet I wonder if you're being fair.

URIAH: In what way, your majesty?

DAVID: To your wife, man, to your wife who, I assume, is very devoted to you.

URIAH: Oh, she is that, Sire.

DAVID: Well then?

URIAH: She is a soldier's wife, your majesty. She understands.

DAVID: I wonder, Uriah. What I mean to say is she is a woman and women are rather delicate creatures, you know.

URIAH: I suppose so.

DAVID: Exotic plants, so to speak. They need special attention.

URIAH: Yes, well, Bathsheba is accustomed to my absences.

DAVID: You're a lucky man, Captain, to have so devoted a wife.

URIAH: I am, your majesty, I am and I treasure her.

DAVID: I'd like to drink a toast to your wife, to Bathsheba. And I insist that you join me. That's an order, Captain, from your commander in chief.

URIAH: Well, Sire, if it is an order...

DAVID: It most certainly is. *(HE pours a goblet of wine which he hands to URIAH.)* Here you are, Captain.

URIAH: Thank you.

DAVID: To Bathsheba!

URIAH: To Bathsheba!

(THEY drink.)

DAVID: Come, come. Drink up, man, drink up.

URIAH: *(HE takes a long swig and coughs.)* It's been a while since I've had anything stronger than water.

DAVID: Doctors prescribe one glass of wine a day, to stimulate the heart. Did you know that?

URIAH: No. No, I didn't.

DAVID: Come, come. Drink up.

(URIAH drains his goblet and DAVID refills it.)

URIAH: That's very good wine.

DAVID: Good enough for a king?

(THEY both laugh.)

URIAH: I can't believe it.

DAVID: What's that?

URIAH: Here I am, in the palace, drinking wine with the great King David. I can't believe it.

DAVID: And I can think of no one more deserving.

URIAH: Drinking wine with the great King David, the greatest warrior that ever lived except, of course, for King Saul and Prince Jonathan. *(HE takes a sip of wine and hiccups.)* I'm not much of a drinker, I'm afraid.

DAVID: You believe in abstinence. And that's very admirable, Captain. Up to a point, that is. King Saul, for example, was a great one for abstinence. He would start fasting sometimes just before going into battle but even he came to realize that too much of a good thing is...just too much of a good thing.

URIAH: That's exactly what I try to tell my men.

DAVID: What's that?

URIAH: Yes, I do! I most certainly do. *(HE takes a sip of wine.)* What a great honor it must have been to fight alongside the great King Saul!

DAVID: It was an experience.

URIAH: What a great warrior!

DAVID: That he was.

URIAH: And the great Prince Jonathan. Did he really kill twenty Philistines all by himself?

DAVID: Well, he did have his armor bearer with him

URIAH: Did he really?

DAVID: And he did take the enemy by surprise.

URIAH: What an inspiration they are! The great King Saul and the great Prince Jonathan! I shall try to follow their example. I shall wipe the enemy off the face of the earth...the Philistines, the Amelakites, the Moabites, the Ammonites...

DAVID: That would take a great deal of wiping.

URIAH: We can do it, your majesty. We can do it, you and I. I've only killed three men so far. Of course, I'm just a novice...

DAVID: But then again that presents a quandary.

URIAH: What's that, your majesty?

DAVID: If we kill off all of our enemies there won't be anyone left to fight.

URIAH: I never thought of that.

> (URIAH takes a swig and DAVID refills his cup. After a
> moment URIAH looks suspiciously at DAVID.)

URIAH: You're not making fun of me are you, your majesty?

DAVID: No, Captain. Murder's not something to be taken lightly.

URIAH: Murder? We're speaking of war, your majesty.

DAVID: And what is war?

URIAH: What is war?

DAVID: Yes, what is war?

URIAH: What is war?

DAVID: Mass murder, is it not? That's what it comes down to, does it not? You know, Captain, when I was an outlaw, fleeing from the clutches of that great warrior, the great King Saul, I was forced to seek refuge among the Philistines. And you know what I found, Captain, to my utter amazement?

URIAH: No, what did you find?

DAVID: I found that they were men, just like you and I.

URIAH: The Philistines?

DAVID: The Philistines. Now isn't that astonishing!?

URIAH: But they're barbarians.

DAVID: And strangely enough that's exactly how they think of us.

URIAH: Yes, but we are the chosen people.

DAVID: Chosen? By whom?

URIAH: By the Lord, our god.

DAVID: And which god is that?

URIAH: Jehovah, the one and only god.

DAVID: Ah yes, but they seem to think that their god, their gods, that is, are the only gods. Now how are we to prove that they are wrong? And how are we to prove that we are right? And does it really matter? If they choose to worship their gods why not let them? We're not really missionaries, are we?

URIAH: Then what are we fighting for?

DAVID: Survival, Uriah. We're fighting to survive.

URIAH: Exactly. And that's why we must keep ourselves pure, your majesty. We must strive for perfection.

DAVID: That's a noble goal indeed, but we are, after all, human, are we not, with all our imperfections and our weaknesses?

URIAH: Not you, your majesty, nor I, your majesty. Women are weak not men.

DAVID: Truly?

URIAH: Oh yes, indeed! Physically, mentally, morally. As a matter of fact I sometimes think that women belong to another race. Not that I don't respect them. My mother, after all, is a woman.

DAVID: And your wife.

URIAH: Exactly.

DAVID: And you love your wife, Uriah, don't you?

URIAH: More than anything in the world. Except, of course, for my God and my country.

DAVID: Are you all right, Captain?

URIAH: Yes. Yes, I'm fine. I just feel a little dizzy, that's all. It's all that wine.

DAVID: Something to eat, that's what you need. Come. We're going to sit you down to a magnificent feast.

URIAH: Fit for a king.

DAVID: And his loyal subject.

URIAH: That's me.

DAVID: That's you indeed. And then I'm going to send you home to your faithful wife because, as you say, she's not as strong as we are.

URIAH: No, indeed.

DAVID: And she needs the arms of a man to protect her, does she not? To keep her warm and safe?

URIAH: That's true, your majesty. That's very true. I have neglected her. I've neglected her shamefully. Poor Bathsheba! And she never complains. Now you take my mother, for example. She's always complaining. But my dear wife, she never complains. And I've neglected her shamefully, shamefully.

DAVID: But we can remedy that, can't we?

URIAH: How's that?

DAVID: By spending the night with her.

URIAH: That's true. I can spend the night with her. I can spend the night with my beautiful wife who never complains.

DAVID: That's right. Come along, come along.

URIAH: Where are we going?

DAVID: We're going to dinner. That's where we're going. And afterwards you're going straight home to your wife.

URIAH: Straight home to my wife.

DAVID: This way, Captain.

> *(DAVID places his arm around Uriah's shoulder. URIAH places his arm around David's shoulder.)*

URIAH: Straight home to my wife who never complains.

DAVID: That's right.

URIAH: My mother complains and I love her, your majesty. I love my wife who never complains.

> *(THEY go off as the lights slowly dim.)*

Scene Three

(The scene is the same. The following morning. JOAB is discovered waiting impatiently. DAVID enters from his bedchamber.)

JOAB: Good morning.

DAVID: Is it?

JOAB: Another night of debauchery?

DAVID: I drank too much.

JOAB: I'm on my way.

DAVID: That city's well protected, you know. We're bound to lose some men if we try to take it.

JOAB: We're bound to lose more if they keep on attacking those outlying villages, and there's no question but they will.

DAVID: I suppose you're right.

JOAB: I'd better get going.

DAVID: The captain was supposed to report to me this morning.

JOAB: He's in the courtyard, champing at the bit.

DAVID: I'd like a word with him.

JOAB: I'll wait outside.

DAVID: Thank you.

305

*(JOAB goes off. DAVID paces about. URIAH enters a
moment later and salutes. DAVID returns the salute.)*

URIAH: Your majesty.

DAVID: Captain. So, you're off to the wars.

URIAH: I shall do my best, your majesty.

DAVID: I'm sure you will.

URIAH: And I want to thank you for the honor you've bestowed upon
me. I shall treasure our meeting for the rest of my life.

DAVID: Good, good. And I hope your meeting last night was just as
memorable.

URIAH: Meeting?

DAVID: With your wife, Captain, with your wife.

URIAH: Yes. Yes, of course.

DAVID: Captain...?

URIAH: Your majesty...I...

DAVID: Go on.

URIAH: I must confess. I just couldn't. The very thought of indulging
myself while my men... I just couldn't. You must forgive me. I hope
you understand.

DAVID: You didn't go home at all?

URIAH: I didn't want to be tempted.

DAVID: I see.

URIAH: Your majesty...I must speak up.

DAVID: Go on.

URIAH: When I was told to report to you personally I was most apprehensive. I was concerned that perhaps I had committed some indiscretion, some stupidity. And secondly... Well, your majesty is a legendary figure ever since you slew that monster when you were just a boy. And, of course, your musical gifts and all the wars you've won, and what you've accomplished for the country. And sometimes famous people, when you meet them in person... The image is somehow tarnished and you come away disappointed and disillusioned.

DAVID: And now that you've met the giant-killer?

URIAH: Your legend, Sire, does not do you justice. The world knows you as a great warrior and a great poet. But nothing has ever been said about your humanity, what a simple and down to earth man you are, how warm how compassionate, how unpretentious. I don't have any brothers, your majesty, but I feel now, if you will allow me...I feel that I have one now. And if I should be blessed with a son I hope you will permit me to name him after you.

DAVID: I'd be honored, Uriah.

URIAH: *(HE embraces him impulsively.)* I beg your pardon, your majesty. Please forgive me.

DAVID: Sit down. Sit down, please.

   (THEY sit.)

URIAH: I'm sorry, your majesty. I got carried away.

DAVID: I'd like to ask your opinion about something and I'd like you to give me an honest answer.

URIAH: I'll do my best.

DAVID: We spoke last night about the difference between men and women. Do you remember?

URIAH: Vaguely.

DAVID: We agreed that women are the weaker sex and, ever since then there's a question that's been puzzling me. Perhaps you can help me.

URIAH: I'd be honored to, if I possibly can.

DAVID: This is purely hypothetical, mind you, but suppose your mother or your wife, for example, were to commit a sin, a sin that would be considered a crime as well, would you be able to forgive her?

URIAH: A sin, you say?

DAVID: That would be considered a crime, a crime punishable by death.

URIAH: My mother, you say?

DAVID: Well, let's just say your wife. I'm speaking hypothetically, of course.

URIAH: Yes, of course. If my wife committed a crime...

DAVID: Punishable by death. Would you be able to forgive her?

URIAH: What sort of a crime are we talking about?

DAVID: Adultery let's say.

URIAH: If my wife committed adultery...

DAVID: Would you be able to forgive her?

URIAH: If Bathsheba committed adultery would I be able to forgive her. *(HE ponders for a moment.)* That's a difficult question to answer, your majesty.

DAVID: Think about it for a moment.

URIAH: Me personally? Would I be able to forgive Bathsheba if she committed adultery.

DAVID: Exactly.

URIAH: I suppose that would be the merciful thing to do.

DAVID: Then you could forgive her.

URIAH: It would be extremely difficult, your majesty, but yes, I think I could. But then, of course, it wouldn't be up to me, now would it?

DAVID: What do you mean?

URIAH: What I mean to say is adultery is a crime. And if Bathsheba broke the law she would have to pay the penalty, wouldn't she?

DAVID: Suppose, let's say, the authorities weren't aware of the incident?

URIAH: But I was?

DAVID: Exactly

URIAH: Well...as a man of honor...

DAVID: You mean to say you'd actually stand by and let your wife stand trial, with the possibility that she might be stoned to death?

URIAH: The law, your majesty, is the law. Besides if Bathsheba committed adultery she wouldn't be the Bathsheba I've loved and treasured as my wife, now would she?. But then, we're speaking hypothetically, of course.

DAVID: Yes. Yes, of course.

   (JOAB reenters.)

JOAB: I'm sorry to interrupt, but it is getting late and we've a long ways to go.

DAVID: Yes. Yes, I'm sorry. *(HE rises.)* Good luck, Captain. *(HE salutes him.)*

URIAH: *(HE rises and salutes DAVID.)* Your majesty.

(JOAB and URIAH start off.)

DAVID: Joab...?

(JOAB and URIAH stop and turn.)

DAVID: I'd like a word with you, in private.

(URIAH goes off.)

DAVID: He never went home last night.

JOAB: I see.

DAVID: If he should find out... Even if he doesn't find out, if I should send her away somewhere until the child is born...

JOAB: He'd still be in the way.

DAVID: He'd actually stand by and let her be stoned to death.

JOAB: I wouldn't doubt it. So...?

DAVID: I have no choice.

JOAB: Why are you telling me this?

DAVID: I want you to see to it that he doesn't come back. Why do you look at me like that?

JOAB: I'm not judging you, if that's what you think. *(HE shrugs.)* It's him or her.

DAVID: It is, isn't it?

JOAB: But please, no crocodile tears.

DAVID: May the Lord forgive me.

JOAB: Tell me something. Is she really worth it?

DAVID: You know, I was thinking about what you said.

JOAB: In regard to what?

DAVID: In regard to my womanizing...

JOAB: Forget it. I spoke out of turn.

DAVID: No, no. You were right. It is unseemly for a man in my position to carry on like that. And I asked myself why. What is it that drives me? What am I looking for? Is it merely pleasure? Variety? It's really a fruitless pursuit, is it not?

JOAB: And did you find the answer?

DAVID: Yes. I've come to realize that I've never really given myself to a woman. Not completely, that is, up until now. Apparently I've been looking for that special one, a woman, that I could respect as an equal, a woman that could challenge me, that could be my friend as well as my lover.

JOAB: And you've finally found her.

DAVID: She's really a remarkable woman, Joab. I can tell her anything...anything at all and she's not shocked, nor is she judgmental. We can almost read each others thoughts. It's nonsense, I know, but it's as if the two of us were actually one, the way a husband and wife should be. There was only one other person I felt this close to.

JOAB: Jonathan?

DAVID: Yes, Jonathan.

JOAB: Some friend! (HE laughs.)

DAVID: You think that's funny?

JOAB: Asking her to sleep with another man.

DAVID: I know, I know. I was awake all night. The thought of her spending the night with him...

JOAB: Well, that won't be a problem anymore, will it? I'll send you word when it's over.

DAVID: Thank you, Joab.

> *(JOAB goes off. DAVID stands looking deeply troubled as the lights fade. The sound of a battle is heard. The noise grows louder and gradually fades.)*

Scene Four

(David's chambers. Late morning. BATHSHEBA is discovered, waiting impatiently. DAVID, a report in his hand, enters from the outside.)

DAVID: I was just going to send for you.

BATHSHEBA: I was beginning to get worried. I haven't heard from you. What have you decided? What are we going to do?

DAVID: There's no need to do anything.

BATHSHEBA: I don't understand.

DAVID: Apparently fate has intervened. I've just received the casualty list.

BATHSHEBA: Is he...?

DAVID: Uriah, I'm afraid, was one of the fatalities.

(BATHSHEBA sits, shaken. (DAVID pours some wine and offers it to her. SHE pushes it away, shaking her head.)

BATHSHEBA: Poor Uriah!

DAVID: He died the way he wanted to, sword in hand.

BATHSHEBA: How did it happen, do you know?

DAVID: He was in the thick of it when they attacked the city. The order was given to retreat. Apparently he wasn't aware of it or he chose to ignore it. He was left to fight on alone and he was overcome.

313

BATHSHEBA: How typical!

DAVID: I'll see to it that he's given a hero's funeral.

BATHSHEBA: You try to prepare yourself for something like this but when it actually happens... Why can't we live in peace with our neighbors? Why can't we just sit down and talk to one another?

DAVID: That would be the reasonable thing to do. Unfortunately men are not always governed by reason.

BATHSHEBA: He was so young.

DAVID: I met him only briefly.

BATHSHEBA: What did you think of him?

DAVID: He was unique.

BATHSHEBA: He died never really knowing what it is to love.

DAVID: He loved the army.

BATHSHEBA: Or was it the image of himself as a great warrior. He spoke so often of you and Saul and Jonathan.

DAVID: He was a fine soldier. You'll miss him, of course.

BATHSHEBA: I missed him while he was alive. I grew used to his absences however, since I always expected him to return. But he won't be coming back anymore, will he? Ironic, isn't it?

DAVID: What's that?

BATHSHEBA: The timing. He'll never know how convenient his death has been.

DAVID: You'll observe the mourning period, of course. And then we'll be married. We can't wait too long.

BATHSHEBA: You don't have to marry me now, do you?

DAVID: What do you mean?

BATHSHEBA: If it's my safety you're concerned about, that's no longer an issue, is it? He was home on leave. Can anyone prove that we didn't spend the night together?

DAVID: Don't you want to be my wife?

BATHSHEBA: Yes, of course, I do.

DAVID: Well, then?

BATHSHEBA: Uriah may have been neglectful, but with him my only rival was the army.

DAVID: You want me to get rid of all my wives? Is that it?

BATHSHEBA: Would you if I asked you to? *(SHE laughs.)* David, I'm only teasing you.

DAVID: I love you.

BATHSHEBA: Do you?

DAVID: You're upset, of course.

BATHSHEBA: It's not only that.

DAVID: What is it then?

BATHSHEBA: I feel guilty somehow.

DAVID: That's nonsense.

BATHSHEBA: I know, I know.

DAVID: I need you.

BATHSHEBA: Do you?

DAVID: You doubt it?

BATHSHEBA: It's just that...

DAVID: What?

BATHSHEBA: We love each other now. But afterwards... Uriah was my husband. We shared a home, a house that is, and occasionally he performed his marital duties, and yet we were strangers. Despite the ceremony, despite the time that we spent together, we were really strangers.

DAVID: And you think it will be the same with us, once you become my wife?

BATHSHEBA: *(SHE shrugs.)* And besides, if you marry me and the child is born so quickly...

DAVID: It's premature. It's not that unusual. I want the boy to be legitimate.

BATHSHEBA: Suppose it's a girl?

DAVID: It won't be, and your son is going to be my heir.

BATHSHEBA: You do have other sons.

DAVID: He's going to be my heir. I promise you, and he's going to be crowned in my magnificent new temple.

BATHSHEBA: Have you heard from Nathan? Has he approved your plans?

DAVID: We're going over the final details this morning, and I hope to start breaking ground some time next week. As a matter of fact, I'm expecting him any minute now.

BATHSHEBA: I'd better leave then.

DAVID: No, stay. I'd like him to meet you.

BATHSHEBA: You think that's wise?

DAVID: You're the widow of a fallen hero. I've called you in to offer the nation's condolences. It's the perfect time.

(NATHAN enters.)

NATHAN: You have a visitor.

DAVID: Come in, come in. I'd like you to meet Bathsheba. She's the wife of one of my captains. The widow, that is. Uriah, I'm sorry to say, was one of our recent casualties.

NATHAN: My condolences.

BATHSHEBA: Thank you.

NATHAN: There's going to be a special service this evening to memorialize all the brave soldiers that have fallen in the recent battle.

BATHSHEBA: Thank you, your Holiness.

NATHAN: I see where the casualty list was a very short one.

DAVID: It was still too long.

NATHAN: Yes, of course.

DAVID: (To BATHSHEBA) You'll excuse us, my dear. Matters of state. (To NATHAN) Excuse me for a moment.

(NATHAN nods. DAVID goes off with BATHSHEBA and returns a moment later.)

NATHAN: She's very beautiful.

DAVID: Why, yes. I suppose she is.

NATHAN: You think I don't notice such things?

DAVID: I'm sure you do. You are, after all, a man as well as a priest.

NATHAN: Ah yes, indeed. A man with all the human frailties mortal flesh is heir to. Apropos, I've been told a very disturbing story, a very unpleasant one, as a matter of fact.

DAVID: Shall we get down to business? This meeting has been a long time in coming.

NATHAN: You have another appointment?

DAVID: No...

NATHAN: Then what's the rush? This story, I'm sure, will interest you.

DAVID: Go on.

NATHAN: It seems that there were these two men, one rich, one poor. The rich man had all sorts of cattle and sheep. The poor man had this one little lamb. He raised it and nurtured it. It grew up with him and his children; shared his food, drank from his cup, even slept in his arms from time to time. It was like one of the family.

DAVID: I'm listening.

NATHAN: One day a traveler came to visit the rich man and, instead of taking one of his flock to serve his guest, the rich man appropriated the poor man's lamb, slaughtered it and fed it to the stranger.

DAVID: Yes, well I'm sure there's a point to be made though, at the moment, it escapes me.

NATHAN: I think you know what I'm getting at. Then shall I be brutally frank? You ordered the death of Uriah because his wife was pregnant and you are the father.

DAVID: I don't know where you heard this fantastic tale.

NATHAN: Never mind where I heard it.

DAVID: Who told you this?

NATHAN: You deny it?

DAVID: Do you really think I'm capable of such an awful crime?

NATHAN: You don't want me to answer that, do you?

DAVID: Well, it isn't true.

NATHAN: I see. Well then, perhaps I have been misinformed.

DAVID: You most certainly have.

NATHAN: There's only one thing to do then.

DAVID: And what might that be?

NATHAN: I'll order an investigation. Not only into the captain's death but into the fact that his wife is pregnant and he hasn't slept with her... How long has it been?

DAVID: Well, there you are. Apparently your informant neglected to tell you that the captain was home on leave shortly before he went into battle.

NATHAN: And he spent the night with her?

DAVID: As far as I know.

NATHAN: I may be mistaken. I'm quite willing to admit it.

DAVID: You most certainly are.

NATHAN: It's a serious charge however and I have no choice but to order an inquiry.

DAVID: Who, may I ask, is making this charge? I think I have a right to face my accuser.

NATHAN: I am your accuser. And until this matter has been cleared up we have nothing further to discuss. *(HE starts off.)*

DAVID: Just a moment.

NATHAN: Yes? I'm waiting.

DAVID: The woman is innocent. The fault's all mine. I fell in love with her and I was carried away.

NATHAN: Love?! How dare you speak to me about love?! What are you? Some schoolboy?

DAVID: She's carrying my child and I intend to make him my heir.

NATHAN: That child is cursed. It will never live that long.

DAVID: Nathan, please...

NATHAN: Do you really think that crimes so awful can go unpunished?

DAVID: I made a mistake.

NATHAN: Mistake?!

DAVID: I was weak.

NATHAN: You call murder a mistake?! You call adultery a mistake?!

DAVID: Up until now my life has been blameless.

NATHAN: The Lord looked with favor on you. He anointed you. He delivered you from the hands of your enemies. He gave you a kingdom to rule. And this is the way you pay him back?

DAVID: I'll do anything. Anything you say. I'll make up for it. I promise you. I'll do penance. I'll do whatever you say. Now, can we get down to business?

NATHAN: What business? What are you talking about?

DAVID: The temple, of course.

NATHAN: Do you really think, in all honesty, that a man like you, a man whose hands are steeped in blood...do you really think that you should be allowed to erect a holy edifice?

DAVID: But everything's underway. I've started to recruit the workmen.

NATHAN: Then stop.

DAVID: I've been amassing all this material. Everything is ready to go. Nathan, please, this is what I've been living for. All through my years as an outlaw, all through my years of exile this is what kept me going. And it's not only for me. It's for the people. There's got to be a proper temple for the people to come and worship. A temple that this kingdom can be proud of.

NATHAN: We are in need of a temple, it's true. And if your heir, whoever he may be, is worthy, he will be allowed to build it. I'll spare the woman, since I hold you entirely responsible. You will be permitted, however, to complete your reign and, if I were you, my son, I'd be thankful for that. The subject is closed. *(HE starts off.)*

DAVID: This is what you've been waiting for, isn't it?

NATHAN: *(HE stops and turns around.)* What are you talking about?

DAVID: You and Samuel, you're both alike. No one dare threaten the supremacy of the church. But what it really comes down to is that no one dare threaten your supremacy, your own ego, your personal power.

NATHAN: Are you quite through?

DAVID: You never had any intention of letting me build that temple. That's the truth, and you know it.

NATHAN: You want the truth, my boy? I'll give you the truth. Samuel was right all along. He was reluctant to give our people a king. He saw what it would lead to. Oh, it's an old, old story...as old as the history of man. We saw it with Saul and now again with you. Power corrupts and absolute power corrupts absolutely.

DAVID: You're a bitter old man, just like Samuel was. I'll take this to the people. They'll support me.

NATHAN: You can take what you like to the people, but I still speak for God.

(DAVID strides off to his bedchamber.)

NATHAN: Don't you dare leave this room while I'm talking to you! "Your brother's blood cries out from the ground" and the mark of Cain is branded on your forehead forever. You and your family will never escape the wrath of the Lord. You hear me? Never! You adulterer! You murderer!

(NATHAN stalks off as the lights come down.)

Scene Five

(A year and a half later. Early morning, the dark just before sunrise. Chanting is heard in the distance. DAVID is discovered, kneeling in prayer. After a moment the chanting comes to a halt and a loud wailing is heard. DAVID looks up and listens. MICHAL enters.)

DAVID: Who's there?

MICHAL: It's me, my dear.

DAVID: Michal, is that you?

MICHAL: One and the same. I've come to console you.

DAVID: Is it over then?

MICHAL: Yes, my dear, it's over.

DAVID: The boy is dead?

MICHAL: Your little son has left this vale of tears. Such a bright little child. And you were so fond of him, weren't you? Poor baby, so innocent, so helpless. And to suffer so needlessly. It's the will of the Lord, I suppose. But it just tore my heart out to see the little thing lying there in agony, gasping for breath. What did he do to deserve such a fate? He's never harmed anyone. He's never committed any crime. And then, for no reason I can think of, these words kept echoing in my mind, "The fathers have eaten sour grapes and the children's teeth are set on edge."

(DAVID sobs.)

323

MICHAL: Yes, my dear, I know, I know. It's bad enough to lose ones' parents or even someone your age, but to lose a child! What could be more tragic?

DAVID: Where's Bathsheba?

MICHAL: Poor dear. She's overcome with grief. She hasn't slept for days. She was telling me that you were going to make the child your heir. Well, that's no problem, is it? You have other sons, haven't you? Why there's your first born, Amnon. A bit of a boor perhaps. But that's not his fault, is it? What I mean to say is he's always been allowed to do as he pleases. And, of course, there's your favorite, the glamorous Absalom. So handsome, so charming, so witty. A little vain perhaps and emotionally unstable some people say, but that's that gossip, isn't it?.

DAVID: What do you want?

MICHAL: I've come to offer my condolences. Isn't that what friends are for?

DAVID: Help me up.

MICHAL: Yes, of course.

> (MICHAL helps DAVID up. HE almost loses his balance
> as SHE guides him to a chair.)

MICHAL: We are getting on, are we not? Well, the years go by and none of us is as young as we used to be.

DAVID: I've been fasting for several days.

MICHAL: Ah yes. Saul loved to fast too, did he not? But that was just before he went into battle, wasn't it? But then you're not going into battle, are you? You're no longer the great warrior, the legendary hero that slew that monster.

DAVID: Thank you for your trouble...

MICHAL: Isn't it strange, the unexpected turn of events? Here I am, back in your arms so to speak. And here you are, visited with one disaster after another. Your beautiful son, dead before he's even had a chance to live. And then that glorious temple of yours. All that planning, all that work and all for nothing.

DAVID: What are you talking about?

MICHAL: Maybe I've been misinformed.

DAVID: I don't know where you get your information.

MICHAL: Then you are going ahead with your plans, for the temple?

DAVID: There's been a slight postponement.

MICHAL: I'm so glad to hear it, since I know how much it means to you, how you've set your heart on it.

DAVID: Have you been speaking to Nathan?

MICHAL: Of course, I've been speaking to Nathan. He's my spiritual advisor.

DAVID: What made you think...?

MICHAL: What?

DAVID: That the temple plans have been aborted.

MICHAL: Well, you know how rumors get started.

DAVID: No, tell me.

MICHAL: I don't think there's any need to tell you anything, dear. I think Nathan has said it all, hasn't he?

DAVID: It was you, wasn't it?!

MICHAL: And what if it was? I'm not saying that it was, but there's always that possibility, isn't there? You think you can play God, don't you? You think you can destroy peoples' lives just to satisfy your whims, your lust, your degeneracy. You think you can murder and destroy and never have to answer for it. Well, now you know, my dear. Now you know what it feels like to have your life torn up by the roots, to have the taste of ashes in your mouth.

(BATHSHEBA enters. MICHAL goes to her and kisses her on the cheek and embraces her.)

MICHAL: Oh, my dear, I'm so sorry.

BATHSHEBA: Thank you, Michal.

(MICHAL smiles beatifically and glides off.)

DAVID: I told you to keep away from her.

BATHSHEBA: She's been so helpful.

DAVID: She's been helpful all right.

BATHSHEBA: What do you mean?

DAVID: She's the one that told Nathan.

BATHSHEBA: Told him what?

DAVID: About your visits here before we were married.

BATHSHEBA: How could she have known?

DAVID: Ever since she came here she's been sneaking about the palace, poking her nose into everything, causing as much trouble as she possibly can.

BATHSHEBA: You said you thought it was Joab.

DAVID: I was wrong. She wanted me to send her back to the man she'd been living with. I refused. And now she's had her revenge. Her father would have been delighted.

(BATHSHEBA sinks into a chair.)

DAVID: Are you all right?

BATHSHEBA: Poor innocent baby.

DAVID: We'll have another, I promise you.

> *(HE kisses her and THEY cling to one another. It's now dawn and the light in the room has become brighter. HE breaks away, starts off then clings to a chair for support.)*

BATHSHEBA: Where are you going?

DAVID: I must get ready.

BATHSHEBA: For what?

DAVID: I'm going to lead the troops.

BATHSHEBA: You can barely walk.

DAVID: I'm perfectly fine. I just need some food, that's all.

BATHSHEBA: You're going to leave me now?

DAVID: I've got to get away. Please...

BATHSHEBA: David...

> *(HE kisses her and goes off to the bedchamber. SHE sits with a sigh. JOAB enters.)*

JOAB: I'm sorry about the boy.

BATHSHEBA: Thank you.

JOAB: Well, his troubles are over.

BATHSHEBA: Yes.

JOAB: Where is he? The troops are all lined up.

BATHSHEBA: He's getting ready to join you.

JOAB: Oh?

BATHSHEBA: It seems we owe you an apology.

JOAB: For what?

BATHSHEBA: We thought it was you that told Nathan.

JOAB: Told him? What?

BATHSHEBA: It doesn't matter since it was Michal all along.

JOAB: You mustn't pay any attention to Michal. She just loves to make trouble. Look, your husband was a casualty of war. That's all you need to know.

BATHSHEBA: Was there ever any doubt?

JOAB: Why no...no, of course not.

BATHSHEBA: Then...?

JOAB: Forget it.

BATHSHEBA: It is true, isn't it? I kept trying to convince myself that it wasn't, that it was just a coincidence, a stroke of fate. But in my heart of hearts I knew. It was just too convenient.

JOAB: I don't know what you're talking about.

BATHSHEBA: He ordered his death, didn't he?

JOAB: Look, what's the point of digging into the past?

BATHSHEBA: Didn't he?!

JOAB: It was your life or his.

BATHSHEBA: God help me, what have I done?!

(DAVID reenters in battle dress, chewing on some food. HE pours himself some wine and drinks.)

JOAB: You're joining us, I understand.

DAVID: I've been away too long.

JOAB: I'll tell the men. *(HE looks hesitantly at BATHSHEBA and goes off.)*

DAVID: No more tears.

BATHSHEBA: No. No more tears. *(SHE strokes his cheek and kisses him.)* My poor dear.

DAVID: There's no point in looking back.

BATHSHEBA: No, you're right.

DAVID: We've got the future to look forward to, years of happiness ahead of us.

BATHSHEBA: You will take care of yourself, won't you?

DAVID: I'm safer on the battlefield, my dear, than I am here at home.

BATHSHEBA: And you will come back to me, won't you?

DAVID: You're not to worry.

BATHSHEBA: I'll be with you every moment, whether my prayers are heard or not.

DAVID: Everything's going to be fine.

(HE kisses her. Cheering is heard in the distance.)

DAVID: I must go.

BATHSHEBA: *(SHE clings to him.)* I love you.

(HE kisses her again and goes off. SHE sits with a sigh.)

BATHSHEBA: But what a price to pay!

(Martial music is heard. MICHAL enters.)

MICHAL: They're getting ready to leave.

(MICHAL goes to the window. The room is now flooded with sunlight.)

MICHAL: Look at them, Bathsheba. Come, look. How splendid they all look in their uniforms!

(The music grows louder. BATHSHEBA covers her face with her hands as the lights come down.)

A SERPENT'S TOOTH

*"How sharper than a serpent's tooth it is
To have a thankless child."*
Shakespeare

CAST OF CHARACTERS

DAVID . . . . King of the Israelites

ABSALOM . . . . David's Son

JOAB . . . . A General

AMNON . . . . David's Eldest Son, Absalom's Step-Brother

TAMAR . . . . David's Daughter, Amnon's Step-Sister

BATHSHEBA . . . . David's Wife

NATHAN . . . . The High Priest

JONADAB . . . . David's Nephew

HUSHAI . . . . A Counselor

AMASA . . . . A General

ABISHAG . . . . A Young Virgin

(NOTE: If so desired the role of AMNON may be doubled with that of AMASA and that of TAMAR with ABISHAG.)

SCENE

Jerusalem and various parts of ancient Israel

ACT ONE

Scene One

(The house of Amnon. AMNON, David's eldest son enters with his cousin, JONADAB.)

JONADAB: What's the matter with you?

AMNON: I just don't feel well.

JONADAB: Have you seen a doctor?

AMNON: He says there's nothing wrong with me. I'm just depressed.

JONADAB: What have you got to be depressed about? You're young. You're healthy. You can do whatever you want to do.

AMNON: No one can do whatever they want to do.

JONADAB: Why don't you just take her?

AMNON: I don't know what you're talking about?

JONADAB: Oh, come, come, cousin. I can read you like a book.

AMNON: And what do you see in this book of yours?

JONADAB: I see a man yearning for what he thinks is forbidden fruit.

AMNON: And what would you advise this man to do?

JONADAB: I've just told you.

AMNON: For one thing she happens to be my sister.

335

JONADAB: Half sister.

JONADAB: And besides, I happen to be in love with her.

JONADAB: Love! Don't talk nonsense. What are you, a silly young school girl?

AMNON: What would you call it then?

JONADAB: Lust, pure and simple. Has she shown any interest in you?

AMNON: On the contrary. She goes out of her way to avoid me?

JONADAB: And you put up with it? The man who will some day inherit a kingdom?

AMNON: I'm not so sure about that.

JONADAB: You are the eldest aren't you?

AMNON: Yes, well, I think the king intends to live forever. I'm serious. I don't know what to do.

JONADAB: It's very simple. Women are all mush underneath. They're sentimental fools. You've got to appeal to the mother in them.

AMNON: And how, exactly, does one do that?

JONADAB: If you're sick, for example, deathly ill...they'll rush to your side with a bowl of soup, a gentle touch...tender loving care.

AMNON: You think she'd fall for a trick like that?

JONADAB: I guarantee it.

AMNON: You don't think she'd be suspicious?

JONADAB: Not if it came from the king. Get the king to send her over.

AMNON: All right. Just for the sake of argument, let's say, she does respond. What then?

JONADAB: You make your move. You pounce. Do I have to draw you a diagram?

AMNON: And what about afterwards? Suppose she complains? Suppose she raises a stink?

JONADAB: They never do. They're too ashamed.

AMNON: I don't know.

JONADAB: Look, forget it.

AMNON: I need time to think.

JONADAB: You do that little thing. *(HE starts off.)*

AMNON: Wait a minute, Jonadab. You're always in a rush. A thing like this demands a little thought.

     (AMNON follows JONADAB off.)

Scene Two

(David's chambers. DAVID enters with NATHAN, the high priest.)

NATHAN: Once and for all, can we drop the subject, please?

DAVID: Will you listen to me for a moment?! I've done my best to walk in the ways of the Lord. I sing his praises continually. I attend all your services faithfully, don't I? And now the Holy Ark has been brought into the city. It's accessible to all. It's well protected and well cared for.

NATHAN: I'm aware of all that.

DAVID: But, Nathan, how can we hold our heads up when our Holy of Hollies is housed in that shabby tent?

NATHAN: Look, David, you've united a kingdom. Our people have never been more prosperous. Your fame is secure.

DAVID: Is that what you think this is all about? My personal glory?

NATHAN: Don't put words in my mouth. Son, listen to me. We all have something to contribute and yours has been a monumental contribution. Not has been, continues to be. But we still have hostile forces to contend with.

DAVID: Our borders have never been more secure.

NATHAN: Don't force me to say it.

DAVID: What?

NATHAN: Your hands are bloody.

338

DAVID: With the blood of our enemies.

NATHAN: You know perfectly well what I'm talking about.

DAVID: One sin, for which I've paid for it dearly.

NATHAN: Your life has been spared. Your dynasty will be preserved. Saul did not get off so easily for a much lesser crime. Your plans have been approved and your heir will be allowed to build your temple for you. And that's the end of it. I don't want to hear anymore. And while we're on the subject of your heirs...

NATHAN: What have they done now?

NATHAN: Instead of worrying about that temple of yours, how about paying some attention to your sons?

DAVID: My sons want for nothing.

NATHAN: Except for a father to take a personal interest in them.

DAVID: I can't be everywhere.

NATHAN: You are a parent as well as a king. And it just so happens that the future of your kingdom rests with your progeny. When was the last time you spoke to Amnon?

DAVID: I don't know.

NATHAN: Well, for your information he's taken to his bed.

DAVID: What's the matter with him?

NATHAN: The doctors are baffled. They can't seem to find the cause, and he's been asking for you. It might behoove you to pay the boy a visit.

   (BATHSHEBA enters.)

BATHSHEBA: Oh, I'm sorry.

NATHAN: Come in, come in. I was just leaving. *(HE goes off.)*

BATHSHEBA: Problem?

DAVID: He refuses to budge.

BATHSHEBA: I thought you'd given up on that temple of yours.

DAVID: I shall never give up on it. In addition to that he gave me a lecture. I don't pay enough attention to my progeny.

BATHSHEBA: What now?

DAVID: Amnon has taken to his bed and they don't know what's wrong with him.

BATHSHEBA: Probably something he drank.

DAVID: You're always running him down. What have you got against the boy?

BATHSHEBA: For one thing, he's no longer a boy. He's grown up...into a boor and a slob.

DAVID: He's not as bright as Solomon, of course.

BATHSHEBA: You're the one that said it.

DAVID: But then, who is?

BATHSHEBA: You look tired.

DAVID: I am tired.

BATHSHEBA: Why don't you take a nap?

DAVID: In the middle of the day?

BATHSHEBA: Why not? After a certain age...

DAVID: What did you want to see me about?

BATHSHEBA: Must there be something special?

DAVID: I'm very busy today.

BATHSHEBA: You're always busy.

DAVID: And nothing to show for it. The fact that we're at peace for a change, the fact that commerce is flourishing, the fact that we're a prosperous and highly respected nation, that has nothing to do with me.

BATHSHEBA: Poor David! No one appreciates him.

DAVID: Tell me something. Do you think I'm a bad father? Tell me the truth. Well?

BATHSHEBA: You spoil them. I know, I know, my dear. It's so much easier to let them have their own way.

DAVID: It isn't that.

BATHSHEBA: What is it then?

DAVID: I spent half my life as a fugitive.

BATHSHEBA: So you want your sons to enjoy the advantages that you never had. But, David, there are times when a parent must say "no". And believe me, in the end, they will thank you for it. No one wants to be resented, I know that, but it's a risk that a father must take. And there's one thing more...

DAVID: And what might that be?

BATHSHEBA: Don't you think it's about time you named your heir?

DAVID: Why? Do you think my departure from this vale of tears is that imminent?

BATHSHEBA: That is not the point. There's this sense of uneasiness, of unspoken rivalry.

DAVID: Good. Keeps them on their toes.

BATHSHEBA: You made me a promise once.

DAVID: When the time comes I will make an announcement and not before. Was there anything else?

BATHSHEBA: Actually I've come to invite you to a little dinner party. Tomorrow's Solomon's birthday.

DAVID: I'm leaving for Hebron tomorrow.

BATHSHEBA: You don't like the boy, do you?

DAVID: I'm fond of all my sons.

BATHSHEBA: He's a remarkable child.

DAVID: So it would appear.

BATHSHEBA: Sometimes he amazes me. Of course he doesn't have the modesty of, let's say, an Absalom, for example, or the wit of Adonijah.

DAVID: Now, now, now.

BATHSHEBA: Just the other day he came up to me... What are you smiling at?

DAVID: I remember when I was the object of all that passion.

BATHSHEBA: You're much too busy these days for that sort of thing...where I'm concerned, at any rate.

DAVID: Come, take a little stroll with me. I've missed our little talks.

BATHSHEBA: I'd love to, my dear, but I have a schedule too, you know.

DAVID: Must I make an appointment?

BATHSHEBA: Why not? That's the only way I can get to see you these days.

DAVID: When are you available?

BATHSHEBA: I'll have to consult my calendar.

DAVID: You do that, and let me know.

BATHSHEBA: If you're still interested by then. *(SHE goes off.)*

DAVID: *(HE smiles and shakes his head.)* Delectable witch.

(DAVID goes off as the lights come down.)

Scene Three

(The house of AMNON. AMNON is discovered reclining. TAMAR enters with a bowl of soup.)

TAMAR: Here you are. It's nice and hot.

AMNON: Thank you. It's very kind of you.

TAMAR: You look so flushed.

AMNON: It's the fever.

TAMAR: You ought to take better care of yourself.

AMNON: I guess I need someone to look after me.

TAMAR: You're such a baby. Well, aren't you going to eat? I took a great deal of trouble preparing that soup.

AMNON: Why don't you feed me?

TAMAR: Now, really!

AMNON: Please? Pretty please?

TAMAR: All right. One spoonful, just to start you off. Open your mouth. Wider. There.

AMNON: That's good. One more.

TAMAR: There.

> *(SHE feeds him a second spoonful of soup. HE takes hold of her wrist.)*

344

AMNON: Your hands are so soft.

TAMAR: I can't feed you if you hold my hand.

AMNON: Won't you rub my temples for me?

TAMAR: First you must finish your soup.

AMNON: I'm really not very hungry.

TAMAR: But you must have some nourishment, if you want to get better.

AMNON: One more spoonful.

(SHE feeds him another spoonful of soup.)

AMNON: Now?

TAMAR: Just one more. *(SHE feeds him another spoonful.)*

AMNON: Now?

TAMAR: You're such a baby. *(SHE sighs, puts down the bowl and massages his temples.)*

AMNON: Mmmm, that feels so good. But you're so far away. Sit down here beside me? I'm not going to bite you. Please.

TAMAR: I can't rub your temples if I sit beside you.

AMNON: Just for a minute. I just want to look at you.

TAMAR: *(SHE sits beside him.)* There.

AMNON: You're so pretty. And your hands are like the petals of a flower. So pink. *(HE takes her hand and examines her fingers, then kisses her fingers.)*

TAMAR: Now, now, now! Amnon. Behave yourself.

AMNON: It's so kind of you to look in on me like this.

TAMAR: I really can't stay very long.

AMNON: I won't keep you long.

TAMAR: As a matter of fact, I should be leaving.

AMNON: Just a little while longer. Please.

TAMAR: If you behave yourself.

>   *(HE kisses the palm of her hand.)*

TAMAR: Amnon!

AMNON: Your eyes are like almonds.

TAMAR: *(Trying to release her hand.)* I really must go.

AMNON: Don't you like me? Just a little bit?

TAMAR: Of course, I like you, Amnon.   But I have things to do.
Amnon, let go of my hand.

AMNON: If you like me, like you say you do, why do you treat me like
this?

TAMAR: I don't know what you mean.

AMNON: You know.

TAMAR: Amnon, please. Let go of my hand.

AMNON: Why don't you lie down here beside me? *(HE pulls her down
beside him and tries to kiss her.)*

TAMAR: Amnon, please!

AMNON: Why not?

TAMAR: You mustn't.

AMNON: Why not?

TAMAR: Because...

AMNON: Because why?

TAMAR: Because you mustn't.

AMNON: Why not? If I love you.

TAMAR: You don't love me.

AMNON: Of course, I love you. I love you very much. You know that I do.

TAMAR: Amnon, please! Let me go! If you really love me, you can speak to the king.

AMNON: Why would I want to speak to the king?

TAMAR: Let me go of me. Please!

AMNON: And suppose I don't? What then?

(SHE breaks away and tries to run off. HE blocks her way.)

TAMAR: Amnon, let me go.

(HE grabs her by the wrist and throws her onto the couch.)

TAMAR: Amnon, please. You mustn't.

AMNON: Mustn't what?

TAMAR: Please, Amnon, please.

AMNON: Just this once. I don't want to hurt you. I just want to love you. That's all. Please, Tamar. Just let me kiss you. Just let me kiss you all over. That won't hurt. Will it? If I kiss you all over? I don't want to hurt you.

(SHE screams. HE covers her mouth with his hand. SHE bites his hand.)

AMNON: Ouch! You little bitch!

(HE slaps her. SHE breaks away. HE catches her and throws her back down on the couch and begins to pull up her gown.)

TAMAR: No! No, please! Help!

(HE slaps her hard. SHE begins to whimper.)

TAMAR: Please! No, please. Amnon, please.

(SHE continues to whimper as HE mounts her, and the lights slowly fade.)

Scene Four

(The house of Absalom. ABSALOM, David's son, enters from the outside hallway with JOAB, David's general.)

ABSALOM: Come in, come in.

JOAB: What did you want to see me about?

ABSALOM: Sit down, sit down.

JOAB: I don't have much time.

ABSALOM: Why is the world in such a rush?

JOAB: We're conducting maneuvers this afternoon outside the city.

ABSALOM: Now that we're neighbors I just thought that we ought to get reacquainted. What are you smiling at?

JOAB: I'm fond of you, Absalom, you know that. But I've known you since you were that high and I can always tell when you want something. So let's not beat around the bush. What can I do for you?

ABSALOM: On the contrary. I just thought that I might possibly be of use to you. I know that you and Amasa are at loggerheads about conscription and other things as well.

JOAB: And...?

ABSALOM: I have the king's ear, you know.

JOAB: That you do.

ABSALOM: And if I were to suggest that it would be a mistake to end conscription even though things are relatively quiet now...

JOAB: Thank you, my boy, but there's no need.

ABSALOM: Oh?

JOAB: We had a showdown yesterday, the king, Amasa and myself and the king has come around to my way of thinking.

ABSALOM: I'm so glad to hear it.

JOAB: Now, what can I do for you?

ABSALOM: I am his favorite, you know.

JOAB: Yes, dear boy, that's not exactly a secret.

ABSALOM: At any rate he is getting on and yet he refuses to name his successor.

JOAB: And you want me to put in a good word for you. Is that it?

ABSALOM: The throne is all but mine.

JOAB: Then you've nothing to worry about.

ABSALOM: There's many a slip, however...

JOAB: It's no use, I'm afraid.

ABSALOM: What do you mean?

JOAB: I've spoken to him a number of times.

ABSALOM: And...?

JOAB: He refuses to budge.

(TAMAR enters looking disheveled. Seeing Joab SHE turns away.)

ABSALOM: Tamar?

JOAB: I've got to go. *(HE starts off.)*

ABSALOM: Yes. Yes, of course.

JOAB: That's all right. I'll see myself out. *(HE goes off.)*

ABSALOM: Tamar, are you all right? Come in, come in.

> *(ABSALOM approaches her and extends his hand. SHE draws away.)*

ABSALOM: What is it? What's wrong?

TAMAR: Nothing.

ABSALOM: Are you all right?

> *(SHE starts to weep.)*

ABSALOM: What is it? What's wrong?

TAMAR: It's all my fault.

ABSALOM: What's happened? Tamar?

TAMAR: It was Amnon, he...

ABSALOM: He what? Did he hurt you?

> *(SHE nods.)*

ABSALOM: Did he...?

TAMAR: I didn't want him to. Honestly I didn't.

ABSALOM: Did he attack you?

> *(SHE nods.)*

ABSALOM: Where was this?

TAMAR: In his bedroom.

ABSALOM: What were you doing in his bedroom?

TAMAR: The king asked me to look in on him. He wasn't feeling well. Oh, Absalom!

ABSALOM: All right, all right. Now just calm down and tell me what happened.

TAMAR: The king sent word. He said that Amnon was ill and that he was asking for me.

ABSALOM: Go on.

TAMAR: I prepared some soup and when I got there...

ABSALOM: Go on.

TAMAR: He dismissed all the servants.

ABSALOM: And you were left alone with him?

TAMAR: *(SHE nods.)* And then he attacked me. He hurt me, Absalom. He hurt me badly. *(SHE cries.)* And then afterwards...

ABSALOM: Go on, go on.

TAMAR: He threw me out. He called in all the servants and he yelled. He yelled, "Get rid of her! Get rid of that slut!" He acted like it was all my fault. I suppose it was.

ABSALOM: Don't be ridiculous.

ABSALOM: No, it's true. I knew how he felt about me. Every time he saw me I could feel him undressing me with his eyes. Oh, Absalom, what am I going to do? Nobody's going to marry me now. What am I going to do?

ABSALOM: Now just keep calm.

TAMAR: You won't tell anyone, will you?

ABSALOM: I'm going to speak to the king about this.

TAMAR: Oh no, please!

ABSALOM: He's got to be punished.

TAMAR: The fault was mine.

ABSALOM: Now stop it! It was not your fault. Amnon did a terrible thing.

TAMAR: No one's going to marry me now. *(SHE weeps.)*

ABSALOM: Everything's going to be all right. Now stop it. You hear me?

TAMAR: Absalom...?

ABSALOM: Yes, dear? What is it?

TAMAR: May I stay here with you? Please? I'll cook for you. I'll take care of the house. Oh, Absalom, please! Don't throw me out. Please don't throw me out.

ABSALOM: I'm not going to throw you out. I'm going to talk to the king.

TAMAR: Oh no, please!

ABSALOM: He committed a crime.

TAMAR: Don't hate me. Please don't hate me.

ABSALOM: I'm not going to hate you.

TAMAR: Then you will let me stay here, won't you? I mean for always. I mean even after you're married. I won't be in the way, I promise you.

ABSALOM: You can stay as long as you like.

TAMAR: You won't change your mind, will you?

ABSALOM: No, I won't change my mind.

TAMAR: You promise?

ABSALOM: I promise. Now come with me.

TAMAR: Where are we going?

ABSALOM: We're going to get you a nice hot bath. I'll call one of the servants to help you.

TAMAR: No!

ABSALOM: A woman, Tamar, a woman. Now you mustn't be afraid. Come on, come on.

> *(SHE rises. HE puts his arm around her shoulder. SHE stiffens and backs away.)*

ABSALOM: I'm not going to hurt you, Tamar. *(HE holds out his hand.)* Come on, dear, come on. Take my hand and we're going to get you a nice hot bath.

TAMAR: *(SHE takes his hand.)* And you won't tell anyone, will you, Absalom?

ABSALOM: That's right, that's right. Come on.

(HE leads HER off as the lights come down.)

Scene Five

(David's chambers. JONADAB is discovered seated. NATHAN enters. JONADAB jumps to his feet.)

JONADAB: Your holiness.

NATHAN: What's happened?

JONADAB: You haven't heard?

NATHAN: Heard what?

JONADAB: I thought it was all over town. If it isn't it will be very shortly. Tamar was raped. That's what she claims, at any rate.

NATHAN: Have you spoken to her?

(JONADAB shakes his head.)

NATHAN: Then...?

JONADAB: According to Absalom. He's with the king right now.

NATHAN: When did this happen?

JONADAB: Yesterday.

NATHAN: Do they know who the culprit is?

JONADAB: Amnon, allegedly.

(NATHAN sighs and shakes his head.)

JONADAB: Yes, I know. He is a boor.

NATHAN: Where's the girl now?

JONADAB: She's staying with Absalom. He's very upset. I'm not surprised, however. What I mean to say is everyone knows how Amnon felt about Tamar.

NATHAN: Oh?

JONADAB: Oh, yes. He talked of nothing else. Why he's absolutely obsessed with her. What does surprise me though...

NATHAN: Yes? Go on.

JONADAB: It's not for me to say but I can't imagine what the king had in mind when he ordered the poor girl to pay Amnon a visit. What could he have been thinking of?

(DAVID enters with ABSALOM.)

NATHAN: Is it true?

DAVID: What?

ABSALOM: Amnon raped my sister.

DAVID: Let's not rush to judgement.

ABSALOM: After what I've just told you?

DAVID: Just calm down.

NATHAN: What sort of state is she in?

ABSALOM: She's hysterical.

NATHAN: Has she been harmed?

ABSALOM: What are you...deaf?

NATHAN: Watch your tongue, young man!

ABSALOM: Didn't you hear what I've just said?

NATHAN: Did he beat her?

ABSALOM: Yes, there are bruises on her body, if that's what you mean. The bruises will heal. That is not the point. I'm just afraid that...

NATHAN: What?

ABSALOM: Her mind will never heal. Don't you understand? She's been violated, mentally as well as physically. She wakes up in the middle of the night and starts screaming. She won't let anyone near her. She's like a frightened child.

DAVID: And the fault is mine.

NATHAN: Now, now, now.

DAVID: That's what he keeps telling me. This would never have happened if I hadn't ordered her to visit him.

NATHAN: No one's to blame. If this is true however...

ABSALOM: If?!

NATHAN: May I finish please?! If this is true Amnon will marry the girl, and that's the end of that.

ABSALOM: I beg to differ with you. Amnon will not marry the girl. She's petrified at the very thought that he might come near her.

NATHAN: Yes, well, time has a way of healing these things.

ABSALOM: She'd kill herself first.

NATHAN: Let's not get melodramatic.

DAVID: I've sent for Amnon. He should be here any minute now.

NATHAN: Exactly. In all fairness to the boy I think we ought to hear his side of the story. First of all, has the girl been examined?

ABSALOM: She has.

DAVID: By a doctor?

ABSALOM: By one of my maids and I've been told in no uncertain terms that my sister was brutally raped.

(AMNON enters.)

DAVID: Well, what have you got to say for yourself?

AMNON: I beg your pardon.

NATHAN: We've been given to understand that you raped your sister?

AMNON: My sister?

DAVID: Don't play the fool with me! We're talking about Tamar.

AMNON: Is that what she said? That I raped her?

DAVID: You deny it then?

AMNON: I most certainly do. I...ah... (HE starts to say something then stops himself.)

DAVID: Go on.

AMNON: Well, it is true that Tamar and I made love.

ABSALOM: Love?!

DAVID: Let him finish please. You've had your say.

AMNON: I never thought she'd make a public issue of it.

DAVID: Then it is true?

AMNON: Yes, but...

NATHAN: Are you trying to say that it was by mutual consent?

AMNON: Does she say otherwise?

DAVID: Never mind what she says. I want you to tell me exactly what happened.

AMNON: She came to my house. She brought me some soup. I asked her to rub my temples for me. I had a terrible headache. And then, well one thing led to another. Never in my wildest dreams... What I mean to say is...

DAVID: What?

AMNON: I thought she was pleased. She certainly seemed to be at first.

NATHAN: At first? What do you mean...at first?

AMNON: I mean...during. And then, well, afterwards she got hysterical. I don't know what came over her. She's always been rather moody. At any rate, I'm sorry to say she made a rather ugly scene, screaming and yelling like some demented shrew. At any rate I had to call in my servants to help me get rid of her. She almost scratched my eyes out. I can show you where she scratched me.

NATHAN: That won't be necessary.

DAVID: You'll marry her.

AMNON: Yes, of course. I'll do whatever you think is right. This whole incident is very painful to me. I've always been fond of Tamar. I have the greatest respect for her. I would never do anything to harm her. *(Almost tearfully)* I'm so sorry. Really I am.

DAVID: All right, all right. *(To NATHAN, ABSALOM and JONADAB.)* Will you excuse us please? *(To AMNON.)* Come with me.

> *(DAVID places his arm around AMNON'S shoulder and leads HIM off.)*

ABSALOM: He's lying. Don't you see?

NATHAN: What's the point of making things worse than they really are? Let him marry the girl.

ABSALOM: He is not going to marry her.

NATHAN: All right, all right. Meanwhile it's time for the evening service. Perhaps you'd care to...

   (ABSALOM turns away in disgust.)

NATHAN: I'll drop by later on and have a talk with her.

ABSALOM: That's very kind of you.

NATHAN: Sarcasm will accomplish nothing. It's all very unfortunate.

ABSALOM: So let's sweep it under the rug.

NATHAN: We'll discuss this later, when you've calmed down. Jonadab?

JONADAB: I think I'm needed here, your holiness.

NATHAN: *(To Absalom)* I'll see you later then. *(HE goes off.)*

JONADAB: Absolutely appalling. However what can you expect? They're two of a kind, the father and his first born. You know, of course the story of the king and Bathsheba, how he got rid of her husband. And if you think he's going to punish...that pig, you can think again.

ABSALOM: He's got to do something.

JONADAB: I may be wrong. I certainly hope so. The girl's an angel. And if there's anything I can do...

ABSALOM: Thank you, Jonadab.

JONADAB: I've always been fond of Tamar. She's a very special girl, so sweet and charming. And Amnon's always been such a boor.

ABSALOM: The king can't ignore this. He can't just close his eyes.

JONADAB: I don't see how he possibly can. If I'm wrong, however, I hope you won't let it rest.

ABSALOM: Don't worry, I won't.

JONADAB: I'm glad to hear you say that. Of course, I do think we ought to wait and see what the king has to say.

ABSALOM: I'd better get back.

JONADAB: I'll walk a ways with you. How is she doing, by the way?

ABSALOM: Not well. Not well, at all.

JONADAB: What an unspeakable monster!

(*JONADAB goes off with ABSALOM as the lights come down.*)

Scene Six

(A room in the women's palace. BATHSHEBA enters with JOAB.)

JOAB: Where is everyone?

BATHSHEBA: Everyone?

JOAB: I thought this was supposed to be a dinner party.

BATHSHEBA: It is. And you're the guest of honor.

JOAB: The only guest, apparently.

BATHSHEBA: I'll try not to bore you.

JOAB: You could never do that.

BATHSHEBA: May I offer you some wine?

(JOAB nods. BATHSHEBA pours two cups of wine and hands him one.)

BATHSHEBA: To your health, General.

JOAB: And yours, your grace.

BATHSHEBA: I'm very angry with you, you know.

JOAB: And that's my cue to ask why?

BATHSHEBA: My son's a great admirer of yours, and he was very disappointed not to see you at his birthday dinner.

362

JOAB: I was otherwise engaged. I did send a present. Didn't I?

BATHSHEBA: Don't you know?

JOAB: My wife took care of it.

BATHSHEBA: You don't like the boy, do you?

JOAB: I hardly know him.

BATHSHEBA: He's going to be our next king.

JOAB: If I'm still around by then, he shall have my undivided loyalty.

BATHSHEBA: What do you mean, if you're still around?

JOAB: He's very young.

BATHSHEBA: In years, perhaps. Nathan, incidentally, has been tutoring him personally.

JOAB: Well, that's a feather in your cap.

BATHSHEBA: You don't think much of his chances, do you?

JOAB: I make it a point not to get involved in politics.

BATHSHEBA: David's given me his word.

JOAB: Then you've nothing to be concerned about.

BATHSHEBA: I thought you were a friend.

JOAB: You've always had...my deepest admiration.

BATHSHEBA: You don't think much of Amnon's chances, after that nasty little incident?

JOAB: I never thought much of Amnon's chances.

BATHSHEBA: Adonijah?

JOAB: Good heavens, no.

BATHSHEBA: Who then?

JOAB: Absalom.

BATHSHEBA: You're not serious.

JOAB: You disagree, of course.

BATHSHEBA: The king is fond of the boy, it's true, though he tries not to show it. But in matters of state he's never let his personal feelings get in the way.

JOAB: What's your objection to Absalom...aside from your personal prejudice?

BATHSHEBA: Absalom does not have the qualities that a king must have.

JOAB: And what, in your opinion, are these qualities?

BATHSHEBA: Emotional stability, for one thing.

JOAB: Well, it's true he does have a temper.

BATHSHEBA: Lack of vanity.

JOAB: And he is conceited, perhaps. But then I don't think you'll find any shrinking flowers here at court.

BATHSHEBA: Vaulting ambition.

JOAB: You've just painted a perfect picture of our king.

BATHSHEBA: And speaking of Absalom, I'm surprised you weren't invited for that sheepshearing festival he's hosting in Baal Hazor.

JOAB: That was strictly a family gathering, for all the brothers, that is.

BATHSHEBA: Including Amnon?

JOAB: Why yes. Yes, of course.

BATHSHEBA: And the king gave his permission?

JOAB: As far as I know. You don't think that Absalom still harbors a grudge, do you? It's been over a year.

BATHSHEBA: Knowing Absalom, what do you think?

JOAB: He is devoted to Tamar, I know. And since that incident the poor girl hasn't been the same.

BATHSHEBA: It's all very unfortunate. I'm absolutely starved. I hope you're hungry too.

(*SHE takes his arm and THEY go off together as the lights come down.*)

Scene Seven

(David's chambers. DAVID and JONADAB are discovered. DAVID is pacing back and forth.)

JONADAB: There must be some mistake. It is quite possible that Absalom still had a grudge against Amnon, but why would he kill everyone of his brothers? It just doesn't make any sense. Of course, Absalom does have a temper, and maybe there was a drunken brawl. When brothers get together it's quite possible. Would you like to me investigate?

DAVID: I've sent Hushai.

JONADAB: Of course, I did think it strange when he made a point of inviting all his brothers. But then again Absalom has always been family oriented. Look at the way he looks after Tamar, poor thing. But then again he is hot headed, isn't he? Well it is just a rumor, isn't it, and you know how malicious some people can be. If it's true however, and I'm sure it isn't, we can just be thankful that young Solomon wasn't included in the invitation. Such a bright young child, and so well behaved. A little frightening at times, I must admit.

DAVID: What could be keeping him? He's been gone for hours.

JONADAB: Hushai is rather slow on his feet these days. Though he is very loyal, I will say that. Can I get you anything, Uncle?

DAVID: No, no. I'm fine?

(HUSHAI, an aged counsellor enters.)

DAVID: Well? What have you heard?

HUSHAI: Amnon's been murdered.

366

DAVID: Only Amnon?

HUSHAI: All the others are safe. That's what I've been told, at any rate.

JONADAB: Thank the Lord!

DAVID: And...who was the culprit?

HUSHAI: It was Absalom, I'm afraid. There was a lot of drinking going on the night before and, in the early hours of the morning when everyone was fast asleep, it seems that Absalom ordered his servants to murder him. There was a great deal of blood apparently and in the excitement some people thought that there'd been a massacre.

JONADAB: Awful! Just awful!

DAVID: And Absalom? Where is he now?

HUSHAI: He's fled the country.

(DAVID sits in despair. NATHAN enters.)

NATHAN: I just heard the news. I can't believe it. Absalom, of all people. I had such hopes for him. What on earth could have possessed him?

JONADAB: He's never forgiven Amnon for that so-called incident with his sister.

NATHAN: But that was years ago.

JONADAB: Just one, your Holiness. However, you'd think by this time...

HUSHAI: The girl has never recovered.

NATHAN: What's that?

HUSHAI: I said the girl has never recovered. She's not right in the head.

JONADAB: Well, there you are.

NATHAN: But to kill one's own brother.

JONADAB: The mark of Cain.

NATHAN: Where is he now? Absalom? Where is he now?

HUSHAI: He's fled the country.

NATHAN: What a tragedy! The brightest and the best. But then again are any of us free from guilt? When blood is shed we are all responsible. *(HE looks directly at David.)* Are we not? The important thing is to learn from our mistakes and to ask the Lord's forgiveness. I'm about to conduct the evening prayer. Perhaps you'd care to join us.

   (DAVID shakes his head.)

NATHAN: I'll come by later on. Jonadab?

JONADAB: Yes. Yes, of course. I'd like to say a prayer for Amnon. And for Absalom as well. I shall ask the Lord's forgiveness for them both. Uncle.

   (JONADAB kisses DAVID on both cheeks and follows NATHAN off.)

HUSHAI: I've never liked that young man.

DAVID: Jonadab?

HUSHAI: Nephew or not, there's something about him.

DAVID: He means well.

HUSHAI: I don't think so.

DAVID: *(After a moment.)* He was the one I was counting on, you know. The only one I could talk to, the only one I had something in common with. All the others...they're like strangers to me.

HUSHAI: There's Solomon, of course.

DAVID: Yes, there's Solomon.

HUSHAI: He's young it's true.

DAVID: He's a cold fish.

HUSHAI: He's a very clever boy.

DAVID: But it's all up here. There's nothing here. *(HE thumps his chest.)* And it's odd, you know, because he's nothing like me at all, and nothing like his mother either. He's impulsive, it's true, but at least with Absalom you know where you stand. I was counting on him. But now, of course, it's out of the question. You were never too fond of him, I know.

HUSHAI: It's difficult not to be fond of the boy. But when it comes to matter of state I think it's dangerous when the heart rules the head.

DAVID: That's why he's my favorite, I suppose. The cart before the horse. The heart before the head. That's always been me. And he is the most intelligent of the lot except, of course, for Solomon. Nathan blames me for the way they all turned out.

HUSHAI: After a certain age we are all responsible for ourselves.

DAVID: I should have forced Amnon to marry her. I should have taken more personal interest.

HUSHAI: Marriage would have been a mistake.

DAVID: *(HE sighs.)* I'd like to be alone for a while.

HUSHAI: Yes, of course. *(HE starts off.)*

DAVID: Thank you, Hushai.

HUSHAI: For what, your majesty?

DAVID: For not passing judgement. For being honest with me. There are not that many here at court.

(HUSHAI bows and goes off. DAVID sinks into a chair and buries his head in his hands as the lights slowly fade.)

Scene Eight

(Five years later. The house of Absalom. ABSALOM is discovered waiting impatiently. TAMAR rushes into the room.)

TAMAR: Fire, fire! *(SHE runs to ABSALOM.)* Fire, fire!

ABSALOM: What is it, dear? What's the matter?

TAMAR: Fire. Fire.

ABSALOM: Now calm down, Tamar. Now just calm down.

TAMAR: There's a fire out there.

ABSALOM: Where?

TAMAR: Out there, in the field.

ABSALOM: Show me. Where? *(HE leads her to the window.)* Now, where's the fire? I don't see any fire.

TAMAR: There was, I tell you.

ABSALOM: All right, all right. But it's not there now. Do you see any fire? Do you?

TAMAR: No. You think I'm seeing things, don't you?

ABSALOM: Now, Tamar.

TAMAR: Maybe I ought to be put away somewhere.

ABSALOM: Now stop it.

371

TAMAR: It's true. I'm crazy like they say.

ABSALOM: No one thinks you're crazy.

TAMAR: The children do.

ABSALOM: They're just teasing you, love. You mustn't pay any attention to the children.

TAMAR: They don't want me here. And they're right. I should have a home of my own.

ABSALOM: This is your home for as long as you like. Now I don't want to hear anymore.

TAMAR: But I did see a fire.

ABSALOM: I'm sure you did. It's that time of year, isn't it? There are all sorts of brush fires now, aren't there?

TAMAR: I suppose so.

(JOAB appears in the doorway unseen by ABSALOM.)

TAMAR: Absalom...?

ABSALOM: *(HE turns and sees JOAB then addresses TAMAR.)* Go to your room. It's all right. Go to your room.

(TAMAR hesitates then runs off.)

JOAB: Are you out of your mind?

ABSALOM: Good morning.

JOAB: What do you think you're doing?

ABSALOM: And how are you this morning?

JOAB: Do you realize what could have happened?

ABSALOM: Would you care for some breakfast? I've just finished mine...

JOAB: And please don't play games with me. Your servants set fire to my crops. They were seen so you needn't deny it. You could have destroyed my entire harvest. I'm waiting for an explanation.

ABSALOM: I've sent you message after message.

JOAB: I've been busy.

ABSALOM: Oh come on, Joab. No one is that busy.

JOAB: All right. I'm here. You've got my attention. What do you want?

ABSALOM: I want you to speak to the king.

JOAB: I've spoken to the king. That's why you're back.

ABSALOM: Yes, I'm back. I've been back for how long now? It's almost two years, and I haven't seen hide nor hair of him. It's as if I didn't exist. I might as well be back in Geshur.

JOAB: Have you tried to see him?

ABSALOM: What do you think? Joab, there are standing orders. I'm not to be admitted to the palace. It's been five years now. Don't you think that's punishment enough? I miss him, Joab. I really do. And he misses me. You know that he does.

JOAB: Quite possibly.

ABSALOM: And neither of us is getting any younger.

JOAB: Absalom, you murdered a man.

ABSALOM: So did you.

JOAB: If you're referring to Abner, he killed my brother.

ABSALOM: And Amnon destroyed my sister. You see what she's like. He listened to you once and I'm grateful to you for that. I really am. But what's the good of his bringing me back, if he won't see me? You and I both know that I'm his favorite. This is just as painful for him as it is for me. Eventually he's going to relent. You know that he is. And when he does he's going to make me his heir, and when that time comes I won't forget you.

JOAB: All right, all right.

ABSALOM: You'll speak to him then?

JOAB: Let me think about it.

ABSALOM: I'm sure he'd like to see his grandchildren, wouldn't he? Remind him of that.

JOAB: I said all right. I'll see what I can do, though it's not so easy to reach him these days.

ABSALOM: You're a good man, Joab. I've always been fond of you and I don't think the king really appreciates how valuable you are.

JOAB: Save it.

ABSALOM: Thank you, Joab.

JOAB: I'm not promising anything.

ABSALOM: When do you think...?

JOAB: Don't rush me. And don't try anything like that again. You hear me? You're a madman.

(JOAB goes off. TAMAR peeks into the room.)

TAMAR: Is he gone yet?

(SHE comes into the room and approaches ABSALOM. Absentmindedly HE puts his arm around her shoulders.)

TAMAR: Absalom?

ABSALOM: What, dear?

TAMAR: Is he a good man?

ABSALOM: That remains to be seen.

(The lights slowly dim.)

Scene Nine

(DAVID's chambers. DAVID enters with JOAB.)

DAVID: Why are you suddenly so interested in Absalom?

JOAB: You miss him and you know it.

DAVID: He's a murderer.

JOAB: "Let him who is without any guilt..."

DAVID: That's enough.

JOAB: He's paid for his sins.

DAVID: He killed his own brother.

JOAB: Half brother.

DAVID: And that makes a difference?

JOAB: It's been five years now, as an outcast, a pariah. I think we can both remember what that was like.

DAVID: Have you seen him?

JOAB: Of course, I see him. He's my neighbor. You have two grandsons now, you know. Two handsome, strapping boys.

DAVID: And Tamar? Does she still live with him?

JOAB: She's like a child.

DAVID: Does he ask about me?

376

JOAB: Continually. He misses you, David. He really does. And, let's face it, you miss him as well. I think it's time to bury the past. Don't you?

DAVID: You say he does ask about me?

JOAB: He's made several attempts to see you but, apparently, he's been barred from the palace.

DAVID: I know of only one.

JOAB: It's been more than once. He's waiting outside.

DAVID: You're pretty sure of yourself.

JOAB: I'm sure of your feeling for the boy.

DAVID: All right. Send him in.

> (*JOAB goes off. After a moment ABSALOM enters. THEY stand looking at one another. DAVID opens his arms. ABSALOM approaches and THEY embrace.*)

ABSALOM: I'm sorry...

DAVID: Let's not talk about it.

ABSALOM: Look at you. You haven't aged at all.

DAVID: Don't look too close. You're a husband now, and a father.

ABSALOM: Two boys. Two beautiful boys and they're anxious to meet their grandfather.

DAVID: It goes so quickly.

ABSALOM: I've missed you.

DAVID: Have you?

ABSALOM: I'd wake up in the morning, a stranger in a strange land and I'd say to myself, "This is the way it was for him, only worse. Because he was a fugitive, hunted like an animal."

DAVID: You were my one shining hope.

ABSALOM: You're disappointed in me, I know. But now that I'm back, I'll make it up to you. I promise.

DAVID: There's only one thing harder than being a king.

ABSALOM: And what is that?

DAVID: Being a father.

ABSALOM: Ah, yes.

DAVID: You understand?

ABSALOM: I'm beginning to.

DAVID: You were the only one. The only one I could talk to.

ABSALOM: Yes, well, there's always Bathsheba.

DAVID: Bathsheba's busy with that campaign of hers.

ABSALOM: What campaign is that?

DAVID: She's determined to make that child wonder of hers the most popular young man in the kingdom.

ABSALOM: *(After a moment)* How are your plans for the temple coming along?

DAVID: The plans are fine.

ABSALOM: Any progress with Nathan?

DAVID: *(HE shakes his head.)* I've given up on Nathan.

ABSALOM: And the temple as well?

DAVID: No, no, no. The temple is going to be built but not by me, I'm afraid. But I see now that it's not important who builds it, as long as it's built. And he's willing to allow my successor to go ahead with the plans. He's promised me that. He's given me his word. I was hoping that might be you. But now...

ABSALOM: What?

DAVID: Why do you think he objects to me?

ABSALOM: I don't know. Why?

DAVID: Because there's blood on my hands.

ABSALOM: But you're a soldier.

DAVID: Yes, well there is this other matter.

ABSALOM: I see.

DAVID: And now you. With Amnon.

ABSALOM: But you are the king...

DAVID: Yes, I'm the king, only Nathan speaks for God.

ABSALOM: But that's ridiculous!

DAVID: I know, I know. But my hands are tied. What difference does it make? You're back. That's the important thing. You must excuse me. It's been a long day. You'll dine with me tomorrow and you'll bring the boys. The prodigal son has returned, and I'm going to kill the fatted calf.

> *(DAVID kisses him and goes off. ABSALOM stands nonplussed. JOAB enters.)*

JOAB: How did it go? Absalom?

ABSALOM: What's that?

JOAB: How did it go?

ABSALOM: He's aged quite a bit, hasn't he?

JOAB: Haven't we all?

ABSALOM: You don't think he's getting senile, do you?

JOAB: What are you talking about?

ABSALOM: It was just a simple question. Everyone's so touchy these days.

JOAB: But you did hit it off.

ABSALOM: Oh everything's fine, except for the fact that I will never succeed him.

JOAB: What do you mean?

ABSALOM: There's blood on my hands. I would never be allowed to build that temple of his.

JOAB: Don't worry. He'll come around. Why do you shake your head?

ABSALOM: Not this time. When it comes to that temple of his nothing or no one will stand in his way. We're so much alike it's frightening.

JOAB: I'll speak to him.

ABSALOM: Forget it. *(HE goes off.)*

JOAB: Absalom...?

> *(JOAB looks deeply concerned as he watches ABSALOM leave.)*

ACT TWO

Scene One

(The house of Absalom. JONADAB enters with AMASA, a general.)

JONADAB: Just the other day, the prince was saying to me, "The army has got to be streamlined, modernized, updated. And General Amasa's just the man to do it." Not that Joab isn't an excellent man, the Lord only knows. In his day, he served the country well.

AMASA: He is a bit old-fashioned, don't you think?

JONADAB: I couldn't have put it better myself.

AMASA: Don't get me wrong. I have the greatest respect for Joab, but he's also... How shall I put it?

JONADAB: A bit of a hothead.

AMASA: Exactly.

JONADAB: Take that incident with Abner, for example. It was nothing but cold-blooded murder.

AMASA: Yes, well, it's the way he went about it. Like a common criminal.

JONADAB: Not very honorable.

AMASA: And then there's the matter of conscription.

JONADAB: Exactly. We're not at war now. Why take men away from their families, from their farms. That's the way Prince Absalom feels, at any rate. You may disagree, of course.

AMASA: Oh no. As a matter of fact, I think the king made a big mistake.

(ABSALOM enters.)

ABSALOM: General, how good of you to come.

JONADAB: I was just telling the general how highly we think of him. How, in his own quiet way, he's made more of a contribution to our military accomplishments than some others I could mention.

AMASA: Yes, well...

JONADAB: There's a time for modesty, but one must give credit where credit is due.

ABSALOM: Exactly. I assume you've brought the General up to date.

JONADAB: Not really, no.

ABSALOM: When I was in exile, general, I vowed that if I should ever return to my native country I would make a trip to Hebron, to give thanks to the Lord. The king has given me permission to do so and I've asked a number of people to join me. It's not only a holy pilgrimage but a sort of back to basics, a communion with our inner selves. It's so easy to lose touch with what is decent and good in our life, modern society being what it is today.

JONADAB: I see.

ABSALOM: As a matter of fact, I've extended an invitation to representatives from each of the twelve tribes, and they've all accepted.

JONADAB: This used to be a God-fearing country and the Prince would like to bring back that sense of decency, that sense of morality that seems to have deserted us.

ABSALOM: Not that the king hasn't done his best.

JONADAB: There's no question about that.

ABSALOM: But he is at the point in his life when he's looking back, when all his thoughts are focused on the past, mired in principles that may have been effective decades ago. Of course, he is getting on and his mind isn't as sharp as it used to be.

JONADAB: The prince has made it his job to keep in touch with the people, with what's happening now.

ABSALOM: That's true. I like to talk to people on the street. Find out what they think, what they feel, what it is they really want, and I can tell you stories...

JONADAB: Oh, yes, indeed.

ABSALOM: Lives disrupted, businesses upset because men have been called away to serve in the military when there's really no need for it. And then there's all those taxes...for what? To build up an arsenal that will never be used. You may disagree, of course.

AMASA: Oh, no, no.

JONADAB: It appears that the general has much in common with our point of view.

ABSALOM: And the point of view of the people.

JONADAB: Exactly.

ABSALOM: We'll be leaving for Hebron two weeks from today and we're hoping that you might be able to join us.

JONADAB: Depending upon your schedule, of course.

ABSALOM: It is short notice and if you find it impossible, we'll be disappointed, of course, but we will certainly understand. But do try to let us know by the end of the week.

JONADAB: I'll see you out.

ABSALOM: And thank you for coming.

JONADAB: You're looking very fit these days. What's your secret?

(JONADAB sees AMASA off and then returns.)

ABSALOM: What do you think?

JONADAB: I think he's hooked.

ABSALOM: I certainly hope so because without the army we are nowhere.

(THEY go off together as the lights come down.)

Scene Two

(DAVID's chambers. NATHAN and HUSHAI are discovered.)

NATHAN: I can't believe it. He's actually declared himself king?

HUSHAI: So it appears.

NATHAN: I used to be fond of the boy. Charming, intelligent, good-hearted. But ever since he came back he's changed. I'd see him in the morning, at the city gate, stopping people, listening to their complaints. And if they didn't have any, he'd provide them. You'd think he was running for office, the way he was carrying on.

HUSHAI: I know, I know.

NATHAN: Was the king aware of all this?

HUSHAI: Aware of it? He encouraged it.

NATHAN: Amazing.

HUSHAI: I tried to warn him. I told him about all the disparaging remarks the prince was making.

NATHAN: And?

HUSHAI: He found it amusing.

NATHAN: And the way he paraded about the city, with all those chariots and all those horses. He had an entourage that was larger than the king's. And he's actually declared himself king?

HUSHAI: That's the word we've received.

385

NATHAN: Why couldn't he have waited? I'm sure David planned to name him as his successor.

HUSHAI: I'm afraid not.

NATHAN: Absalom was his favorite.

HUSHAI: There's the question of the temple, you see.

NATHAN: What about the temple?

HUSHAI: Would you have given permission for Absalom to go ahead with the plans?

NATHAN: He's obsessed with that temple of his. As if that could make up for... Yes, well...never mind.

(DAVID enters.)

HUSHAI: Any word?

DAVID: Not yet. We're waiting to hear from the scouts that Joab sent out.

NATHAN: Are you aware of the fact that he's declared himself king?

DAVID: Yes, Nathan, I'm aware of it.

NATHAN: He's probably been planning this for months.

DAVID: Years, I would say.

NATHAN: And yet you gave him permission to go to Hebron.

DAVID: It never occurred to me...

NATHAN: You were warned, I understand.

DAVID: People were always running him down.

NATHAN: Did it ever occur to you to ask why?

DAVID: They were jealous of him, that's why. He's a brilliant, gifted young man. No matter what he's done, you can't take that away from him.

NATHAN: He was always just a little too ambitious.

DAVID: You say that now, but you were fond of him, too and so was everyone. There were so many good qualities, it was difficult to see beyond them. I've been deceived. What can I say? It's not the first time, and it probably won't be the last.

NATHAN: It might, I'm afraid, be the last.

(JOAB enters.)

DAVID: Well?

JOAB: At this very moment he's marching on the capitol, he and Jonadab.

DAVID: There you are. He's the one, that Jonadab. He's the one that's behind all this. He's a wily, deceitful young man. He, too, had me fooled.

JOAB: David, you and I both know that Absalom could not possibly be persuaded to do anything he didn't want to do.

DAVID: How large a force does he have?

JOAB: It's not only the size of his army...

NATHAN: He has an army?

JOAB: Oh, yes indeed. Led by that stalwart general who opposed conscription, who stood for peace and prosperity.

NATHAN: Amasa, too?

JOAB: In addition to that, wherever he goes, he is welcomed with open arms. Apparently he's the savior come to rescue the country from a tyrant.

NATHAN: What are we going to do?

JOAB: We have three alternatives. We can stay and fight, we can surrender or we can run.

DAVID: Suppose we make a stand? What are the odds?

JOAB: That's difficult to say. There'll be a lot of bloodshed. I can tell you that.

    (BATHSHEBA enters.)

BATHSHEBA: Is it true that an army is approaching the city?

JOAB: Very rapidly.

BATHSHEBA: Led by Absalom?

JOAB: And Jonadab and Amasa.

BATHSHEBA: Amasa?! *(SHE turns to David.)* What do you intend to do?

DAVID: We're going to retreat.

BATHSHEBA: You're going to run away, without a fight?

DAVID: I said we are going to retreat.

BATHSHEBA: You're going to abdicate? Is that it?

DAVID: Don't talk nonsense.

BATHSHEBA: Then what?

DAVID: We need time.

BATHSHEBA: Time for what?

DAVID: To gather our forces. To get organized.

JOAB: I'll alert the men. *(HE goes off.)*

NATHAN: I'd better make preparations. The ark has got to be readied for travel.

DAVID: The ark stays here.

NATHAN: But...

DAVID: The ark stays here. Leave some priests behind to stand guard.

(NATHAN sighs, hesitates and then goes off.)

BATHSHEBA: David...

DAVID: It won't be easy, I know.

BATHSHEBA: But the shame of it, the humiliation.

DAVID: I've been a fugitive before.

BATHSHEBA: You're a little older now, my dear. And what about the rest of us?

DAVID: We'll manage. Don't worry.

BATHSHEBA: I can't believe that you're just giving up.

DAVID: I am not giving up.

BATHSHEBA: That's what it amounts to.

DAVID: I will not subject this city to a civil war. Not again. Brother against brother. Nine years of it. Not again. The people will turn to me, eventually.

BATHSHEBA: The people! Who, in God's name, are the people? A bunch of sheep who believe what you tell them to believe. Why did you take him back, that murderer?

DAVID: I'm putting you in charge of the women. Take only what you can carry.

BATHSHEBA: Carry where? Hushai, talk to him. We can't run away. We're not criminals. It's that monstrous young man that's the criminal.

DAVID: Now stop it! *(HE takes hold of her shoulders.)* I need you now, now more than ever. Tell me that I can count on you. Please.

(SHE sighs. HE kisses her. SHE sighs and goes off.)

HUSHAI: I'd better pack a few things. *(HE starts off.)*

DAVID: Hushai...

HUSHAI: Your majesty?

DAVID: Just a moment.

HUSHAI: Yes?

DAVID: I want you to stay behind. Absalom has always been fond of you. He respects you and he trusts you. He's got Jonadab whispering into one ear. Perhaps you can whisper into the other.

HUSHAI: If you think it can do any good.

DAVID: And perhaps you can find some way of getting word to us, about what they're up to.

HUSHAI: I'll do my best, your majesty.

DAVID: Thank you, my friend.

HUSHAI: You'll be back here soon. I know it.

(DAVID embraces him and goes off. HUSHAI sits with a sigh. The lights dim to a spot on HUSHAI. The sound of marching feet and cheers are heard. The lights come up slowly. HUSHAI is seated in the same spot. ABSALOM enters with JONADAB. HUSHAI rises.)

ABSALOM: Hushai?!

HUSHAI: Greetings, your majesty.

JONADAB: Well, well, well!

ABSALOM: What a pleasant surprise!

JONADAB: Yes, isn't it? You got left behind.

HUSHAI: I stayed behind, of my own accord.

JONADAB: Did you really?

HUSHAI: I served David well...

JONADAB: You most certainly did.

HUSHAI: Just as I intend to serve his successor.

ABSALOM: You're a sight for sore eyes, my dear old friend.

JONADAB: When did this sudden change of heart take place?

HUSHAI: There was no change of heart. I've been trying for quite some time to persuade the king to accept the prince as his successor.

JONADAB: If that's your story, you stick to it. *(HE goes off.)*

ABSALOM: Don't pay any attention to him. It's so good to see you, Hushai. Tell me, how did my father take it?

HUSHAI: David's not the man he used to be.

ABSALOM: You do understand. I knew that you would That's why I had to step in. When I think of my father, the way he used to be. He was like a god. And now... I guess the time will come for us all, but when it does for me, I hope I'll have sense enough to step down. I really think, if it weren't for that...witch...

HUSHAI: You mean Bathsheba?

ABSALOM: Yes, the glamorous Bathsheba. The power behind the throne. She's got him under her thumb, she and that little monster of hers. Can you imagine what this country would be like with that little prodigy at the helm?

HUSHAI: There's no danger of that apparently.

ABSALOM: Not while I'm alive, at any rate. Oh, I know what people say about me. Vain, self centered, egotistical. And where would I be if I weren't? Standing in the shadow of that old colossus. Everyone pretending that he's still the hero that he was. Look at the way he handled the rape of my sister. And even years ago, when Abner was murdered. To this very day, that murderer is still his right hand man. Well, things are going to be different now. I know my limitations. Don't think I don't. A king is only as good as the men that advise him. And of all the people at court, you were the only one...the only one that showed any sense.

HUSHAI: You do have Jonadab.

ABSALOM: Oh, he's clever all right, but he's just a little too intense, a little too eager. He makes me very uneasy. I've got such plans, Hushai. Such wonderful plans. I can't wait to get started.

(*JONADAB reenters.*)

ABSALOM: Well?

JONADAB: The palace is deserted.

ABSALOM: Amazing.

JONADAB: The king, however, did leave a souvenir behind. Actually ten souvenirs, to be exact.

HUSHAI: Ten concubines, to look after the palace.

JONADAB: And its inhabitants, perhaps?

HUSHAI: As to that, I couldn't say.

JONADAB: *(To Absalom)*Why not?

ABSALOM: What are you getting at?

JONADAB: What more fitting symbol? You've replaced your father in more ways than one.

ABSALOM: You're mad.

JONADAB: All ten in one fell swoop. Unless, of course, you're not man enough.

ABSALOM: All ten of them, at once?

JONADAB: Well, you may need a moment or two to catch your breath.

ABSALOM: The man is mad.

JONADAB: You're always bragging about what a great lover you are.

ABSALOM: I never bragged about what a great lover I was.

JONADAB: I suppose you could take them one day at a time, but it wouldn't make the same statement.

ABSALOM: He's really serious.

JONADAB: There are two things in life I'm serious about, sex and politics. And when you combine the two, they're unbeatable. Of course, I wouldn't want to embarrass you.

ABSALOM: You don't think I'm up to it?

JONADAB: Who's to say, until you're put to the test?

ABSALOM: I haven't even had my dinner yet.

JONADAB: I know, I know.

   (THEY both laugh.)

ABSALOM: You're a devil. You know perfectly well, I can resist anything...but a challenge.

JONADAB: And there are two of them there, I know you've had your eye on.

ABSALOM: That little brunette?

JONADAB: As ravishing as ever.

ABSALOM: *(To Hushai)* He's impossible.

JONADAB: I tell you what. We'll spread a tent on the roof, just in case you get an attack of modesty, and, of course, we'll prepare a lavish lunch, for sustenance.

ABSALOM: Let's go, before I lose my nerve.

JONADAB: As long as you don't lose...

ABSALOM: My stamina?

> *(THEY go off, laughing. AMASA enters.)*

AMASA: Hushai?!

HUSHAI: Greetings.

AMASA: You stayed behind.

HUSHAI: Apparently.

AMASA: That may not be the wisest move you've ever made. However, now that you're here...you're very welcome, indeed. I need someone to help me talk some sense into those two madmen. Where are they off to now?

HUSHAI: They're heading for the roof.

AMASA: What for?

HUSHAI: A political move.

AMASA: What kind of a political move?

HUSHAI: Fornication apparently. The king left some concubines behind, to look after the palace.

AMASA: Is that what this is all about? I don't believe it. How did I ever let myself get into this mess?

> (AMASA shakes his head, sighs and goes off. HUSHAI watches him leave, then goes off quickly.)

Scene Three

(The countryside. BATHSHEBA is discovered seated on a large rock. A low rumble of thunder is heard. NATHAN enters.)

NATHAN: What are you thinking?

BATHSHEBA: You don't want to know.

NATHAN: This too shall pass.

BATHSHEBA: That ought to keep me warm tonight.

NATHAN: He needs all the support that we can give him.

BATHSHEBA: Support? For what? So we can wander about the countryside like beggars? Look at us, Nathan. Just look at us! Aren't you ashamed? Aren't you humiliated?

NATHAN: I'm proud of him.

BATHSHEBA: Proud?.

NATHAN: This may be our king's finest hour.

BATHSHEBA: I've never heard such rot in all my life.

NATHAN: Sometimes, my dear, it takes courage not to fight.

(There's a loud clap of thunder. DAVID enters.)

DAVID: We're going to rest here for a moment. *(HE sits.)*

NATHAN: Are you all right?

DAVID: Yes, yes. I'm fine.

BATHSHEBA: I'm glad to hear it.

(A low rumble of thunder is heard.)

BATHSHEBA: It's going to rain any minute now.

DAVID: We'll have to find some shelter.

BATHSHEBA: Where? There's not a house in sight.

DAVID: I know this area. On the other side of that hill there's a farm house.

BATHSHEBA: We'll be soaking wet by then.

DAVID: I'm sorry, my dear.

BATHSHEBA: Sorry? You're not the least bit sorry. You think all this..this deprivation is good for the soul.

NATHAN: Now, now, now.

BATHSHEBA: I will not be silent any longer. People are laughing at him behind his back. Is this a king? Is this a leader? A man that let's himself be mocked and spit at?

NATHAN: All right.

BATHSHEBA: It is not all right. That horrible man! That vicious man!

DAVID: What man?

BATHSHEBA: By the side of the road, the one that stood there and cursed at you. *(SHE turns to Nathan.)* This terrible man, he just stood there cursing the king, and throwing stones at him. Joab wanted to strike him down but he stopped him.

DAVID: You don't kill a man for throwing a stone.

BATHSHEBA: What he did was treason. Don't you understand? You're a king, in case you've forgotten!

NATHAN: You mustn't let it upset you, my dear. The king has many loyal followers.

BATHSHEBA: Where are they? Tell me that.

(JOAB enters.)

JOAB: We'd better keep moving, if we're going to beat that storm.

BATHSHEBA: What sort of a general are you? Why don't you do something?

DAVID: Bathsheba!

BATHSHEBA: David, we can't keep on running like this. *(SHE turns to Joab.)* Give me a sword. If no one else has the courage, I'll stand up to that little nonentity. That unspeakable monster. David please... *(SHE breaks down and sobs.)*

DAVID: *(HE places his arm around her.)* It's all right, my love. It's going to be all right. *(HE turns to the others.)* She's tired. We've got to find a place to spend the night.

(DAVID and BATHSHEBA go off together.)

NATHAN: She's right though. We've got to take a stand eventually.

JOAB: I'm expecting some word from the palace any minute now, and meanwhile we are gathering more men.

(JOAB goes off. A clap of thunder is heard as NATHAN follows him off.)

Scene Four

(DAVID'S chambers. ABSALOM enters with JONADAB.)

JONADAB: We've got to strike now while the iron is hot.

ABSALOM: I don't want a civil war. Not if we can help it.

JONADAB: Look, the sooner we move, the less bloodshed there's going to be.

ABSALOM: He's a tired, old man.

JONADAB: Exactly. And they're not going to risk their lives for a tired old man. All we've got to do is to let them know that we want the king, and that's all we want. We have ten thousand men. What am I talking about? We have over twelve thousand men.

ABSALOM: But we don't know what they have.

JONADAB: They're on the run, we know that. And why do you think that is?

ABSALOM: I'd like to hear what Hushai has to say.

JONADAB: Who's running this show? Are we, you and I, or is it that antiquated fossil?

(HUSHAI enters.)

ABSALOM: Jonadab thinks that we ought to move right now.

JONADAB: Take them by surprise. Before they have a chance to get organized.

399

ABSALOM: What do you think, Hushai?

HUSHAI: I'm not so sure about that.

JONADAB: Why not?

HUSHAI: Do you know how many men they have?

ABSALOM: Exactly.

HUSHAI: Their force is almost twice as large as ours.

JONADAB: Now how do you know that?

HUSHAI: I was here when they left. Remember? And I'm sure they've picked up more along the way.

JONADAB: If their force is so large why did they leave?

HUSHAI: David didn't want any bloodshed within the city.

ABSALOM: And neither do I.

HUSHAI: In addition to that, the king is still a popular figure and to attack him directly would be a mistake.

JONADAB: Then there's nothing for us to do but lie down and die.

ABSALOM: Will you listen to the man!?

JONADAB: I'm listening, I'm listening but I don't like what I hear.

HUSHAI: I suggest that we start building up our forces. Send word throughout the country. Start recruiting from the various tribes. And then when we've put together a sizable army, at least large enough to match theirs, then we can make our move.

ABSALOM: That makes sense to me.

JONADAB: Oh sure. And it gives them time to recruit more men as well.

HUSHAI: It's risky, that's true. But to move right now would be disastrous.

JONADAB: Don't you see what he's up to? He's working for them. He was left behind to sabotage.

ABSALOM: Oh, come now.

JONADAB: He was always close to the king.

ABSALOM: So were you. So was I. So were we all.

JONADAB: Then, do as you please. I've had my fill of it. *(HE stalks off.)*

ABSALOM: He's so...hotheaded.

HUSHAI: Maybe he's right.

ABSALOM: No, he's not. He's just stubborn that's all, and he's been getting stranger by the day. He gets up in the middle of the night and paces back and forth. He's even started talking to himself. Yesterday afternoon I heard these two men arguing. I came into the room and there he was, all alone, arguing with himself. I'm just afraid that he's going to crack up completely, if he hasn't already. I made a big mistake teaming up with him. I'd better see what he's up to.

(ABSALOM goes off. AMASA enters.)

AMASA: Have you any idea what's going on?

HUSHAI: We've just had a meeting

AMASA: That's nice to know. And may I ask what's been decided, if anything?

HUSHAI: They've decided to start recruitment.

AMASA: Whose idea was that?

HUSHAI: What's that?

AMASA: Jonadab's, no doubt. Something's got to be done about that man. Why they asked me to join them, I'll never know, since they never consult me. Where's the prince?

HUSHAI: He went to look after him.

AMASA: They don't need a general. They need a keeper.

   (AMASA goes off. HUSHAI hurries off in the opposite direction.)

Scene Five

(A farmhouse. DAVID is discovered lost in thought. NATHAN enters.)

NATHAN: How is she?

DAVID: She's asleep. She's right, I suppose. We've got to make a stand.

(JOAB enters.)

DAVID: Well?

JOAB: Hushai has persuaded them to postpone their attack. They're going to start recruiting.

DAVID: Which means they'll be unprepared.

JOAB: Exactly.

DAVID: Then we've got to strike now.

JOAB: No doubt about that.

DAVID: All right. We'll split three ways. You'll take charge of the right flank. Abishai will take the left. And I'll take the center.

(JOAB and NATHAN look at one another.)

DAVID: What? *(HE looks from one to the other.)* What?

JOAB: It's too dangerous.

DAVID: Of course, it's dangerous.

403

JOAB: For you, I mean.

NATHAN: Suppose you're taken?

DAVID: I belong back here with the women. Is that what you're trying to say?

JOAB: Please. Let's not get emotional about it.

NATHAN: It takes more courage, sometimes, to admit the truth.

JOAB: It's you we're fighting for, and we don't want to be burdened with having to worry about your safety.

DAVID: All right, all right. But I want your word. You're not to touch the boy. Not a hair of his head. Is that understood?

JOAB: If the shoe were on the other foot...

DAVID: I don't care.

JOAB: All right, all right.

DAVID: All right what?

JOAB: I said all right. *(HE goes off.)*

DAVID: That's not good enough!

NATHAN: David, David, calm down.

DAVID: I don't trust that man. I never have.

NATHAN: You're not questioning his loyalty, are you?

DAVID: Some men fight because they have to. And there are others who love the taste of blood. They can't wait to take up the sword and hack a man to pieces. The boy is not responsible. He's been misled. Jonadab can be very persuasive. Besides, if there's anyone to blame it's me. You've said so yourself.

NATHAN: Isn't it about time you stopped making excuses for him?

DAVID: If he harms one hair of that boy's head...

BATHSHEBA: *(Offstage)* David...?

DAVID: He'll have me to answer to.

BATHSHEBA: *(Offstage.)* David?!

NATHAN: She's calling you.

>*(DAVID goes off. NATHAN sits, deeply troubled as the lights come down.)*

Scene Six

(DAVID'S chambers. ABSALOM enters with AMASA.)

AMASA: We've got to go out to meet them. We have no choice.

ABSALOM: What do you think of our chances?

AMASA: We've lost the element of surprise for one thing.

ABSALOM: Do they outnumber us?

AMASA: I haven't the vaguest idea. Where's Hushai?

ABSALOM: He's gone to find Jonadab. He seems to have disappeared.

AMASA: Typical.

ABSALOM: Maybe we shouldn't have waited.

AMASA: Well, it's too late now.

(HUSHAI enters.)

ABSALOM: Well, have you found him?

(HUSHAI nods.)

ABSALOM: And?

HUSHAI: He's dead.

ABSALOM: Dead?

HUSHAI: He hung himself.

406

AMASA: Too bad he waited so long. I've never trusted that man. He's always been two-faced. Someone's been sending out word to your father and it's obvious now. It must have been him all along. I'll assemble the troops. *(HE goes off.)*

ABSALOM: I'm not superstitious, but somehow or other this gives me a very uneasy feeling.

HUSHAI: It's not too late.

ABSALOM: For what?

HUSHAI: To give over.

ABSALOM: Surrender?!

HUSHAI: He loves you, son.

ABSALOM: You're mistaken, Hushai. It's not me he loves. It's the little boy he used to dandle on his knee, until he saw that I had a mind of my own, until he saw that I was not his baby. That was the end of the loving parent. Suddenly I was his rival. I was a threat. It's true, Hushai, and you know it.

HUSHAI: He loves you still, and he would never do you any harm..

ABSALOM: You're so kind, Hushai, so good. You refuse to think evil of anyone. But my father's an egotistical, self-centered tyrant. He would sacrifice us all to fulfill what he sees as his destiny.

HUSHAI: You're mistaken.

ABSALOM: He refuses to admit that he's mortal, that one of these days he's going to die. He's still the boy that slew Goliath, the glamorous comrade of the great Prince Jonathan. He resents us all, all of us that will survive him. It's true whether you're willing to admit it or not. And do you know whom he resents the most? His favorite's little boy, young Solomon. And do you know why? Because he's cleverer than he is. As a matter of fact, he's cleverer than all of us.

HUSHAI: But you're still his favorite.

ABSALOM: And yet he'll never let me succeed him.

HUSHAI: He may have a change of heart, now that he sees you have a following.

ABSALOM: Don't you understand? I've got blood on my hands. I'd never be permitted to built that precious temple of his. That's all he lives for, that precious temple of his. He really believes that that's going to be his salvation, that that's going to erase the memory of his sins, his adultery, his homicide.

HUSHAI: We may be outnumbered, son.

ABSALOM: Pray for me, Hushai. *(HE embraces HUSHAI and goes off.)*

HUSHAI: I wish I could, dear prince. I wish I could.

(The lights come down as the sound of battle is heard.)

Scene Seven

(A tent near the Jordan River. DAVID is discovered pacing about. BATHSHEBA sits nearby.)

BATHSHEBA: You'll wear yourself out.

DAVID: It must be over by now.

BATHSHEBA: And then what?

DAVID: What do you mean?

BATHSHEBA: What do you intend to do?

DAVID: What are you talking about?

BATHSHEBA: About that son of yours.

DAVID: Let's wait and see, shall we?

BATHSHEBA: I'm sure you've given the matter a great deal of thought.

DAVID: All I can think about right now...

BATHSHEBA: Is what's happening to that precious Absalom of yours. How you're going to throw your arms about that devoted son. "Come home. All is forgiven."

DAVID: Why do you hate him so?

BATHSHEBA: David...

DAVID: What?

BATHSHEBA: The man is a traitor.

DAVID: And...?

BATHSHEBA: Treason is punishable by death.

DAVID: That would teach him a lesson, wouldn't it?

BATHSHEBA: If we should happen to lose the battle, if you should happen to be taken prisoner what do you think he would do with you?

DAVID: Let me ask you this, my dear. If this were your son, what would you do?

BATHSHEBA: My son would never betray his king. But, yes, if he were mine I would still let the law take its course. If you'd been firm with Amnon, if you'd been firm with all of them this would never have happened.

> *(NATHAN enters.)*

DAVID: Well?

NATHAN: It's all over with. We've beaten them.

BATHSHEBA: The Lord be praised!

DAVID: And Absalom?

BATHSHEBA: That's all he cares about.

NATHAN: I don't know. There were many casualties, on both sides.

DAVID: Where's Joab?

NATHAN: I haven't seen him. They've captured Amasa.

DAVID: Bring him in.

> *(NATHAN goes off and returns a moment later with AMASA who falls on his knees.)*

AMASA: Your majesty.

DAVID: Why, Amasa? Why?

AMASA: They were very persuasive.

NATHAN: What did they promise you?

AMASA: It wasn't that. They led me to believe that their cause was just.

DAVID: Where are they now?

AMASA: Jonadab took his own life.

DAVID: And my son?

AMASA: You haven't been told? He's dead, your majesty.

DAVID: How did it happen?

AMASA: I'm sorry.

DAVID: How did it happen?

AMASA: I ordered a retreat. Somehow or other, the prince got left behind. His hair got caught in some low-lying branches. His mule went on without him and left him hanging in midair.

DAVID: Go on.

AMASA: I started back to rescue him, but by that time he was surrounded by your men.

DAVID: And?

AMASA: Joab ordered your soldiers to kill him. No one obeyed.

DAVID: Go on.

AMASA: Joab took his sword and plunged it into the prince's heart. The rest of the men closed in on the prince...and that's all I could see. Afterwards they took the body and threw it into a pit.

NATHAN: Is this true?

AMASA: On my honor.

(BATHSHEBA snorts.)

AMASA: I wasn't the only witness.

(DAVID goes off. After a moment a wild, subhuman cry is heard.)

DAVID: (Offstage) Absalom! Oh, Absalom, my son, my son! (HE sobs heartrendingly.)

(NATHAN starts off.)

BATHSHEBA: Let him be.

DAVID: (Offstage) Oh, Absalom, my son, my son!

NATHAN: How could he do such a thing?

BATHSHEBA: He's a soldier. It was war.

NATHAN: He's a brute.

AMASA: It's true. He loves the taste of blood. The man's a beast. He always has been and he always will be.

NATHAN: To kill a man like that, in cold blood.

AMASA: That's his specialty, you see.

BATHSHEBA: You're a fine one to talk.

(JOAB enters.)

JOAB: Where is he? Where's that madman? *(HE goes off.)* What are you, crazy? Have you gone out of your mind?

(DAVID reenters, followed by JOAB.)

DAVID: Don't come near me.

JOAB: You can be heard all over the camp.

DAVID: Stay away from me, or I won't be responsible.

JOAB: These men have risked their lives to protect you. Some of them have died. And this is the way you treat their memory?

DAVID: Give me a sword! Someone give me a sword!

JOAB: I don't care what you think of me. But you go out there and you apologize. You hear me?! You apologize to all those men who are devoted to you.

NATHAN: All right. That's enough.

JOAB: Don't interfere!

NATHAN: A man has a right to mourn his own son.

JOAB: Not if that son is a traitor, and not if that man is a king.

DAVID: No. He's right.

JOAB: You go out there and you talk to them. You hear me? You tell them how proud you are of them. Wailing and whining like some senile old woman.

NATHAN: I said, that's enough.

(DAVID goes off. JOAB follows him.)

NATHAN: Unspeakable.

AMASA: There's no stopping him now.

NATHAN: We can't go on like this. He has got to name an heir, or this is only the beginning. There are others waiting in the wings.

BATHSHEBA: What are you talking about?

AMASA: He's right, you know. Only they're not waiting any longer.

NATHAN: What do you mean?

AMASA: There's this man named Sheba. He's succeeded in raising an army. Before you know it he'll be marching on the capitol.

> *(The cheering of the men can be heard in the distance. NATHAN goes off followed by BATHSHEBA. AMASA sits uneasily as the lights come down.)*

ACT THREE

Scene One

(Several weeks later. David's chambers. Sunset. DAVID enters with NATHAN.)

NATHAN: Who is this man, Sheba?

DAVID: He's a Benjamite. That's all I know.

NATHAN: Is his claim legitimate?

DAVID: No, it is not.

NATHAN: All of Israel is ready to follow him.

DAVID: The people of Judah are still with me.

NATHAN: Nevertheless...

DAVID: I sent Amasa to look into it.

NATHAN: Amasa? After the way he betrayed you?

DAVID: It was a mistake, perhaps.

NATHAN: I should think so.

DAVID: At any rate, I haven't heard from him so I sent Joab to see what was keeping him.

NATHAN: You're speaking to him then?

DAVID: For the moment.

415

NATHAN: David, you've simply got to name an heir.

DAVID: I fully intend to.

NATHAN: When?

DAVID: Nathan, please.

NATHAN: Can't you see what's happening? This country is falling apart.

>   *(JOAB enters, a bloody sack slung over his shoulder. HE tosses the sack at David's feet.)*

DAVID: What's that?

JOAB: You sent me to take care of him, didn't you? There's his head.

DAVID: Whose head?

JOAB: Sheba's. Whose did you think?

NATHAN: It's over then?

JOAB: Apparently.

NATHAN: Were there many casualties?

JOAB: None whatsoever.

DAVID: How did you manage that?

JOAB: A little diplomacy.

NATHAN: Really?

JOAB: Yes, really. Which goes to prove, despite rumors to the contrary, that I do have certain social graces.

DAVID: What happened?

JOAB: We pursued him until he took refuge in the city of Abel Beth Maacah. This charming woman came out. She said the townspeople didn't want any trouble. She asked me what we wanted. I told her that all we wanted was the head of the rebel leader. She went back into the city and the next thing you know the head of Sheba came flying over the wall.

DAVID: And Amasa? What took him so long?

JOAB: I never did find out. Before I had a chance to question him he met with an accident.

NATHAN: What sort of an accident?

JOAB: He ran into my sword. I can't imagine what he was thinking of. *(HE turns to David.)* I'm sure you'll bury him with full military honors. He was, after all, a great patriot. And now, if you'll excuse me I'd like to wash up. *(HE starts off.)*

DAVID: Joab...!

JOAB: Your majesty?

DAVID: Take that with you...please.

(JOAB picks up the sack, winks at NATHAN and goes off.)

NATHAN: Something has got to be done about that man. You can't let him go about murdering people. Of course, in this case...I mean he was, after all, a traitor.

(HUSHAI enters.)

DAVID: Amasa's dead. Did you know?

HUSHAI: Yes, I've heard all about it.

DAVID: What have you heard?

HUSHAI: When Joab arrived Amasa went to greet him.

DAVID: And?

HUSHAI: Joab approached him as if to embrace him then he grabbed hold of him and sunk his dagger into his abdomen.

NATHAN: Abner all over again.

HUSHAI: He left the body in the middle of the road. Finally one of the men passing by dragged the corpse to one side.

NATHAN: The man is unspeakable.

DAVID: *(To HUSHAI)* Help me up. It's my leg again.

HUSHAI: You should have it looked after, your majesty.

DAVID: I'm not going to spend my remaining days being fussed over by one doctor after another.

　　　(HUSHAI helps DAVID up and THEY start off slowly.)

NATHAN: Have you given any thought...?

DAVID: Not now. Please!

　　　(HUSHAI and NATHAN exchange glances. HUSHAI shrugs as HE and DAVID go off. NATHAN shakes his head and follows them off as the lights come down.)

Scene Two

(A room in the Palace of the Women. BATHSHEBA enters with ABISHAG, a pretty young girl.)

BATHSHEBA: The king is dying.

ABISHAG: But...

BATHSHEBA: But what?

ABISHAG: He just took part in a battle.

BATHSHEBA: Where he collapsed and almost died. He's bedridden now.

ABISHAG: I see.

BATHSHEBA: Good. Now, he may ask you to lie beside him, but I can assure you, he's perfectly harmless. Just try to keep him warm. That's all. And don't go getting any wild ideas.

ABISHAG: I understand.

BATHSHEBA: See that you do. Any and all visitors...any and all conversations, you report to me. Is that understood?

ABISHAG: Yes, your grace.

(NATHAN enters.)

NATHAN: Is this the girl?

(BATHSHEBA nods.)

419

NATHAN: You've instructed her?

(BATHSHEBA nods.)

NATHAN: Wait outside.

(ABISHAG bows and goes off.)

NATHAN: She's very pretty.

BATHSHEBA: He can still see.

NATHAN: Now that Sheba's been disposed of we now have Adonijah.

BATHSHEBA: Yes, I know.

NATHAN: He is next in line, you know.

BATHSHEBA: I'm aware of that.

NATHAN: And he's parading about the city with his entourage.

BATHSHEBA: It's Absalom all over again.

NATHAN: He's organized a gathering at En Rogel. He's invited a number of people to join him including Joab. If Joab accepts the invitation...

BATHSHEBA: We are in serious trouble.

NATHAN: Exactly.

BATHSHEBA: Leave it to me.

(THEY go off.)

Scene Three

(DAVID's bedchamber. DAVID is discovered, sitting up in bed. ABISHAG sits beside him, her hand in DAVID's.)

ABISHAG: Here, let me fix your pillow.

(SHE makes him more comfortable.)

DAVID: Thank you. *(HE holds her hand.)* Where was I?

ABISHAG: You mustn't talk too much.

DAVID: Why not?

ABISHAG: You must save your strength.

DAVID: For what? I can't fight anymore. I can't make love. But worst of all, I have no more songs to sing. *(HE kisses her hand.)* Such a sweet, lovely hand. Ten years ago you would have been my favorite. Five years ago. Maybe two.

ABISHAG: For how long?

DAVID: What's that?

ABISHAG: Nothing.

DAVID: I heard you, you little baggage. Yes, it's true. I am a fickle man. However, once I love, I love forever. Believe it or not.

ABISHAG: *(After a moment)* What are you thinking, your majesty?

DAVID: Poor Michal.

421

ABISHAG: Saul's daughter?

DAVID: Yes, Saul's daughter. She was the first, you know. She risked her life to save me. Defied her father. But then she deserted me. I never forgave her for that. I nurse my grudges, you see.

ABISHAG: But you were a fugitive, weren't you?

DAVID: What has that got to do with it?

ABISHAG: We're all of us human.

DAVID: The daughter of a king has no right to be human. You disagree.

ABISHAG: Who am I to disagree with his majesty?

DAVID: You'd be loyal to your husband, wouldn't you?

ABISHAG: As loyal as I possibly could.

DAVID: *(HE laughs.)* You little minx.

> *(JOAB enters.)*

ABISHAG: You have a visitor.

JOAB: David?

DAVID: Yes? What is it?

JOAB: It's Joab.

DAVID: So it is.

JOAB: I've come to pay my respects.

DAVID: I'm not dead yet.

JOAB: I'm off to En Rogel tomorrow.

DAVID: En Rogel?

JOAB: Your son's invited me to join him there, your son Adonijah. He is your eldest now, you know. Is there any message you'd care to send him?

DAVID: What's that?

JOAB: Is there any message you'd like to send to Adonijah?

DAVID: Tell him...

JOAB: Yes?

DAVID: I wish him good health.

JOAB: I'll see you when I get back.

DAVID: Not if your stay's a long one.

> *(JOAB starts off.)*

DAVID: Oh, Joab...

JOAB: Your majesty?

DAVID: Have a good trip.

JOAB: Thank you. *(HE goes off.)*

DAVID: Now there's a piece of work for you.

ABISHAG: You don't like him, do you?

DAVID: A grave understatement, my dear.

ABISHAG: If you don't like him, why do you put up with him?

DAVID: He knows where all the bodies are buried.

> *(BATHSHEBA enters.)*

BATHSHEBA: I'm sorry I'm late.

(BATHSHEBA nods to ABISHAG who leaves very quietly.)

BATHSHEBA: Are you comfortable?

DAVID: As comfortable as a dying man can be.

BATHSHEBA: Do you really intend to die?

DAVID: I haven't quite made up my mind.

BATHSHEBA: Wasn't that Joab that just left here?

DAVID: The great soldier himself. He's on his way to En Rogel. He's going to join Adonijah.

BATHSHEBA: He's declared himself king, you know, Adonijah. Did you know that?

DAVID: No.

BATHSHEBA: David...

DAVID: All day long I've been thinking...

BATHSHEBA: What, dear?

DAVID: Jonathan.

BATHSHEBA: What about him?

DAVID: I keep asking myself, did I seek his friendship in order to steal his throne? That's what Saul accused me of, you know, and Abner.

BATHSHEBA: You were anointed by Samuel before you even met them.

DAVID: That's true. I keep forgetting. I was responsible for the rift between them, though, Saul and Jonathan. Swifter than eagles, stronger than lions. But Saul was a wounded bird.

BATHSHEBA: And Jonathan?

DAVID: Jonathan was perfection. His love, for me, was more wonderful than the love of women.

BATHSHEBA: More wonderful than ours?

DAVID: You gave me something none of the others did.

BATHSHEBA: And what was that?

DAVID: You gave me peace, strangely enough, when you think of what we went through. What a price we paid!

BATHSHEBA: I pray every day for God to forgive us.

DAVID: I'll find out shortly, whether he has or not. I've been a bad father, I know that. And you were right. I wanted them to love me. Absalom, Amnon, Tamar. All of them. But I failed them miserably, even your young Solomon.

BATHSHEBA: He loves you, David. As much as you'll let him. He's not demonstrative, perhaps. But he's bright, and honest and straightforward, and his hands are clean. He can build your temple for you. David...

DAVID: Yes, my dear?

BATHSHEBA: You gave me your promise, in case you've forgotten.

DAVID: Where is he now?

BATHSHEBA: He's waiting outside, and you needn't worry about Adonijah. Solomon's prepared to deal with him. Shall I send him in?

DAVID: In a moment. I want a word with you first.

BATHSHEBA: I'm listening.

DAVID: You're to see to it that he carries out my plans for the temple.

BATHSHEBA: I will. I promise.

DAVID: And Joab...

BATHSHEBA: What about him?

DAVID: No matter what happens, he must be held accountable. He murdered Abner. He murdered Amasa, and he murdered my Absalom. He must be held accountable.

BATHSHEBA: I'll see to it.

DAVID: *(HE sighs.)* Help me into that chair.

> *(SHE helps him into a chair and makes him comfortable.)*

DAVID: Do I look all right?

BATHSHEBA: *(SHE straightens his robe and his hair.)* You look fine.

DAVID: Like a dying man.

BATHSHEBA: Vanity, vanity.

DAVID: Stop fussing and send him in.

> *(SHE kisses him on the forehead and goes off. DAVID arranges his garments, making sure they're draped properly. After a moment HE looks toward the doorway.)*

DAVID: Solomon? Come in, come in.

> *(A shadow appears in the doorway as the lights slowly dim.)*

QUEEN OF PERSIA

CAST OF CHARACTERS

AHASUERUS . . . . King of Persia

BIGTHA . . . . The King's Chamberlain

MEMUCAN . . . . The Prime Minister

HAMAN . . . . A Persian Lord

MORDECAI . . . . A Jewish Merchant

ESTHER . . . . Mordecai's Young Cousin

HEGAI . . . . The Keeper of the Women

SCENE

Shushan, the capital of ancient Persia

ACT ONE

Scene One

(A moonlit evening. A terrace outside the king's chambers. Music and raucous male laughter is heard offstage. BIGTHA, the king's chamberlain, enters from the interior, crosses and goes off. A moment later AHASUERUS, the king, enters a bit unsteadily from the interior followed by MEMUCAN, his prime minister.)

MEMUCAN: I suggest you call him back. Did you hear what I said?

AHASUERUS: *(HE sits with a thud.)* You'd like that, wouldn't you?

MEMUCAN: What on earth are you talking about?

AHASUERUS: You're jealous.

MEMUCAN: I may be jealous but, at least, I'm sober.

AHASUERUS: You admit it then.

MEMUCAN: Yes, I admit it.

AHASUERUS: Say it.

MEMUCAN: Vashti is the most beautiful woman in the world, bar none.

AHASUERUS: Oh, no. You don't get away that easily.

MEMUCAN: Look, I just want to save you the embarrassment. What are you smiling at?

AHASUERUS: That's for me to know and you to ponder.

431

MEMUCAN: She's not going to come. And even if she did... You're going to hate yourself in the morning.

(A burst of laughter is heard.)

MEMUCAN: Do you really want to subject your wife, your queen, to those brutes in there? What are you trying to prove? Everyone agrees that Vasthi is the most beautiful woman in the world.

AHASUERUS: Not everyone. And besides that's not the point.

MEMUCAN: What is?

AHASUERUS: I want to prove...

MEMUCAN: What?

AHASUERUS: That I am the master.

MEMUCAN: Well, of course, you are. You're the king.

AHASUERUS: Of my household. I am not... It's a vulgar phrase and I refuse to repeat it. Suffice it to say that...I am the master.

(BIGTHA reenters out of breath.)

AHASUERUS: Well?

BIGTHA: Her highness begged me to inform you, your majesty...

AHASUERUS: Yes? Go on.

BIGTHA: Her highness begged me to inform you, your majesty...

AHASUERUS: Get to the point.

BIGTHA: She's indisposed.

MEMUCAN: Well, there you are. Thank you, Bigtha.

AHASUERUS: Just a moment.

BIGTHA: Your majesty?

AHASUERUS: Where exactly was the queen when she begged you to inform me that...she was indisposed.

BIGTHA: She was...

AHASUERUS: I'm listening.

BIGTHA: She was at the table, your majesty.

MEMUCAN: Well, that doesn't mean anything.

AHASUERUS: And what exactly was she doing when she begged you to inform me that she was indisposed?

BIGTHA: She was...

AHASUERUS: Yes? She was...what?

BIGTHA: She was holding a goblet of wine in her hand.

MEMUCAN: She could still be...

AHASUERUS: Bigtha?

BIGTHA: Your majesty?

AHASUERUS: Did the queen look indisposed to you?

BIGTHA: Well, I...

AHASUERUS: Did the queen look ill? Bigtha?

BIGTHA: Not really, your majesty.

MEMUCAN: She may have misunderstood.

AHASUERUS: Bigtha...

BIGTHA: Your majesty?

AHASUERUS: You go back there and you tell the queen that his majesty demands her presence here at once. Is that perfectly clear?

BIGTHA: Your majesty. *(HE bows and starts off.)*

AHASUERUS: That is a royal command. You hear me?

BIGTHA: Your majesty. *(HE bows again and scurries off.)*

AHASUERUS: If you have something to say, say it. Well?

MEMUCAN: Nothing. *(HE starts back in.)*

AHASUERUS: How dare you turn your back on me?

MEMUCAN: May I be dismissed?

AHASUERUS: No, you may not. I'd like to know what you're thinking.

MEMUCAN: Now? This very minute?

AHASUERUS: You were staring at me.

MEMUCAN: I'm sorry. That was rude of me.

AHASUERUS: What were you thinking?

MEMUCAN: I'm thinking that this feast of yours has been going on for quite some time now.

AHASUERUS: You're not enjoying yourself?

MEMUCAN: That's not the point.

AHASUERUS: What is?

MEMUCAN: This is costing a lot of money. Especially all those expensive favors you're showering everyone with.

AHASUERUS: You feel slighted?

MEMUCAN: I wasn't thinking of myself.

AHASUERUS: What were you thinking of?

MEMUCAN: The royal coffers are not exactly bottomless. However I am not in charge of the treasury...

AHASUERUS: Exactly, you are not in charge of the treasury, nor are you aware of certain protocol.

MEMUCAN: Like what?

AHASUERUS: As king of the most powerful nation in the civilized world, I have a certain position to maintain.

MEMUCAN: You also have a budget, whether you like it or not.

(BIGTHA reenters.)

AHASUERUS: Well? Where's the queen?

BIGTHA: Where I left her, your majesty.

AHASUERUS: And where was that?

BIGTHA: At the table, your majesty.

AHASUERUS: Did you give her my message?

BIGTHA: I did.

AHASUERUS: And what was her response?

BIGTHA: Her exact words were...

AHASUERUS: Go on, go on.

BIGTHA: "He's drunk again."

AHASUERUS: That's what she said?

(BIGTHA nods.)

AHASUERUS: In front of everyone?

BIGTHA: I'm afraid so, your majesty. I tried to speak to her in private but her highness wouldn't budge. "Speak freely," she said. "We're among friends," she said.

AHASUERUS: I suppose there were all sorts of clever comments.

BIGTHA: I'm not quite sure. There was so much laughter.

AHASUERUS: You go back there and you tell the queen that an apology is in order. Well? What are you waiting for?

(BIGTHA nods, bows and goes off.)

MEMUCAN: I'm thirsty. I need some more wine. Won't you join me?

AHASUERUS: If you're thirsty, go ahead.

MEMUCAN: What are you going to do?

AHASUERUS: I'm going to sit right here until this matter is settled. I'm not as drunk as you think I am.

MEMUCAN: Nor are you...

AHASUERUS: Nor am I what? Go on. Say it. Nor am I what?

MEMUCAN: You're in an argumentive mood and no matter what I say, you'll take it the wrong way.

AHASUERUS: I see. There's a wrong way and a right way and I'm sure to take the wrong one. You think you're so very clever. Everything you say, everything you do is right. Maybe you should be the king and I should be the prime minister. Isn't that what you're thinking?

MEMUCAN: You're putting the queen in a very awkward position.

AHASUERUS: I'm putting her in an awkward position? I',m putting her in an awkward position?

MEMUCAN: It's unbecoming for the queen to display herself in front of that drunken mob in there and if she disobeys a royal command she's in deep trouble.

AHASUERUS: You know, even as a boy you were never likeable. The only reason I appointed you prime minister was because I felt sorry for you. The fact of the matter is you are a very destructive person.

MEMUCAN: You want me to flatter you. Is that it?

AHASUERUS: No, I don't want you to flatter me.

MEMUCAN: What do you want?

AHASUERUS: I want the truth.

MEMUCAN: No, you don't. As a matter of fact, you're afraid of the truth.

AHASUERUS: And what might that be?

MEMUCAN: You can never be another Cyrus. You can never be another Darius. Your dreams of glory can never be fulfilled. Not in the way you'd like them to be at any rate.

AHASUERUS: And what is that supposed to mean?

MEMUCAN: You cannot found an empire since your grandfather beat you to it.

AHASUERUS: So there's nothing for me to do. Is that it? Is that what you're trying to tell me?

MEMUCAN: On the contrary. There's a great deal for you to do.

AHASUERUS: Like what?

MEMUCAN: Like keeping this massive empire in some sort of order. It's not a very glamorous prospect, I warrant you, but it's something that's got to be done, if you want to hold on to what your predecessors acquired, that is.

(*Laughter is heard offstage. BIGTHA reenters.*)

AHASUERUS: Well? What did she say?

BIGTHA: Her exact words were...

AHASUERUS: (*Impatiently*) Oh, please!

BIGTHA: "Tell his majesty," she said, "his apology is accepted."

(*HAMAN, a courtier, enters from the interior.*)

AHASUERUS: Yes? What is it?

HAMAN: The company is anxiously awaiting the arrival of the queen.

MEMUCAN: The queen is indisposed.

AHASUERUS: The queen is not indisposed. She refuses to come. I gave a royal command and she disobeyed it.

(*Laughter is heard offstage.*)

HAMAN: That's a very serious offense, your majesty. To defy the king and, even more to the point, for a wife to disobey her husband. Think of what an example that sets.

MEMUCAN: (*Mockingly*) Off with her head!

HAMAN: You find that amusing, prime minister?

AHASUERUS: (*To Haman*) What would you advise me to do?

HAMAN: That's not for me to say, your majesty.

AHASUERUS: I'm asking you. What would you advise me to do?

HAMAN: To allow her to continue as queen, under the circumstances... Can you imagine what sort of a message this would send to the women of Persia?

MEMUCAN: For one thing it would encourage the women of Persia to maintain their self respect, even when their husbands demand otherwise. I think we should be grateful to the queen.

AHASUERUS: Don't listen to him. I do think execution, however, would be a little drastic, don't you?

MEMUCAN: I was only joking.

AHASUERUS: What do you think, Haman?

HAMAN: Divorce and exile, I think, would be appropriate.

AHASUERUS: Divorce and exile.

HAMAN: That's one suggestion.

MEMUCAN: Two. *(To Ahasuerus)* May I speak with you in private?

AHASUERUS: Say what you have to say. I have no secrets.

MEMUCAN: Vashti may not be blessed with a giant brain and, through no fault of her own, she's terribly spoiled but I will say this for her; she's one of the few people here at court that's really straightforward with you.

AHASUERUS: You being one of the others, I suppose. Bigtha, send for the scribes. I want to announce my divorce.

BIGTHA: *(HE bows and starts off.)* Your majesty.

AHASUERUS: And Bigtha...

BIGTHA: Your majesty?

AHASUERUS: After that you can tell the queen to start packing. She's leaving for Egypt in the morning.

BIGTHA: Your majesty...

AHASUERUS: And as for you, my friend, you can escort her. Unless you'd prefer Syria. As a matter of fact I need a good man in Syria. Yes, you can leave for Syria in the morning. *(To Bigtha)* What are you waiting for?

BIGTHA: Your majesty. *(HE bows and scurries off.)*

AHASUERUS: Haman, how'd you like to be my new prime minister?

HAMAN: Your majesty...?!

AHASUERUS: Yes or no?

HAMAN: I'd be greatly honored, your majesty.

AHASUERUS: You're it.

> *(MEMUCAN strides off.)*

AHASUERUS: Well, that settles that.

HAMAN: Are you quite sure...?

AHASUERUS: Are you questioning my decision?

HAMAN: I wouldn't be doing my duty if I didn't.

AHASUERUS: You're a good man, Haman, a good man.

HAMAN: My sons and I are at your service, your majesty.

AHASUERUS: How many sons do you have, by the way?

HAMAN: Ten, your majesty. Ten strapping boys.

AHASUERUS: Ten sons! I envy you. The queen has yet to give me an heir.

HAMAN: Another good reason for the divorce.

AHASUERUS: That's true. But now I've got no one to give me an heir. *(HE sits despondently.)* Absolutely no one. Legitimate, that is.

HAMAN: There are many lovely women in the kingdom, your majesty.

AHASUERUS: So there are. I've got the entire civilized world to choose from, haven't I?

HAMAN: You most certainly have. We can send scouts throughout the kingdom to bring you the most beautiful virgins.

AHASUERUS: What a brilliant idea! Speak to Hegai. Have him organize a search.

HAMAN: I'll see to it at once, your majesty. *(HE starts off.)*

AHASUERUS: Haman...

HAMAN: Your majesty?

AHASUERUS: What's that? Nothing.

HAMAN: Your majesty. *(HE bows and goes off.)*

>   *(Raucous laughter is heard. Silence. Then a romantic melody. AHASUERUS sighs and sits looking lost and forlorn as the lights come down.)*

Scene Two

(Early morning. The house of Mordecai, a Jewish merchant. MORDECAI enters with ESTHER, his young cousin and ward.)

ESTHER: Now I want you to behave while I'm gone.

MORDECAI: Yes, mother.

ESTHER: I'm serious. No more lawsuits. Is that perfectly clear?

MORDECAI: That's not up to me.

ESTHER: Mordecai! You are impossible.

MORDECAI: I will not be bullied. I will not be taken advantage of just because I'm a Jew. We have to stand up for our rights otherwise people will walk all over us.

ESTHER: That's all very well, but you go out of your way to antagonize people.

MORDECAI: You know nothing about the outside world, how business is conducted, how much cheating and swindling goes on.

ESTHER: *(SHE sighs.)* All right. Now I've given the maid instructions and you're to listen to her. She has a copy of your diet and you're to stick to it. You hear me?

MORDECAI: Yes, I hear you.

ESTHER: And make sure you dress warmly. We don't want you catching cold again. If I'm lucky I should be back home in about a year or so.

442

MORDECAI: Nonsense! You won't be coming back at all unless, of course, you start to order the king about.

ESTHER: Everyone knows this charade is just an excuse for him to bed all the beautiful virgins in the kingdom. How long has this farce been going on?

MORDECAI: He's got to choose a wife eventually.

ESTHER: Why?

MORDECAI: Because he's got to have an heir. A legitimate one, that is.

ESTHER: Well I fervently hope that I'm not the one to give it to him. Look at the way he treated the queen.

MORDECAI: They say that he's changed quite a bit. And as queen you could do a lot for our people.

ESTHER: And you really think he's going to choose a Jewess?

MORDECAI: Now, Esther, we went over all this. He does not have to know...

ESTHER: No! I'm sorry. I will not lie.

MORDECAI: Now who's being stubborn?

ESTHER: I'm not ashamed of who I am.

MORDECAI: Who's asking you to be ashamed? But sometimes, my dear, to get along the world...

ESTHER: You're a fine one to talk.

MORDECAI: All right, all right. Do as you please. If you're not questioned about your religion, however, there's no need to bring it up, is there? Is there?

ESTHER: *(SHE goes to the door.)* It's getting late. Where are they?

MORDECAI: They'll be here soon enough. Now remember, don't be uppity and do as you're told. Remember what happened to the queen. I think I hear a carriage.

ESTHER: Oh, Mordecai! *(SHE clings to him.)*

MORDECAI: Now, now.

ESTHER: I don't want to go.

MORDECAI: Now, now, now, my child, we have no choice. Just think of all the good you might be able to do.

(HEGAI, the keeper of the women, enters.)

HEGAI: Well, is she ready?

MORDECAI: She's all packed.

HEGAI: Packed?

MORDECAI: Just her clothes and her personal belongings.

HEGAI: I told you, nothing. Everything will be provided.

ESTHER: *(To Hegai)* Must I go?

MORDECAI: She's a little apprehensive.

HEGAI: Don't you want to be queen of Persia?

ESTHER: Not really, no.

HEGAI: I see. What do you want?

ESTHER: I want to stay here and take care of my cousin.

HEGAI: Don't you want a husband?

ESTHER: Eventually, I suppose. But when I marry I would like to have some say in the matter.

HEGAI: Well, well, well!

MORDECAI: She doesn't really mean that. What I mean to say is...

HEGAI: What?

ESTHER: What he means to say is I've been taught to think for myself.

MORDECAI: But she's very well behaved. Really she is.

HEGAI: She'd better be. I won't put up with any nonsense. Come along now, come along.

MORDECAI: Might I have a word with you?

HEGAI: What is it?

MORDECAI: In private?

HEGAI: *(To Esther)* Wait in the carriage.

    (ESTHER hesitates and goes off.)

MORDECAI: You look like a very intelligent man.

HEGAI: Get to the point.

MORDECAI: She's used to little luxuries.

HEGAI: She'll have everything she needs.

MORDECAI: And she's very naive. She knows nothing about the outside world. About human nature. If you could keep an eye on her I'd greatly appreciate it. *(HE produces a little bag of coins which HE offers to Hegai.)*

HEGAI: What's that?

MORDECAI: For your trouble.

HEGAI: I haven't had any as yet.

MORDECAI: In this case you might have.

HEGAI: I'll know how to deal with it.

MORDECAI: No offense.

HEGAI: None taken.

MORDECAI: She's all I have in the world.

HEGAI: Don't worry. She'll be well looked after.

MORDECAI: Thank you.

HEGAI: Don't thank me. That's my job.

MORDECAI: Could I possibly see her from time to time?

HEGAI: Absolutely not.

MORDECAI: Just to look in on her.

HEGAI: No. However I can't stop you from passing by the palace of the
women and her looking out the window...occasionally.

MORDECAI: Thank you.

HEGAI: But don't make a pest of yourself.

MORDECAI: I won't. I promise.

> *(HEGAI goes off. MORDECAI stands thoughtfully for a moment
> then walks quickly to the door and stands looking out. HE waves
> to the departing carriage as the lights come down.)*

Scene Three

(Early evening. The king's chambers. HEGAI enters followed by ESTHER.)

HEGAI: Come along, come along.

ESTHER: Is this where I meet the king?

HEGAI: This is it. Now there's nothing to be nervous about. The king is a man just like any other man.

ESTHER: That's what I'm afraid of.

HEGAI: Don't be too clever. Just remember what happened to the queen. Just be yourself. I take that back.

ESTHER: I want to go home.

HEGAI: This is going to be your home from now on in.

ESTHER: And what makes you so sure of that?

HEGAI: Have you looked in the mirror lately?

ESTHER: There are many girls just as pretty as I am. Well, almost, at any rate, and when he finds out that I'm a Jewess...

HEGAI: Will you stop harping on that?!

ESTHER: I don't care...

HEGAI: Now you listen to me. You were born beautiful. You had nothing to do with it so it's nothing to brag about. The same goes for being a Jew. It's not an accomplishment. It's a fact of nature. No one's

447

asking you to lie about it. Just take that chip off your shoulder. It's most unbecoming.

ESTHER: I don't know what to do. I don't know how to behave. I don't know what to say.

HEGAI: Just use your common sense. Women can easily get the upper hand if they play their cards right.

ESTHER: I'm not good at using my so-called feminine wiles.

HEGAI: Nonsense! You're a master. Why do you look at me like that? Yes, I am a eunuch. That doesn't mean... Never mind. The fact of the matter is I had my reasons for holding you back all this time.

ESTHER: And what might that be?

HEGAI: The king is getting tired of all this, and I think he's just about ripe for the plucking. Now it's up to you. You can spoil it all and I'll send you back to your cousin, or you can use the gifts that your god has given you and fulfill your destiny.

ESTHER: And you think my destiny...?

HEGAI: Is to be queen of Persia. You're bright, you're ambitious and...

ESTHER: And what?

HEGAI: Never mind. You're spoiled enough as it is.

(BIGTHA enters.)

BIGTHA: Is this the one?

(HEGAI nods.)

BIGTHA: *(To Esther)* Turn around.

(ESTHER turns around.)

BIGTHA: Not bad. Not bad at all. Have you instructed her?

HEGAI: I've done my best. *(HE turns to Esther.)* Bigtha's a friend. Do as he says...and good luck. *(HE goes off.)*

BIGTHA: Let's see you bow.

(ESTHER bows and rises.)

BIGTHA: No, no, no! You don't get up until you're told to.

ESTHER: I'm sorry.

BIGTHA: Just remember that. And when do you speak?

ESTHER: When I'm spoken to.

BIGTHA: Just answer questions. Don't volunteer any information unless you're asked. Is that understood?

ESTHER: Yes, your majesty.

BIGTHA: I'm not his majesty.

ESTHER: I was just practicing.

BIGTHA: And don't be impertinent!

(SHE sighs.)

BIGTHA: Now what?

ESTHER: Nothing.

BIGTHA: And when and if you're dismissed you exit backwards. Is that understood?

(ESTHER nods. AHASUERUS enters. ESTHER bows.)

BIGTHA: Esther, your majesty.

(AHASUERUS nods. BIGTHA bows and goes off. AHASUERUS sits.)

AHASUERUS: You may rise.

ESTHER: *(SHE rises.)* Thank you...your majesty.

(Music is heard. ESTHER looks about, startled.)

ESTHER: What's that?

AHASUERUS: Music. Don't you like music?

ESTHER: Yes. It's very nice.

AHASUERUS: You may sit.

ESTHER: Must I?

AHASUERUS: You prefer to stand?

ESTHER: To begin with.

AHASUERUS: Where are you from?

ESTHER: What's that?

AHASUERUS: I said...

ESTHER: Right here, in Shushan. I'm sorry. I'm rather nervous.

AHASUERUS: What are you nervous about?

ESTHER: It's not every day one meets a king.

AHASUERUS: Would you care for some wine?

ESTHER: Is that permitted? Yes, please. *(Half to herself.)* That might help.

AHASUERUS: What's that?

ESTHER: Nothing. I would like some wine.

(AHASUERUS pours a goblet of wine and offers it to her. ESTHER approaches him and takes the wine.)

AHASUERUS: Aren't you going to drink it?

ESTHER: Am I supposed to drink alone?

AHASUERUS: *(HE smiles and pours some wine for himself.)* So, what shall we drink to?

ESTHER: Your health, your majesty.

AHASUERUS: To my health.

(THEY drink.)

AHASUERUS: Wouldn't you care to sit down?

ESTHER: Where would you like me to sit?

AHASUERUS: Anywhere your little heart desires.

ESTHER: I'll sit here, if that's all right.

(HE nods and SHE sits a short distance away.)

AHASUERUS: Are you comfortable?

ESTHER: Not really.

AHASUERUS: What's the matter?

ESTHER: I feel awkward and out of place and...

AHASUERUS: And what?

ESTHER: I wish I was back home.

AHASUERUS: With ma<u>mah</u> and pap<u>ah</u>?

ESTHER: No. They're both dead.

AHASUERUS: Oh, I'm sorry.

ESTHER: That's all right. They died a long time ago.

AHASUERUS: Whom do you live with?

ESTHER: My cousin. He's a widower and he adopted me.

AHASUERUS: What does he do...for a living?

ESTHER: He's a cloth merchant.

AHASUERUS: Is he successful?

ESTHER: I suppose so.

AHASUERUS: Don't you know?

ESTHER: We live well, if that's what you mean. We have two servants, though I do most of the work. Like my cousin says, "If you want something done properly, do it yourself."

AHASUERUS: And what exactly do you do?

ESTHER: I cook and I sew. The servants do the cleaning and I inspect. I also paint, I play the lute.

AHASUERUS: Do you sing?

ESTHER: That's debatable. I do write poetry though.

AHASUERUS: You can write?

ESTHER: Oh, yes. And I can read as well. My cousin taught me to read and to write and to think for myself.

AHASUERUS: Did he really?

ESTHER: Some men find that intimidating.

AHASUERUS: Well, it is unusual.

ESTHER: I don't see why it should be. Women are, after all, human beings.

AHASUERUS: Well, there is a difference between a man and a woman.

ESTHER: I'm shocked to hear it.

AHASUERUS: Are you making fun of me?

ESTHER: I'm sorry. I didn't mean to be impertinent. Oh, dear!

AHASUERUS: What's the matter now?

ESTHER: I was warned not to be impertinent. But I'm sure you want me to be myself.

AHASUERUS: Who else would you want to be?

ESTHER: Exactly.

AHASUERUS: You're very unusual.

ESTHER: I know. It's frightening, isn't it? Not that you're afraid of me. I'm the one that's afraid of you. I mean, after all, if I displease you, you could chop my head off.

AHASUERUS: I wouldn't want to do that.

ESTHER: Or, if I were your wife, you could banish me. I'm sorry, I'm sorry. I shouldn't have said that.

AHASUERUS: We all make mistakes.

ESTHER: I'm very good at that. Making mistakes, I mean.

AHASUERUS: I was drunk, you know.

ESTHER: I'm sorry, I...

AHASUERUS: That's all right. I miss her very much.

ESTHER: Why don't you call her back?

(HE shakes his head.)

ESTHER: Why not?

AHASUERUS: It would set a precedent.

ESTHER: Aren't kings allowed to make mistakes?

AHASUERUS: Unfortunately not.

ESTHER: That's awful.

AHASUERUS: I also lost my best friend.

ESTHER: That's even worse. Friends are even more important.

AHASUERUS: Especially those who tell you the truth.

ESTHER: That's one thing I'm very good at.

AHASUERUS: Are you?

ESTHER: Too good, I'm told.

AHASUERUS: Have you enjoyed your stay here at the palace?

ESTHER: Not really, no. Oh, the fault's all mine. Hegai has gone out of his way to make me comfortable. It's just that...

AHASUERUS: Just that what?

ESTHER: I feel so useless. All I've done for over a year is bathe and purify myself and douse myself in oils and scents and spices. I smell like a perfumery.

AHASUERUS: What would you like to do?

ESTHER: I'd like some responsibility.

AHASUERUS: Like what? A child, perhaps?

ESTHER: Of my own? Well yes, eventually, I suppose. But then again children do grow up and leave the nest, so to speak.

AHASUERUS: A husband, perhaps.

ESTHER: And husbands die. What I mean to say is women do live longer. It's a scientific fact. So why is it that women are limited to the family? Men have families and they do other things as well. Not that I don't think the family isn't important.

AHASUERUS: I'm glad to hear it.

ESTHER: But women do have something more to offer.

AHASUERUS: Like what?

ESTHER: A different sensibility. A different sense of values.

AHASUERUS: For one so young you seem very knowledgeable.

ESTHER: There is an advantage to being young.

AHASUERUS: And what might that be?

ESTHER: Our minds are less clouded by all sorts of emotions.

AHASUERUS: I see.

(There is an awkward pause then ESTHER breaks the silence.)

ESTHER: It must be very exciting to be in charge of the entire world.

AHASUERUS: Persia is not the entire world.

ESTHER: The entire civilized world.

AHASUERUS: The life of a king can be very dull. One must stand...or sit, if one is lucky...for hours at a time reviewing parades, listening to long discussions. One must attend all sorts of dreary functions and preside at endless ceremonies.

ESTHER: Do you have to? I mean you're the king. You can do as you please.

AHASUERUS: No one can do as they please, especially if you're king. Every word you say, every move you make is carefully scrutinized and blown completely out of proportion. Do you realize that I'm responsible for one hundred and twenty seven provinces, and each one has its own special problems. It's all very petty and uninspiring. I'd much rather be out in the field with my men.

ESTHER: But you do have a court full of ministers...

AHASUERUS: Such as they are. How would you like to be the next queen of Persia?

ESTHER: Is that a rhetorical question...or...

AHASUERUS: Or what?

ESTHER: A proposal of marriage?

AHASUERUS: It's a simple question. Just answer yes or no.

ESTHER: It's not simple at all. It's a question that demands a great deal of thought.

AHASUERUS: You've had over a year to think about it, haven't you?

ESTHER: I've never given it any serious thought.

AHASUERUS: Well, think about it.

ESTHER: I most certainly will.

AHASUERUS: And...what's your answer?

ESTHER: I said I'll have to think about it.

AHASUERUS: You do that little thing.

(AHASUERUS claps his hands together twice. BIGTHA appears.)

AHASUERUS: See that the young lady is escorted back to her quarters.

ESTHER: I'm sorry. I didn't mean... I'm sorry.

BIGTHA: *(To Esther)* Come along. *(Under his breath)* Bow.

ESTHER: *(SHE bows.)* I'm terribly sorry. I hope you're not offended.

BIGTHA: Come along.

ESTHER: It's not Hegai's fault. He told me what to do. If I did anything wrong, the fault's all mine.

BIGTHA: Come along, come along. *(HE starts off.)*

ESTHER: *(SHE bows and starts to follow BIGTHA off, turning her back to the king.)* Oh, I'm sorry.

> *(ESTHER backs out of the room with BIGTHA. AHASUERUS paces about then stands thoughtfully, listening to the music. BIGTHA reenters.)*

BIGTHA: Well?

AHASUERUS: I may be making a big mistake. But it won't be the first time, will it?

BIGTHA: A charming young lady.

AHASUERUS: Her charms are quite obvious. It's also obvious that she has a mind of her own. Say a prayer for me, Bigtha...and start the preparations for the wedding.

> *(BIGTHA scurries off. AHASUERUS stands lost in thought as the lights come down.)*

Scene Four

(Late morning. The queen's chambers. MORDECAI is discovered waiting impatiently. HEGAI enters.)

HEGAI: Yes? What is it?

MORDECAI: I must see the queen.

HEGAI: She's not the queen as yet. What do you want with her?

MORDECAI: It's a personal matter.

HEGAI: What are you doing here? Do you want to spoil everything? I said you could pass by the window from time to time, but you pass by every day. People are beginning to get suspicious.

MORDECAI: It's on my way to the shop.

HEGAI: Well, you can't see her now. The wedding's about to begin. If there's going to be a wedding, that is.

MORDECAI: What do you mean?

HEGAI: She's hysterical. She says she doesn't want to go through with it.

MORDECAI: Why not?

HEGAI: She won't even talk to me. That's the gratitude I get.

MORDECAI: Let me speak to her. She's always listened to me.

HEGAI: If you think it'll do any good. Wait here.

458

(HEGAI goes off. MORDECAI sighs, sits then rises and paces about. ESTHER enters in her wedding gown, followed by HEGAI.)

ESTHER: Oh, Mordecai! *(SHE runs to Mordecai and clings to him.)* Oh, Mordecai!

MORDECAI: *(To Hegai)* Let me speak to her...in private.

HEGAI: There isn't much time. *(HE goes off.)*

ESTHER: Oh, Mordecai! *(SHE weeps.)*

MORDECAI: What is it? What's the matter?

ESTHER: I can't go through with it. I just can't.

MORDECAI: Why not?

ESTHER: I will not marry a man under false pretenses. You were the one that taught me to be open and honest and now you tell me to conceal my heritage.

MORDECAI: Do you really think the king would marry you if he knew the truth?

ESTHER: Exactly. A marriage built on lies... What sort of a future does it have? I don't understand it. Why is there this feeling against the Jews?

MORDECAI: Jealousy, my dear. Jealousy, pure and simple.

ESTHER: But why? Why are they so jealous of us?

MORDECAI: Because we're successful, that's why. Because we're intelligent, that's why. Because we're more civilized. The rest of the world worships idols.

ESTHER: Well, if I can't be open and honest with my husband...

MORDECAI: Have you lied to him?

ESTHER: Well, no. Not exactly.

MORDECAI: I was married to your cousin for over twenty years and when she died there were all sorts of things I discovered about her that I knew nothing about. The king chose you from among the most beautiful young ladies in the kingdom. He must be very much in love with you.

ESTHER: He may be attracted to me physically but we know nothing about each other.

MORDECAI: That comes with time. And the physical is very important, my dear.

ESTHER: And once we get to know one another we may hate each other. Oh, Mordecai, I want to go home. It was all so simple before I came here.

MORDECAI: You would have married in any case.

ESTHER: Yes, but it would have been someone of our own faith. Oh, look at you! Look how thin you've gotten! Have you been eating properly. And look at that robe!

MORDECAI: What's wrong with this robe?

ESTHER: It's filthy.

MORDECAI: It was just washed.

ESTHER: Not very well, apparently.

MORDECAI: Now listen to me. We don't have very much time and I have something very important to tell you. But first you must promise me you won't get upset.

ESTHER: What's the matter? Are you ill? I knew it.

MORDECAI: It has nothing to do with me. As a matter of fact, what I have to tell you concerns the king. I had something to do in my shop this morning and just as I was closing up I happened to overhear these two men. Their names are Harbona and Teresh. They're members of the king's personal guard. They're planning to slip into his chamber one night this week and murder him.

ESTHER: But why?

MORDECAI: Maybe it's political. I don't know. The important thing is you must warn him, at once.

ESTHER: Why don't you? I'll introduce you to him. Why not? This would be the perfectly opportunity. He keeps asking me about you. And, I mean, you must admit it's very peculiar that my only living relative won't even take the time to show up at my wedding. I've told him all about you...how clever you are and how well educated.

MORDECAI: Some other time.

ESTHER: But he's going to ask me where I got this information.

MORDECAI: Tell him. There's no need for him to know that we're related. I'm simply a merchant that you've dealt with. I'm sure your friend, the eunuch, will agree with me.

ESTHER: You mustn't refer to Hegai as a eunuch. He's very sensitive about that.

MORDECAI: What shall I call him?

ESTHER: He has a name.

(HEGAI reenters.)

HEGAI: The king is coming. Quickly, quickly. Come this way. Hurry up.

MORDECAI: Good luck!

(MORDECAI kisses her and follows HEGAI off. AHASUERUS enters a moment later.)

AHASUERUS: So, there you are. What's the matter? Is there anything wrong?

ESTHER: You're not supposed to be here. Don't you know that it's bad luck for the groom to see the bride before the wedding?

AHASUERUS: You're not superstitious, are you?

ESTHER: Of course not. But why tempt fate?

(THEY smile.)

AHASUERUS: That's better. What are you so nervous about?

ESTHER: I don't know.

AHASUERUS: Well, if it's any consolation to you I'm just as nervous as you are. Maybe even more so.

ESTHER: Why should you be nervous? You've been through all of this before.

AHASUERUS: Exactly.

ESTHER: You can always divorce me and send me into exile.

AHASUERUS: That's nothing to joke about.

ESTHER: You must have loved her very much.

AHASUERUS: Once you're in love, my dear, you never stop loving. Not that you can't love someone else as well.

ESTHER: Why did you choose me? You could have married anyone.

AHASUERUS: I don't know.

ESTHER: There must have been a reason.

AHASUERUS: I'm curious, I guess. I want to find out more about you. Why you think the way you do. Why you behave the way you do.

ESTHER: Is that a good reason to marry someone?

AHASUERUS: I can't think of a better one. Can you?

ESTHER: Well, yes.

AHASUERUS: Name it.

ESTHER: Well, I should think that you'd want to find your bride...attractive.

AHASUERUS: Oh, that!

ESTHER: You don't think that's important?

AHASUERUS: Do you?

ESTHER: Why yes, of course.

AHASUERUS: I'm glad to hear it. Frankly, my dear, when it comes to women I'd rather be out there fighting the Greeks. At least in a war the battle lines are clearly drawn and the enemy is right out there in front of you.

ESTHER: Are we enemies, you and I?

AHASUERUS: Well, of course, we are. Men and women are natural born enemies. Even the act of love... It's aggressive, just like a battle. As a matter of fact there are some species where the female actually devours the male. The praying mantis, for example. After she's been impregnated by the male the female has him for dinner. I swear it.

ESTHER: *(After a moment)* Your majesty...?

AHASUERUS: Not your majesty. Not anymore.

ESTHER: What shall I call you?

AHASUERUS: Muley.

ESTHER: Muley? Why Muley?

AHASUERUS: When I was a boy my nurse called me Muley. She said I was as stubborn as a mule. What are you thinking?

ESTHER: Have there been many attempts on your life?

AHASUERUS: Why do you ask?

ESTHER: I have my reasons.

AHASUERUS: We're all of us sitting targets, all of us in public life, that is. Are you worried about my safety?

ESTHER: I've just been warned about a plot to kill you. Two men, two of your personal guards, Harbona and Teresh, are planning to slip into your chamber one night next week...

AHASUERUS: Who told you this?

ESTHER: What difference does it make?

AHASUERUS: I'd like to know.

ESTHER: A merchant.

AHASUERUS: What's his name?

ESTHER: Mordecai.

AHASUERUS: A Jew?

ESTHER: Why yes, I suppose he is.

(HEGAI reenters.)

AHASUERUS: Hegai...?

HEGAI: Your majesty?

AHASUERUS: Have we had any dealing with a Jew named Mordecai?

HEGAI: Mordecai. Mordecai. I believe he's a cloth merchant. His shop is just outside the palace gate I believe.

AHASUERUS: Must we give all our business to the Jews? Aren't there enough Persian merchants to go around?

HEGAI: Has he done anything wrong?

ESTHER: Nothing at all, except to save the king's life.

AHASUERUS: Now, now, now. You mustn't upset yourself. I'll have this Jew brought in for questioning.

ESTHER: What about the men who are plotting to kill you?

AHASUERUS: I'll have them brought in as well. Don't worry. Why was the queen allowed to be upset like this?

ESTHER: I'm not the queen as yet and I'm not upset. I'm angry. A man comes here to save your life and instead of gratitude you reprimand Hegai for dealing with a Jew.

AHASUERUS: All right, all right.

ESTHER: It is not all right. I don't understand your attitude. You behave as if this Jew was the criminal and not those treacherous guards.

AHASUERUS: For your information, my dear the Jews own half my kingdom.

ESTHER: Exactly half? You've got it all figured out?

AHASUERUS: Come, come, come.

ESTHER: And if you are in debt whose fault is that?

AHASUERUS: I'm not blaming anyone, my dear. You've led a very sheltered life. You know nothing of the world. When dealing with the Jews one must be cautious. They are notoriously unscrupulous.

ESTHER: That is a generality and like most generalities is groundless.

(Music is heard.)

AHASUERUS: I must go. The wedding is about to begin. Now look, child, if he is innocent no harm will come to this Jew of yours. You have my word. Come, give your king a little kiss. Your husband-to-be? Just a little peck.

(SHE pecks him on the cheek.)

AHASUERUS: Ah well, I guess that will have to do...for now. Look after her Hegai.

HEGAI: Your majesty.

(AHASUERUS takes HEGAI aside.)

AHASUERUS: I want to have a little talk with you afterwards.

HEGAI: Certainly, your majesty.

(AHASUERUS goes off.)

ESTHER: What did he say to you?

HEGAI: Nothing.

ESTHER: Hegai?!

HEGAI: What was that all about it?

ESTHER: I'm not going through with it.

HEGAI: What's the matter now?

ESTHER: You heard him. You heard the way he spoke about the Jews. I'm going to tell him right now.

HEGAI: Good. And then afterwards perhaps you'd like to assemble all the guests and make a general announcement.

ESTHER: Oh, Hegai, how can I possibly marry a man that feels the way he does about my people?

HEGAI: The Jews are one small segment of your people and if they're not very popular there must be a reason for it.

ESTHER: And what might that be?

HEGAI: They're clannish, they're proud, they're arrogant and your cousin is the worst of the lot.

ESTHER: My cousin is a very kind man, a very intelligent man.

HEGAI: Oh, yes, I know very well how intelligent your cousin is. Everyone in the city knows how intelligent he is. He spends half his life in court trying to prove how intelligent he is. Your cousin happens to be the rudest, most insensitive man in the kingdom.

ESTHER: People take advantage of him because he's a Jew.

HEGAI: There are ways...

ESTHER: He wants justice and he has every right to stand up for his rights.

HEGAI: Your cousin is smug and intolerant and so are you.

ESTHER: How can you say that?

HEGAI: So the king isn't perfect. What of it? Do you know anyone in the world that is?

ESTHER: You don't understand. *(SHE turns away from him.)* Oh, what's the use?!

HEGAI: And what is that supposed to mean? Never mind. I know perfectly well what you meant. Hegai is a eunuch and everyone knows that eunuchs are incapable of love.

ESTHER: I never said that.

HEGAI: No, but that's what you meant, isn't it?

(The music offstage has become a march. BIGTHA enters.)

BIGTHA: What's the matter? What's holding things up?

HEGAI: She's coming. She's coming.

BIGTHA: Well, hurry it up. We can't wait all day. *(HE goes off.)*

ESTHER: *(After a moment)* I'll go through with it on one condition...and one condition only.

HEGAI: And what might that be?

ESTHER: That you never leave my side.

HEGAI: That may prove a little awkward at times.

(THEY both giggle. ESTHER kisses HEGAI on the cheek. HEGAI bows low. ESTHER takes a deep breath and starts off. As the music grows louder ESTHER, her head erect, seems to grow taller. HEGAI stands watching her leave as the lights slowly dim.)

ACT TWO

Scene One

(The office of the prime minister. HAMAN is seated at his desk. MORDECAI appears in the doorway.)

HAMAN: Come in, come in.

MORDECAI: Your lordship.

HAMAN: You know who I am?

MORDECAI: Yes, of course. You're the new prime minister.

HAMAN: Hardly new. I've been prime minister for over a year now. You know why you're here?

MORDECAI: I can guess, your lordship. I've told the police everything that I know.

HAMAN: The police?

MORDECAI: In regard to that incident a few weeks ago.

HAMAN: This has nothing to do with the police. You're well acquainted with the police, I gather.

MORDECAI: I wouldn't say well acquainted. I have had some difficulties now and then and I've had to turn to the police for their assistance.

HAMAN: Rather often, I gather.

MORDECAI: Unfortunately. You see, your lordship, because of my religion people think they can take advantage of me.

HAMAN: Your religion being...?

MORDECAI: I'm a Jew.

HAMAN: A most ancient tribe. I've had many friends among the Jews.

MORDECAI: Have you really?

HAMAN: That was some time ago.

MORDECAI: Then you understand our predicament.

HAMAN: And what might that be?

MORDECAI: The prejudice we must endure.

HAMAN: Actually I felt the prejudice came from your side of the fence. That was my experience at any rate. You realize, of course, that you Jews are unique.

MORDECAI: In what sense, your lordship?

HAMAN: Oh come, come. You're a law unto yourselves.

MORDECAI: We have our religious observances.

HAMAN: And your loyalty to the throne?

MORDECAI: Is my loyalty being questioned?

HAMAN: Do you accept the divinity of our king?

MORDECAI: He certainly has the right to consider himself divine.

HAMAN: You haven't answered my question.

MORDECAI: It's not for me to question our sovereign.

HAMAN: You still haven't answered my question. Do you accept the divinity of the king?

MORDECAI: I'm a loyal subject and there's absolutely no reason to question my loyalty.

HAMAN: If I were to invite you to dinner would you sit down and dine with me?

MORDECAI: Are you inviting me to dinner?

HAMAN: You have an annoying habit of answering my questions with a question.

MORDECAI: I'm sorry.

HAMAN: Would you sit down and dine with me if I were to invite you to dinner?

MORDECAI: I'd be honored, your lordship.

HAMAN: And would you share our food?

MORDECAI: We have certainly dietary laws, you see...

HAMAN: You'd risk offending your prime minister for these senseless, antiquated rules. Is that it?

MORDECAI: They may be antiquated but they were instituted for some very good reason.

HAMAN: Is that the mysterious secret of your success? These antiquated rules of yours?

MORDECAI: Mysterious secret?

HAMAN: I'm referring to this wealthy Jewish empire within our Persian empire?

MORDECAI: I know of no Jewish empire. Some Jews are good business men and some are not.

HAMAN: You Jews have no country of your own. Don't you feel any loyalty to this nation that supports you so lavishly?

MORDECAI: I don't understand why you question my loyalty. The great king Cyrus himself adopted the god of the Jews as one of the official gods of Persia. Surely, your lordship, there's room enough in this empire for all sorts of beliefs.

HAMAN: You think I'm being narrow-minded, do you? You think that we should tolerate views that come into conflict with the very soul of this establishment?

MORDECAI: I know of no conflict, your lordship.

HAMAN: Persia, too, has it's unique observances such as showing respect for figures of authority. They may seem trivial to you, these observances, just as your special rules may seem odd to us, but you are the guests, so to speak, of this empire, and when one is someone's guest it behooves one to show a certain respect to one's host. Or am I wrong?

MORDECAI: Respect is a two way street.

HAMAN: You think someone should kneel to you? Is that it?

MORDECAI: Certainly not. Why would any right thinking man ask another to humble himself for no good reason?

HAMAN: Respect for authority is no good reason? Respect for the office of authority is no good reason to show respect?

MORDECAI: There are many ways of showing respect, your lordship. Superficial gestures such as saluting and kneeling and the like are...

HAMAN: Are what?

MORDECAI: Superficial gestures.

HAMAN: Thank you so much for sparing me this most interesting interview.

MORDECAI: Am I excused?

HAMAN: For the present.

MORDECAI: May I ask what prompted you to summon me?

HAMAN: I pass by your shop every day and never once have you knelt in my presence. As a matter of fact you make it a point of turning away and busying yourself with something, pretending not to notice me.

MORDECAI: Is that the reason I've been summoned here?

HAMAN: I said you're excused.

> (*HAMAN busies himself with some papers. MORDECAI hesitates, waiting for some clarification, then realizes that there's none forthcoming.*)

MORDECAI: Your lordship.

> (*MORDECAI goes off. HAMAN looks up then sits drumming his fingers on his desk as the lights slowly dim.*)

Scene Two

(The queen's chambers. Early afternoon. ESTHER stands looking out the window. HEGAI enters holding an expensive robe draped over his arms.)

ESTHER: Well?

HEGAI: He refused it.

ESTHER: What's he doing out there? Why is he dressed like that?

HEGAI: He's in mourning.

ESTHER: Apparently. But why?

HEGAI: I haven't the vaguest idea. All I know is that he's making a spectacle of himself and that's all we need.

ESTHER: Bring him in.

HEGAI: I don't think that's a good idea.

ESTHER: I don't care what you think.

HEGAI: Things are bad enough as they are.

ESTHER: I want to see him.

HEGAI: But...

ESTHER: Hegai, please!

(HEGAI heaves a deep sigh and goes off. ESTHER goes to the window and looks out. After a moment SHE starts to pace about.

474

MORDECAI enters dressed in sackcloth, his head covered with ashes. HE is followed by HEGAI.)

ESTHER: Thank you, Hegai. I said thank you, Hegai.

(HEGAI glares at Mordecai and goes off.)

MORDECAI: You sent for me?

ESTHER: Won't you sit down?

MORDECAI: I prefer to stand.

ESTHER: I'm sorry I've neglected you, Mordecai, but things are at sixes and sevens here. The king and I had a disagreement. Well, I guess it was a little more than that. We're not speaking to one another and I've been confined to the palace.

MORDECAI: What was this disagreement about?

ESTHER: Leading a double life, my dear, has not been easy. Every time I've been to visit you I've had to make up some sort of story, and the king's grown very suspicious. He's begun to doubt that you exist at all. In addition to that... Well, I have been speaking my mind, telling him what I think, making suggestions about reform. He calls it interfering. He even resents my charity work.

MORDECAI: But you've become very popular.

ESTHER: He resents that too. At any rate, I lost my temper and I said if he felt that way that maybe we shouldn't see each other anymore, and maybe he should divorce me like he did the queen and...I said all sorts of things, and he was furious, and he said that I could not leave the premises. So I'm a prisoner here in the palace. He treats me like a piece of property. He has no respect for my opinion. He has no respect for me as a person.

MORDECAI: You must be patient with him.

ESTHER: It'll work itself out in time, I suppose. It has to, one way or another. In the meanwhile I'm stuck here, and I'm bored, bored, bored.

MORDECAI: You haven't heard?

ESTHER: Heard what?

MORDECAI: *(HE reaches inside his garment and produces a tattered parchment which he hands to Esther.)* Read it.

ESTHER: *(SHE reads the document.)* I can't believe it. I knew the king had no use for the Jews. But this...

MORDECAI: It's not the king.

ESTHER: It has the king's seal. This is a royal decree.

MORDECAI: It's Haman's doing.

ESTHER: The prime minister? You must be mistaken.

MORDECAI: I have it on good authority.

ESTHER: I find that hard to believe.

MORDECAI: Nevertheless it's true.

ESTHER: Haman's a sensitive, intelligent man. As a matter of fact, I consider him a friend, one of the few friends I have here at court.

MORDECAI: In that case you must speak to him at once.

ESTHER: If it's really him then...

MORDECAI: I assure you it is.

ESTHER: The only trouble is...

MORDECAI: What?

ESTHER: The king is very possessive and very jealous. It's ridiculous, I know, but he's even jealous of my friendship with Haman.

MORDECAI: Then you must speak to the king. At this very moment this decree is being distributed to every province in the kingdom. We are all of us doomed.

ESTHER: But he won't see me.

MORDECAI: Have you tried?

ESTHER: Yes, of course, I've tried. After our last quarrel I thought, "This is foolish. It can't go on like this." so I sent him a note. He never answered. I sent him another, and when I didn't hear from him I went to his chambers.

MORDECAI: And?

ESTHER: I was turned away.

MORDECAI: Then you must speak to Haman.

ESTHER: You don't understand. It would only antagonize the king.

MORDECAI: You've got to do something. And don't forget, my dear, you're still one of us. Or have you forgotten?

ESTHER: No, I have not forgotten and I will do something. I promise you.

MORDECAI: Everyone thinks you've deserted us. They think that you've made yourself scarce in order to save your own skin. I said they were wrong, that there must be a reason for it. But what was I to think? Your visits come to a sudden end and then...this decree.

ESTHER: How could you doubt me?

MORDECAI: Time was passing, and the thirteenth of Adar is less than a month away.

ESTHER: I'll come up with something. I promise you. Go home. Go home and pray for us.

MORDECAI: I knew you wouldn't let us down. God be with you. my child.

(MORDECAI kisses her and goes off. ESTHER paces restlessly. After a few moments HEGAI reenters.)

ESTHER: *(SHE holds up the edict.)* Did you know about this?

HEGAI: I heard rumors.

ESTHER: And you said nothing?

HEGAI: It was just a rumor. And besides I figured you'd find out soon enough.

ESTHER: When it was too late?

HEGAI: Now calm down.

ESTHER: Who's responsible for this edict? Is it the king or is it Haman?

HEGAI: It's your cousin.

ESTHER: Mordecai? What are you talking about?

HEGAI: His shop is just outside the palace gate. Haman passes by every day. Your cousin refuses to kneel. He insists it violates his personal rights. The man is impossible. At any rate someone reported him to Haman. Haman called him into his office and shortly after that this edict was issued.

ESTHER: And you think there's a connection?

HEGAI: I know there is.

ESTHER: I don't think Haman's that petty.

HEGAI: Your cousin certainly is. As soon as I laid eyes on him I knew he was trouble. And as far as Haman is concerned he's just as arrogant. In addition to that he has this obsession about the Jews.

ESTHER: It's a royal decree.

HEGAI: According to Bigtha the royal treasury stands to gain a fortune, so the king was easily persuaded.

ESTHER: And the king is willing to slaughter all the Jews in order to fill the royal coffers?

HEGAI: Well, he is in debt. He's still paying off that year long feast he gave. And besides he's been told that the Jews are a threat to the government, that they've organized a plot. Haman has all sorts of documents and witnesses, or so I've been told.

ESTHER: If there are witnesses you know that they've been bribed, and if there are documents you know they're false.

HEGAI: Quite possibly.

ESTHER: Haman is a brilliant man, a visionary.

HEGAI: And a fanatic. Both the prime minister and your cousin. It's these idealists. They're the ones that cause all the trouble.

ESTHER: I've got to get in touch with Haman. I'll send him a note.

HEGAI: That would be a mistake.

ESTHER: Suppose I give a dinner, invite the king and suggest that Haman might join us.

HEGAI: And how are you going to reach the king?

ESTHER: The day after tomorrow the king sits in the inner court. Anyone may approach him there.

HEGAI: If he doesn't extend his scepter toward you, if he doesn't acknowledge your presence you'll be led away...and executed.

ESTHER: That's an ancient law and it's never really been enforced.

HEGAI: It most certainly has and not too long ago.

ESTHER: I'll just have to take that chance.

HEGAI: You are not responsible for that idiot cousin of yours.

ESTHER: But I am, you see. And besides do you really think that I could stand by and watch my people be slaughtered?

HEGAI: It's a lost cause, I tell you. Please, don't throw your life away for nothing.

ESTHER: At least it will let me know.

HEGAI: Know what?

ESTHER: If the king is really in love with me.

HEGAI: The king was in love with Vashti. Give me a day or two. I'll have a talk with Bigtha. He owes me a favor.

ESTHER: I can't wait a day or two. I want you to call in the dressmakers. If I'm going to face the king I want to look my best.

HEGAI: I'll do nothing of the sort.

ESTHER: Very well. *(SHE goes off.)*

HEGAI: You're not supposed to leave your quarters. Esther, please! Don't do anything foolish.

(HEGAI follows her off as the lights come down.)

Scene Three

(Early evening. The queen's chambers. HAMAN is discovered pacing impatiently. HEGAI enters.)

HEGAI: I'm sorry to keep you waiting my lord. Her highness will be joining you very shortly.

HAMAN: I'm early it seems.

HEGAI: No, no, no. You're just in time.

HAMAN: I did receive word that we were expected a little earlier.

HEGAI: That's right. The queen was anxious to have a word with you.

HAMAN: How long has this been going on? This little contretemps between the two of them?

HEGAI: I'm not quite sure what you're referring to.

HAMAN: You know perfectly well what I'm referring to. How could you possibly permit her highness to do anything so rash? Appearing unannounced in the inner court. Risking her life like that. She's young and impulsive, but surely you should have known better.

HEGAI: I'm merely a servant, my lord.

HAMAN: Nonsense! You're her friend and her confidante.

HEGAI: You're quite mistaken, my lord. And now, if you'll excuse, I have some chores I must attend to.

(HEGAI goes off. HAMAN continues to pace about. ESTHER enters.)

481

ESTHER: I'm sorry to keep you waiting. You're staring at me.

HAMAN: You've lost some weight.

ESTHER: It's unbecoming.

HAMAN: Is this some sort of special diet that you're on? What are you laughing at?

ESTHER: I don't know. I really don't know.

HAMAN: I'm very angry with you.

ESTHER: You're not going to scold me, are you?

HAMAN: When you act like a foolish child what else am I to do ? Risking your life like that!

ESTHER: Risking my life?

HAMAN: Oh, come, come. We know each other too well for you to play games with me. You may not be aware of it but you have me to thank for your being here. The king was so engrossed that he wasn't even aware of your presence. As a matter of fact the guards were ready to haul you away and they would have if I hadn't nudged him in time.

ESTHER: How can I every repay you?

HAMAN: Don't you dare flirt with me, you vixen! It's no joking matter. I am really very upset.

ESTHER: It's an old barbaric law. No one takes it seriously.

HAMAN: The fact of the matter is we are barbarians still.

ESTHER: I suppose the king is furious.

HAMAN: Please!

ESTHER: What?

HAMAN: It's bad enough when the two of you are speaking. When you have these little tiffs he becomes absolutely impossible. However, I will not complain. I swore to myself I would never complain. I knew perfectly well what I was letting myself in for when I accepted this thorny position.

ESTHER: Then why did you accept it?

HAMAN: Ambition, my dear. Overweening ambition. Not to mention conceit. Oh, yes. I'm the first to admit it. I actually believe that I can persuade almost anyone to do almost anything I want them to do.

ESTHER: I really think you can.

HAMAN: With help, perhaps. I've been counting on you to keep things on an even keel. And this is the way you reward my trust. Barging brazenly into the lion's den as if you were attending an afternoon tea. It's caused quite a scandal, you know. Not only have you tarnished your unblemished reputation...

ESTHER: Oh, dear!

HAMAN: Oh, dear indeed! Not only have you shocked the local gentry but I thought the king was going to have a heart attack. He turned absolutely white.

ESTHER: He seemed to control himself remarkably well, I thought. As a matter of fact, unless I'm mistaken, I had the feeling that he was actually glad to see me.

HAMAN: He dotes on you and you know it.

ESTHER: He has a strange way of showing it.

HAMAN: Let's give the devil his due. The man is really trying. It's the case of an unremarkable man, living in unremarkable times, married to a most remarkable young lady.

ESTHER: Then the fault's all mine.

HAMAN: A good deal of it, yes. However it's pointless to beat your lovely bosom in repentance. You were clever enough to catch him. Reeling him in, however, is going to take monumental patience.

ESTHER: Do you really think he's in love with me?

HAMAN: Why should he be any different from the rest of us?

ESTHER: Then why does he spend so much time with his concubines?

HAMAN: It's merely a matter of conjecture, of course, but I suspect he runs to them merely to lick his wounds.

ESTHER: Then I don't know what to say, how to behave.

HAMAN: You must realize by now that a marriage can offer one just so much. Don't burden it with impossible dreams. Romance is for story books.

ESTHER: Then what's the answer?

HAMAN: One must look elsewhere for fulfillment.

ESTHER: *(Feigning shock)* What are you suggesting?

HAMAN: I'll ignore that.

ESTHER: Seriously, Haman, it's a man's world and you know it.

HAMAN: Don't fool yourself, my child. The master is just as much the slave as the servant.

ESTHER: Your marriage is a happy one, isn't it?

HAMAN: My marriage fills a certain void. I have a devoted wife and ten strapping sons, but a man needs more than a family.

ESTHER: And a woman?

HAMAN: There are some people, both men and women who live life on an animal level. And then there are those of us, like you and I, that live for other things. Shall we call it glory? I have my governmental duties. You have your charities.

ESTHER: Not since I've been confined to the palace.

HAMAN: He'll get over it. And when he does, when you return to the role of Lady Bountiful, you shall find the royal treasury filled to overflowing.

ESTHER: Oh? And where is this sudden windfall to come from?

HAMAN: Never mind where. I ask only one thing of you, just one thing, my dear young lady, my lovely friend.

ESTHER: And what might that be?

HAMAN: Forget about those precious Jews of yours. Don't look so innocent. You know perfectly well that the Jews are a bone of contention between you and the king. I know you mean well but your compassion is sadly misplaced. I know, I know. It's very tempting to champion the underdog. In this case, however, the underdog is equipped with fangs and claws and well able to look after itself.

ESTHER: The Jews, my dear Haman, are like anyone else. Some are strong, some are weak.

HAMAN: The Jews are predatory beasts, blood sucking vampires. Let me ask you this. If you had a child and, when you approached its cradle, you found a serpent lying there, would you be more concerned about the child or the serpent? I love this kingdom and I hope one day to see our children and our grandchildren living in peace and harmony. And there's only one way to achieve this peace and harmony and that's by removing this parasite...this leech that's been draining the life of this empire for lo these many years.

ESTHER: What exactly have they done, these Jews?

HAMAN: Oh come, come. You know perfectly well that the Jews have a strangle hold on our financial and business institutions. Powerful monopolies that dominate our economic system.

ESTHER: And you resent the hard-earned success of these firms.

HAMAN: I have nothing against these people personally. I grew up among them. Some of them were my friends, as much as any non-Jew can befriend a Jew.

ESTHER: But surely there's room enough in this world for more than one religion.

HAMAN: What has religion got to do with it? Unless by religion you're referring to these man-made institutions that do nothing but succeed in separating one man from another, that set up barriers between brothers. I know you share my vision of a world without walls, without chains. A world where one man can reach out to another without fear, without mistrust, without suspicion.

ESTHER: And you think by eliminating the Jews we can achieve this world?

HAMAN: It's a beginning.

ESTHER: And once we've eliminated the Jews who's next? The Syrians? The Egyptians? The Babylonians? No, no, no. Let me finish. It's Persia for the Persians. I understand perfectly. But even here in Shushan, the very heart of this magnificent empire, how many true Persians will you find? When it comes right down to it...what is Persia?

HAMAN: Persia is a dream.

ESTHER: Can you think of one single dream that's worth a human life?

HAMAN: An insect has life. A rodent has life.

ESTHER: The Jews are an ancient culture, a civilized race. Surely they have something to offer.

HAMAN: Civilized? Have you read their literature? Have you read their so-called holy books? Adultery, my dear. Incest. Daughters coupling with fathers. Lust. Fratricide. An eye for an eye. A god so heartless that he demands they be prepared to offer their only son as a living sacrifice.

ESTHER: They also believe in loving their neighbor, in honoring their parents. It seems to me that if we're to achieve this greatness you've been extolling it behooves us to set an example for these people instead of butchering them.

HAMAN: Life is a battle for survival.

ESTHER: And the Jews are the enemy.

HAMAN: Exactly.

ESTHER: Suppose, my dear, Haman, you were to find that the queen of Persia herself was a Jewess?

HAMAN: Oh come, come!

ESTHER: Just suppose. What then?

HAMAN: My dear child, life is difficult enough without having to deal with hypothetical conundrums.

ESTHER: If I were a Jewess would you stand by and watch me being slaughtered? I insist on an answer.

HAMAN: Very well, if you insist. I would.

ESTHER: Are you serious?

HAMAN: With great reluctance.

ESTHER: You're not really serious, are you?

HAMAN: I was never more serious in my life. Look at you. You're trembling all over. Why must you be so intense about everything? Here. Sit down. Let me get you some wine.

(HAMAN helps ESTHER into a chair as AHASUERUS enters.)

AHASUERUS: Am I interrupting?

HAMAN: Her highness and I were having a rather heated debate.

AHASUERUS: Perhaps I'd better leave.

HAMAN: Nonsense. As a matter of fact the queen and I were discussing the Jews.

AHASUERUS: Is that why you brought us here? To discuss the Jews?

ESTHER: Among other things.

AHASUERUS: When you know it's a waste of time.

ESTHER: Why do you say that?

AHASUERUS: Because it's a royal decree and a royal decree is divine. It cannot be reversed.

ESTHER: And royal charity?

AHASUERUS: It's a pity that this cousin of yours, if he exists at all, never taught you that charity begins at home. And here I thought that this mad, reckless gesture of yours was an act of love.

ESTHER: There are some acts of love, your majesty, that are not performed in the dark.

HAMAN: Let's drop the subject of the Jews, I beg of you. At least for tonight.

AHASUERUS: It was my understanding that this invitation of yours included a dinner. Or was I mistaken about that as well?

ESTHER: I'm really not feeling very well. Could we possibly postpone our little dinner until tomorrow?

AHASUERUS: What's the matter with you?

ESTHER: It's nothing really. It's just that...I haven't been sleeping well.

AHASUERUS: You're not the only one. Haman? *(HE strides off.)*

HAMAN: Till tomorrow.

(HAMAN goes off. ESTHER sits despondently. HEGAI reenters.)

HEGAI: What's the matter? What's wrong?

ESTHER: Everything.

HEGAI: I told you it was pointless. And that cousin of yours is certainly no help.

ESTHER: What has he done now?

HEGAI: He's still out there, making a spectacle of himself. Take a look. Go on. Take a look.

(THEY both go to the window and look out.)

HEGAI: And there goes Haman.

ESTHER: Oh dear! *(SHE walks away from the window.)* Did he kneel?

HEGAI: What do you think?

(ESTHER sighs.)

HEGAI: What are you going to do?

ESTHER: They're coming back tomorrow.

HEGAI: And?

ESTHER: I don't know. I really don't know. *(SHE starts to sob and clings to HEGAI.)* What am I going to do, Hegai? What am I going to do?

(HE pats her reassuringly as the lights slowly dim.)

ACT THREE

Scene One

(Later that evening. The King's chambers. AHASUERUS is discovered gazing out over the city. BIGTHA enters carrying a large volume. AHASUERUS sits with a sigh. BIGTHA sits beside him and opens the book.)

AHASUERUS: Tell me something, Bigtha.

BIGTHA: Your majesty?

AHASUERUS: How long have you been married?

BIGTHA: Longer than I care to remember, your majesty.

AHASUERUS: Does it get any easier?

BIGTHA: With time, your majesty.

AHASUERUS: Tell me the truth. Does your wife still interest you?

BIGTHA: My wife and I have made our peace, your majesty.

AHASUERUS: Is there really such a thing?

BIGTHA: It comes about much sooner than you might think.

AHASUERUS: This business of man and woman…it's a terrible burden isn't it?

BIGTHA: A sweet one, nevertheless.

490

AHASUERUS: In retrospect, perhaps. Women call it love when 'it's nothing more than animal coupling. What is it that attracts one man to one particular woman? The poets have one answer for it. The scientists another. Who's right, do you think?

BIGTHA: I find the subject of love, like religion unfathomable.

AHASUERUS: *(HE rises, walks toward the window and looks out.)* Look at them out there. Fast asleep. Why not? What have they got to worry about? *(HE turns to BIGTHA.)* Have I been a bad king, Bigtha? You don't have to answer that. *(HE paces about.)* I don't understand this obsession of hers with the Jews? What have the Jews ever done for Persia? Can you tell me that? And now they're plotting to overthrow me. And she expects me to turn the other cheek. Have you ever heard anything so ridiculous?

BIGTHA: Women are an enigma.

AHASUERUS: You can say that again. *(HE sits and sighs.)* All right. What are you going to read me tonight?

BIGTHA: I thought we might look at the book of records, your majesty.

AHASUERUS: That ought to put me to sleep. And to risk her life like that! You must admit that did take courage. Amazing. Absolutely amazing.

BIGTHA: Indeed.

AHASUERUS: Vashti was headstrong too but, now that I look back, rather shallow. Women have no right to have a brain. They have so many advantages to begin with. *(HE sighs.)* All right, let's begin.

BIGTHA: *(HE reads from the book of records.)* "In those days, while Mordecai, the Jew, stood near the king's gate, two of the king's chamberlains, Harbona and Teresh by name, of those who kept the door, were bitter and sought to lay hands on the king. And the thing was known to Mordecai, the Jew, who told it unto Esther, who was then betrothed to the king and Esther certified the king thereof."

AHASUERUS: Let me see that.

(BIGTHA hands the volume to AHASUERUS, who looks over the passage.)

AHASUERUS: Why would a Jew want to save my life? If they're planning to overthrow me, that is? Does that make sense to you? I see nothing about a reward. Didn't the Jew receive some sort of a reward?

BIGTHA: Not that I know of, your majesty.

AHASUERUS: Well, Jew or not, he should receive some sort of a reward, don't you think? I mean after all he did save my life.

BIGTHA: I think so.

AHASUERUS: Now there's a poser for you. How does one reward someone for saving one's life? The life of a king, to boot.

BIGTHA: Good question.

AHASUERUS: Go fetch someone, one of my advisers.

BIGTHA: Your majesty.

(BIGTHA rises, bows and goes off. AHASUERUS rises and paces about. BIGTHA reenters almost immediately followed by HAMAN.)

HAMAN: Your majesty, I hope I'm not disturbing you. I've come on a matter of extreme gravity.

AHASUERUS: Ah, Haman!

HAMAN: I've been up all night and I'm very upset.

AHASUERUS: What a coincidence! So am I, and I'm deeply puzzled. Perhaps you can offer a solution.

HAMAN: Why yes. Yes, of course. But...

AHASUERUS: Can it wait?

HAMAN: Why yes, of course.

AHASUERUS: I would like your considered opinion. A man who saves the king's life... He should be rewarded, don't you think?

HAMAN: Yes, of course.

AHASUERUS: Now the question is how does one reward a man who saved the life of a king?

HAMAN: Who saved the life of the king. Ah, yes. I understand. *(HE smiles modestly.)* Well, your majesty...

AHASUERUS: Yes?

HAMAN: You're putting me in a rather awkward position.

AHASUERUS: What's that? I see your point. However I'm sure you'll have no trouble in being objective. You certainly seem to have a handle on things.

HAMAN: Thank you, your majesty. Now let me see. How does one reward a man who saved the king's life?

AHASUERUS: Take your time.

HAMAN: I've always been of the opinion that a good deed is its own reward.

AHASUERUS: Yes?

HAMAN: However, when it comes to the king himself I do think something special is in order.

AHASUERUS: Money, perhaps?

HAMAN: Yes, well, money, after all, is merely just...money. But when it comes to honor... Now that's another matter entirely. With that in mind, if his majesty has no objection, I would dress this man in royal robes. I would place him upon one of his majesty's royal steeds. I would have this man led through the streets of the capital by one of the most eminent lords in the kingdom; and, as they passed through the streets, I would have this lord announce loudly and clearly, "Thus shall it be done to the man whom the king delights to honor." That's merely a suggestion, of course.

AHASUERUS: And, might I say, an excellent one. And you are just the man for the job, my dear Haman.

HAMAN: I'm very flattered.

AHASUERUS: I'd like you to seek out a Jew named Mordecai and I'd like you, yourself, to do the honors. He has a little shop just outside the palace gate.

HAMAN: The Jew? Mordecai?

AHASUERUS: Yes. The Jew named Mordecai. He's a cloth merchant.

HAMAN: Yes, I know the man. As a matter of fact...

AHASUERUS: What's that?

HAMAN: Nothing.

AHASUERUS: At any rate I'm sure you'll agree that you're one of the most eminent lords in the kingdom.

HAMAN: I'm afraid I don't understand.

AHASUERUS: What is it that you don't understand?

HAMAN: Why on earth would you want to honor this Jew?

AHASUERUS: For the simple reason that this Jew saved my life.

HAMAN: There must be some mistake.

AHASUERUS: I quite agree. Perhaps you'd care to examine the records?

HAMAN: Why yes, I most certainly would.

AHASUERUS: Bigtha.

(BIGTHA hands the volume to HAMAN, pointing to the pertinent passage.)

HAMAN: Remarkable.

AHASUERUS: Yes, isn't it?

HAMAN: Perhaps there's some mistake.

AHASUERUS: Hardly, since I personally provided the entry.

HAMAN: Yes, well, I'm sure there must be some very simple explanation.

AHASUERUS: I certainly hope so, my friend. I certainly hope so.

HAMAN: What I mean to say is...

AHASUERUS: Yes?

HAMAN: Apparently this matter was kept hush-hush.

AHASUERUS: I was under the impression that you were on top of things.

HAMAN: One can't be everywhere, your majesty.

AHASUERUS: A flaw, unfortunately, that can be fatal. I think you'd better get started. It's almost morning.

HAMAN: Under the circumstances, your majesty... What I mean to say is...what with this new edict, nerves are strained and tempers are running high.

AHASUERUS: And you think you might be at risk exposing yourself like that.

HAMAN: Exactly.

AHASUERUS: That's something to think about. Isn't it Bigtha?

BIGTHA: Your majesty?

AHASUERUS: Alert my personal guards. They're to accompany the prime minister wherever he goes. They're not to leave his side. Is that understood?

BIGTHA: Your majesty. *(HE bows and goes off.)*

AHASUERUS: That ought to do the trick. Don't you think? Well...?

HAMAN: Your majesty. *(HE bows and starts off.)*

AHASUERUS: Good luck. And incidentally...

HAMAN: *(HE stops and turns.)* Your majesty?

AHASUERUS: You borrowed my signet ring to authorize that now rather questionable edict. You never did return it.

HAMAN: Yes. Yes, of course. *(HE takes the signet ring from his finger and gives it to AHASUERUS.)*

AHASUERUS: Don't forget this evening.

HAMAN: What's that?

AHASUERUS: We're dining with the queen. Don't be late.

HAMAN: Yes. Yes, of course. *(HE starts off.)*

AHASUERUS: And Haman...?

HAMAN: Your majesty?

AHASUERUS: What was it you wanted to talk to me about?

HAMAN: It can wait, your majesty.

(HAMAN bows and goes off as BIGTHA reenters.)

AHASUERUS: *(Under his breath)* I'm sure it can. *(HE turns to Bigtha.)* Bigtha.

BIGTHA: Your majesty?

AHASUERUS: I should like to examine all the evidence in regard to this so-called Jewish conspiracy.

BIGTHA: Your majesty.

> *(BIGTHA smiles, bows and goes off. AHASUERUS stands lost in thought as the lights slowly fade.)*

Scene Two

(The queen's chambers. The following evening. ESTHER and HEGAI are discovered.)

HEGAI: I wouldn't start celebrating if I were you.

ESTHER: What do you think it means?

HEGAI: The king decided to reward someone who saved his life. That's what it means.

ESTHER: You mean he doesn't intend to do anything in regard to the edict?

HEGAI: He's conducting an investigation.

ESTHER: Then he's going to discover that this Jewish plot is fiction.

HEGAI: Don't you understand? A royal edict is irreversible. This doesn't change anything in regard to the Jews.

ESTHER: Does he know that Mordecai's my cousin?

HEGAI: No.

ESTHER: And what of Haman? Will he continue as prime minister?

HEGAI: I don't know.

ESTHER: I wonder what's keeping them.

HEGAI: The king was up all night, I know that. And he spent the entire day examining the evidence. Who knows what sort of mood he's in.

ESTHER: And Haman?

HEGAI: I don't know. I don't know anything more than you do.

(AHASUERUS enters. HEGAI bows and goes off.)

ESTHER: Haman's not with you?

AHASUERUS: He'll be here shortly. Until then you'll have to put up with me. Or would you like me to leave and return when he gets here?

ESTHER: Don't be ridiculous.

AHASUERUS: That's how you think of me, isn't it? That I'm ridiculous?

ESTHER: I don't want to fight. I don't want to argue.

AHASUERUS: That's fine with me.

AHASUERUS: For the life of me I don't know what you see in Haman.

ESTHER: You were the one who appointed him prime minister.

AHASUERUS: He's efficient and he's clever but there's something about him that makes my blood run cold. What do you two have in common? Can you tell me that?

ESTHER: He treats me like an equal, for one thing. He listens to me and he respects what I have to say.

AHASUERUS: And I don't?

ESTHER: You resent the very fact that I dare speak my mind.

AHASUERUS: I deal with matters of state all day long. Must I continue these discussions in the privacy of my bedroom?

ESTHER: I'm sorry. I cannot divorce my mind from my body nor would you really want me to. You have your concubines for mindless love, if that's what you need.

AHASUERUS: All right, all right.

ESTHER: You're not jealous of Haman, are you?

AHASUERUS: Kings are never jealous.

ESTHER: Yes, dear.

AHASUERUS: It's just that I've had a number of complaints from some of my ministers.

ESTHER: About what?

AHASUERUS: About your interference.

ESTHER: I will not remain silent when I have something to contribute. I am the queen. I am your wife and I demand to be heard, and you should support me instead of running me down.

AHASUERUS: And racing about the city like some commoner. It's not only unseemly it's downright dangerous.

ESTHER: I feel safer among the people in the street than I do here at court.

AHASUERUS: And as far as my concubines are concerned they're completely open with me. They have no mysterious relatives. They have no hidden past. I know nothing more about you than I did the day we first met. You never speak about your family. You never speak about your friends. You're always running off to your cousin's home, if it really exists. If he really exists.

ESTHER: He most certainly does.

AHASUERUS: Then why haven't I met him in all this time?

ESTHER: I've told you.

AHASUERUS: You've told me nothing. Where do you really go? And what do you really do there?

ESTHER: He's an older man and he needs looking after?

AHASUERUS: He couldn't possibly be bedridden since he's always off somewhere.

ESTHER: I never said that he was.

AHASUERUS: Oh, now look. A cousin who refuses to attend the wedding of his only living relative? Forget that I'm the king, but a cousin who's not even interested in meeting your husband?

(HAMAN enters, dirty and disheveled.)

AHASUERUS: What is that awful smell?

HAMAN: Your majesty. Your highness. I'm sorry I'm late.

AHASUERUS: *(HE waves the air away from his nose.)* Is that you?

HAMAN: The streets of our fair city, your majesty. I intend to have a long talk with the minister of sanitation. In addition to that I was pelted with garbage by several ruffians and thugs. *(To Esther)* I must apologize for my appearance. I had hoped to bathe and change before coming here but the guards insisted on bringing me here directly. *(HE turns to Ahasuerus.)* Under orders, I presume.

AHASUERUS: It might interest you to know, my dear Haman, that I've spent the entire day examining all the evidence. I'm referring to this so-called Jewish conspiracy of yours.

HAMAN: Conspiracy?

AHASUERUS: You intend to deny it?

HAMAN: I can't imagine what you're referring to.

AHASUERUS: Are you going to deny that you informed me about a Jewish plot to overthrow the government?

HAMAN: I never said there was a plot.

AHASUERUS: You most certainly did.

HAMAN: I said that they're well organized. I said they posed a threat. And so they do. And so they are. The Jews are a law unto themselves and as long as they exist the government of Persia lives under a cloud.

AHASUERUS: From what I've been told, my dear Haman, this is nothing but a personal vendetta.

HAMAN: I don't know where you've gotten this information.

AHASUERUS: You have nothing personal against the Jews? You have nothing personal against one Jew in particular?

HAMAN: If you're referring to this Mordecai then you're quite mistaken. It's true that it was his refusal to pay his respects to the office of prime minister that made me aware of this Jewish threat. But believe me, your majesty, I would welcome the Jews with open arms if they accepted our laws, if they accepted his majesty's divinity.

AHASUERUS: Will you tell me please what we're going to accomplish by slaughtering innocent men, women and children?

HAMAN: Innocent, your majesty?

AHASUEҡUS: What are they guilty of?

HAMAN: Pride, your majesty. Greed, your majesty. The Jews are a stiff-necked people, interested only in personal gain. And perhaps you're not aware of the havoc they cause...the rivalry, the dissension, the unrest. We need go no farther than this very room. There used to be faith among the three of us. There used to be understanding. And now what do we have? Doubt, suspicion, mistrust.

AHASUERUS: And whose fault is that?

HAMAN: Mine, your majesty. I admit it freely. I am guilty as well. I am guilty of being an idealist, your majesty, of believing in an utopia.

AHASUERUS: Utopia, my foot! I simply do not understand how a man of principle, how a distinguished man like yourself could stoop to such deception.

HAMAN: I know of no deception, your majesty. It was a matter of semantics apparently. If you will walk through the streets of the capital however, if you will poll the man on the street, then you will understand what you've accomplished with this new decree. The people have never been more united. The people have never been more proud to call themselves Persian. They are no longer ashamed to salute the Persian flag, to be called patriotic. Even the queen will attest to that.

ESTHER; I'm afraid I've never understood this business of patriotism, my dear Haman. I've never understood how one country can be considered better or more beautiful simply because we happen to be living in it.

HAMAN: In a world fraught with danger, in a world where enemies abound a country must be prepared to defend itself, be prepared to fight to the death to protect the fatherland.

ESTHER: Perhaps we would not be surrounded by enemies if we were not so insular, if we were not guilty of the very crimes you lay at the foot of the Jews.

HAMAN: I would dearly love to continue this discussion, your highness, but obviously it's purely academic since a royal decree is divine and cannot be rescinded. And might I add, your majesty, when I mentioned the money the royal treasury would inherit you were not so fastidious. Couldn't we possibly sit down and eat? I've been on my feet all day and I am famished.

AHASUERUS: Yes, let's eat. I'm hungry too. We can talk about this later.

ESTHER: But time is running out.

AHASUERUS: Nonsense.

ESTHER: But...

AHASUERUS: I said that's enough. That smell is awful. Haman, why don't you go home and bathe.

HAMAN: Thank you, your majesty. I'm most grateful. I'm sure this can all be settled amicably. *(HE starts off.)*

ESTHER: Just a moment.

AHASUERUS: What now?

ESTHER: I think there's something you both ought to know.

AHASUERUS: Couldn't it possibly wait?

ESTHER: You said just a minute ago that you don't know much about me. That I haven't been open with you.

AHASUERUS: Yes, well...this is hardly the time.

ESTHER: Unfortunately the time is long overdue. You see, gentlemen, I happen to be a Jewess.

AHASUERUS: You mean you've adopted the god of the Jews? Now what made you go and do a thing like that?

ESTHER: I mean that I am a Jewess. I was born a Jew and raised as a Jew.

HAMAN: I know how much her highness empathizes with that unfortunate race...

ESTHER: It's the truth, my dear Haman, and you know it.

HAMAN: I know nothing of the sort.

AHASUERUS: *(HE turns to Haman.)* Is she telling the truth or isn't she?

HAMAN: It's the first I've heard of it.

AHASUERUS: *(HE turns to Esther.)* I don't believe you.

ESTHER: I think you do.

AHASUERUS: Why have you waited so long to tell me this?

ESTHER: Would you have married me if you had known?

AHASUERUS: I have nothing against the Jews. I may have spoken disparagingly about them from time to time, but then I've spoken disparagingly about many things. Have I ever done the Jews any harm? Well? Have I?

ESTHER: Then I was mistaken.

AHASUERUS: You most certainly were, and it was foolish of you to conceal your heritage like that. The Jews are an ancient race and a noble one and all this might have been avoided if you'd just spoken up. Well, my dear prime minister, what have you to say to this?

HAMAN: Not a thing except that this is probably the best kept secret in the history of Persia, and I see no reason why it can't continue to be.

ESTHER: I don't think my friends and my neighbors will continue to be so cooperative.

HAMAN: What difference does it make? Who would dare raise a hand against the queen?

ESTHER: You don't expect me to stand idly by while my people are being slaughtered, do you?

AHASUERUS: But what can we do?

ESTHER: I don't know what you're going to do, but I'm going to join my people, even if it means my death.

HAMAN: Your majesty...your highness, I'm at the point of exhaustion. I didn't sleep at all the night before. I had an impossible day. My feet are killing me and I've got the most violent headache imaginable.

AHASUERUS: Forget your headache, my dear Haman, because I've got a great cure for that. I suggest you put on your thinking cap and come up with something. Well?

HAMAN: *(Wearily)* Well what?

AHASUERUS: The Jews, you fool! The Jews!

HAMAN: There's only one fool in this room and... I'm sorry. I'm terribly sorry. I'm awfully tired.

AHASUERUS: I suggest you get your affairs in order as quickly as possible. My guards are outside the door and they will escort you. *(HE turns his back on Haman.)*

ESTHER: I beg of you, do something. I'll intercede for you, Haman. I'll beg the king to spare you.

HAMAN: There's nothing to be done, my dear. *(HE faces the king, head erect.)* I have served your majesty to the best of my ability. I have served this empire to the best of my ability.

AHASUERUS: You are a cold, vicious, destructive man.

HAMAN: Quite possibly, your majesty. *(HE looks contemptuously at the king.)* I sincerely hope that my successor is someone worthy of you. *(HE starts off majestically, falters, recovers his balance and goes off, head high.)*

AHASUERUS: He built this special gallows, you know, for the sole purpose of hanging this innocent Jew. He's going to be the first one to try it out.

ESTHER: And that will solve everything, won't it?

AHASUERUS: Your people will be avenged, at any rate. To say nothing of this merchant of yours, this Mordecai.

(HEGAI enters.)

ESTHER: You've never met him, have you, this man who saved your life?

AHASUERUS: No.

ESTHER: Then perhaps it's time.

(ESTHER nods to HEGAI who goes off and reenters with MORDECAI dressed in an elegant robe.)

ESTHER: Mordecai, your majesty...my cousin.

MORDECAI: *(HE bows.)* Your majesty.

AHASUERUS: I suppose I should have known.

ESTHER: *(To Mordecai)* The decree cannot be reversed.

AHASUERUS: You must understand, my dear fellow, a royal edict is divine. There's absolutely nothing that I can do about it.

MORDECAI: Perhaps there is, your majesty.

AHASUERUS: What would you suggest?

MORDECAI: Another edict.

AHASUERUS: Calling for what?

MORDECAI: Giving permission to the Jews to arm themselves; giving permission to the Jews to defend themselves.

AHASUERUS: Yes, well...that certainly seems the fair thing to do.

MORDECAI: We should see to it at once.

AHASUERUS: Yes, well, tomorrow will be soon enough. Let's sit down to dinner first. I'm absolutely starved. And besides, we have a lot of catching up to do.

MORDECAI: Your majesty.

AHASUERUS: *(HE places his arm around Mordecai's shoulder.)* I'd like to learn more about your customs, Mordecai. The Jews have always fascinated me.

(AHASUERUS leads MORDECAI off.)

ESTHER: But gentlemen...

(ESTHER sighs, shakes her head and follows them off as the lights come down.)

Scene Three

(The king's chambers. Early morning, some months later. HEGAI is discovered holding a folded robe. BIGTHA enters.)

BIGTHA: Good morning.

HEGAI: Good morning. Her highness will be wanting this robe when she gets up. *(HE hands the robe to Bigtha.)*

BIGTHA: Thank you.

HEGAI: The king is back sooner than expected.

BIGTHA: So it appears.

HEGAI: This war with the Greeks...does there seem to be any end in sight?

BIGTHA: The king doesn't seem to think so.

HEGAI: It's amazing. An illiterate group of shepherds keeping the greatest kingdom in the world at bay.

BIGTHA: From what I can gather they are not completely illiterate. And don't forget, they're fighting to protect their homes and their families.

HEGAI: Why don't we just forget about them?

BIGTHA: They seem to have this rather insidious form of government which seems to be gaining in popularity. They call it democracy.

HEGAI: Democracy?

BIGTHA: Everyone, it seems, has a say in the government.

HEGAI: I should think that would result in chaos.

BIGTHA: Obviously not. Interestingly enough they have no eunuchs.

HEGAI: Oh?

BIGTHA: They do have slavery however.

HEGAI: I see.

(MORDECAI enters holding a document in his hand.)

BIGTHA: Good morning, your lordship.

MORDECAI: His majesty's expecting me. Is he up?

BIGTHA: Oh, yes. I'll let him know that you're here.

MORDECAI: Thank you.

(BIGTHA goes off.)

HEGAI: Congratulations, Prime Minister.

MORDECAI: It was only a temporary appointment.

HEGAI: I've heard otherwise.

MORDECAI: Then you know more than I.

HEGAI: Impossible.

(HEGAI goes off. AHASUERUS enters a moment later.)

AHASUERUS: Good morning, Mordecai.

MORDECAI: Good morning, your majesty, and welcome home. I hope I'm not too early.

AHASUERUS: No, no, no. On the battlefield one becomes accustomed to rising with the sun.

MORDECAI: You asked for my report...in regard to the Jews.

AHASUERUS: Yes, yes. Yes, of course.

MORDECAI: *(Consulting the document he holds.)* The new decree, you may recall, gave permission for the Jews to arm themselves and to defend themselves against their enemies. The clash took place on the thirteenth day of Adar, as scheduled. The Jews, of course, were victorious. Seventy five thousand of their enemy perished in the conflict. Unfortunately the conflict continued, in the capital, for a second day, and three hundred more of their enemy perished on that second day. I'm pleased to report that there was no looting, on the part of the Jews, that is. Haman's ten sons were killed in the fighting and we thought it prudent to display their bodies on the gallows inaugurated by their father.

AHASUERUS: Oh? And what did her highness have to say about that?

MORDECAI: She was not too happy about it.

AHASUERUS: They're never satisfied, are they? Well, how would you like to continue as my prime minister...on a permanent basis, that is?

MORDECAI: I'd be honored, your majesty.

AHASUERUS: Good. And it might interest you to know that I've decided to adopt your Jehovah as one of our official gods. There is a precedent for it, you know. My grandfather, Cyrus...

MORDECAI: Yes, I know.

AHASUERUS: Do you think it would please your cousin?

MORDECAI: I'm sure it will.

AHASUERUS: She's not very easy to please.

(ESTHER enters.)

ESTHER: Good morning.

AHASUERUS: Good morning.

(THEY kiss.)

AHASUERUS: I'd like you to meet our new prime minister.

ESTHER: Congratulations.

MORDECAI: Thank you. Well, as the new prime minister I'd better be about my business. I'll leave this report for you to look over at your leisure. Again, welcome home.

AHASUERUS: Thank you, Mordecai.

> *(MORDECAI bows and goes off. AHASUERUS glances at the report and sets it down. Romantic music is heard softly in the background.)*

AHASUERUS: Did you miss me?

ESTHER: Did you miss me?

AHASUERUS: Every moment of the day.

ESTHER: Was that me or your creature comforts?

AHASUERUS: Would you be offended if I said that you are one of my creature comforts?

ESTHER: You said you had a surprise for me.

AHASUERUS: I've decided to adopt your Jehovah as one of our official gods. What do you say to that?

ESTHER: It's become quite fashionable these days to become a Jew.

AHASUERUS: I suspect that you don't really believe in this Jehovah of yours.

ESTHER: I'm not quite sure what I believe in.

AHASUERUS: You must believe in some sort of a god.

ESTHER: Why?

AHASUERUS: Surely you don't think that we created ourselves?

ESTHER: I don't believe in adoring whatever mysterious life force there may or may not be, merely out of fear and ignorance. Nor do I believe in praying for special favors I'm not so sure that I deserve.

AHASUERUS: What do you believe in?

ESTHER: I believe in doing the best I can with what I'm given.

AHASUERUS: But without the gods we're no better than the beasts of the field.

ESTHER: The beasts of the field do not go to war. The beasts of the field do not go about killing their own kind in the name of their gods, in the name of their country. *(SHE sits thoughtfully.)*

AHASUERUS: What are you thinking?

ESTHER: I'm thinking how frightening it is that our lives are so dependent on luck, on chance. Suppose I hadn't been summoned to the palace. Suppose you hadn't taken a fancy to me. Suppose Mordecai hadn't overheard those two men plotting to kill you.

AHASUERUS: Perhaps your Jehovah had something to do with it.

ESTHER: I'm not ruling it out.

AHASUERUS: *(HE sits beside her and kisses her.)* I'm still waiting for the surprise you said you had for me.

> *(SHE beckons to him with her finger. HE leans over and she whispers in his ear.)*

AHASUERUS: When?

ESTHER: Four months, according to the doctors.

(HE lifts her into the air and whirls her about, laughing triumphantly, then kisses her and sets her down.)

AHASUERUS: It will be a boy. It must be.

ESTHER: I shall do my best.

AHASUERUS: From here on in everything is going to be fine. Just you wait and see.

ESTHER: Except, perhaps, for the war with the Greeks?

AHASUERUS: Yes, well... At any rate, I promise you one thing.

ESTHER: And what might that be?

AHASUERUS: No harm will ever come to your Jews again.

(The music in the background comes to a halt.)

AHASUERUS: But just between the two of us, you must admit, my dear, they are a pretty shrewd lot. Come, confess it.

ESTHER: *(SHE sighs, smiles then slips her arm into his.)* Shall we take a walk around the garden?

(THEY start off slowly as the music resumes and the lights come down.)

Photo by Marty Beim

About The Author

As an actor Norman Beim has performed on Broadway, Off Broadway, toured nationally and has appeared on television and in films. He has also directed a number of stage productions. His plays have been performed nationally and internationally and won a number of awards. His debut novel, Hymie And The Angel, was published last year. Mr. Beim is a member of The Dramatists Guild, Actors Equity, The Screen Actors Guild, AFTRA and The Bronx Council of the Arts. He lives in New York City.